Martin Luther King, Jr., and the
Sermonic Power of Public Discourse

STUDIES IN RHETORIC AND COMMUNICATION
General Editors:
E. Culpepper Clark
Raymie E. McKerrow
David Zarefsky

Edited by Carolyn Calloway-Thomas
and John Louis Lucaites

Martin Luther King, Jr., and the Sermonic Power of Public Discourse

The University of Alabama Press   Tuscaloosa and London

∞

The paper on which this book is printed meets the minimum
requirements of American National Standard for Information
Science-Permanence of Paper for Printed Library Materials,
ANSI Z39.48-1984.

Library of Congress Cataloging-in-Publication Data

Martin Luther King, Jr., and the sermonic power of public discourse / edited by
    Carolyn Calloway-Thomas, John Louis Lucaites.
        p. : cm.—(Studies in rhetoric and communication)
    Includes bibliographical references and index.
    ISBN 0-8173-0689-7
    1. King, Martin Luther, Jr., 1929–1968—Oratory.   I. Calloway-
Thomas, Carolyn.   II. Lucaites, John Louis.   III. Series.
E185.97.K5M32   1993
323'.092—dc20   92-21236

British Library Cataloguing-in-Publication Data available

Contents

Acknowledgments

The origins of this volume can be traced to two scholarly conferences held in 1988, the year that marked the twenty-fifth anniversary of two of Rev. Martin Luther King, Jr.'s most famous rhetorical efforts: "Letter From Birmingham Jail" and "I Have a Dream." The first conference, "Martin Luther King, Jr.: The Power of Oratory," was cosponsored by the Speech Communication Association and the Martin Luther King, Jr., Center for Nonviolent Social Change and was held in January at the King Center in Atlanta, Georgia. The second conference was the annual meeting of the Southern Speech Communication Association held in Memphis, Tennessee, in April, which hosted a plenary session on King's oratory. The importance of King's leadership in the civil rights movement had long been recognized and, indeed, frequently attributed in large degree to his abilities as an orator. Surprisingly, however, very little systematic or sustained scholarly attention had been devoted to the study of either the rhetorical forms or functions of his public advocacy (a situation, we are happy to report, that has begun to change in the past five years). The scholars and critics who participated in these forums honored the memory of Dr. King as one of America's great leaders by searching for and probing the rhetorical insights in his public speeches and writings that might lead to an enriched understanding of the role that public advocacy plays in effecting social and political change. What emerged in those presentations was an unstated but virtually unanimous recognition of the centrality of the sermonic forms and functions of King's discourse. As those who made formal presentations revised and developed their oral remarks to accommodate the demands of the written word, the organizing theme of this volume emerged.

It is perhaps a cliché, but nonetheless true for it, that no project of this sort can succeed without the help of others. In this case, we would like to acknowledge the assistance of Herman Hudson, Martha C. Kraft professor and dean of Afro-American Affairs, and Morton Lowengrub, dean of the College of Arts and Sciences, at Indiana University. Our colleagues in the Department of Speech Communication have been exceptionally supportive of the project. Shawn Parry-Giles served as an able research assistant, and we wish to thank her for her help in generating the bibliography and checking footnotes. Marsha Houston, professor of Speech Communication at Tulane University, deserves special thanks for her work in organizing the Atlanta conference and her continued interest in the project. Finally, we wish to express our deepest appreciation to our chairperson, James R. Andrews, for his sustained support and encouragement for this project since its inception.

Copyright Acknowledgments

We gratefully acknowledge the right to quote from the following materials:

Excerpt from "Letter from Birmingham Jail" from *Why We Can't Wait* by Martin Luther King, Jr. Copyright © 1963, 1964 by Martin Luther King, Jr. Reprinted by permission of HarperCollins Publishers.

Martin Luther King, Jr., *I Have A Dream*. Copyright © 1963 Martin Luther King, Jr. Reprinted by permission of Joan Daves Agency.

Martin Luther King, Jr., *A Time to Break Silence*. Copyright © 1968 Estate of Martin Luther King, Jr. Reprinted by permission of Joan Daves Agency.

Martin Luther King, Jr., *Final Speech in Memphis*. Copyright © 1968 Estate of Martin Luther King, Jr. Reprinted by permission of Joan Daves Agency.

Eugene "Bull" Connor Papers, Birmingham Public Library, Birmingham, Alabama. Used by permission.

Introduction

Carolyn Calloway-Thomas
John Louis Lucaites

When Rev. Martin Luther King, Jr., proclaimed his "dream" before the American people on 28 August 1963, he boldly joined the canonized group of great American orators, taking his place alongside the likes of Daniel Webster, Abraham Lincoln, Frederick Douglass, and Franklin Delano Roosevelt. There can be little question that this particular expression of King's dream marks a great moment in American history; too frequently, however, we equate King's greatness as an orator—and by extension as a national political and moral leader—with this one speech, almost as if he had mystically emerged from the shadows of the Lincoln Memorial to crystallize and articulate the demands of the civil rights movement. Such an account comports well with America's romanticized conception of the selfless hero who arrives in the nick of time to save the community from whatever evil it faces.[1] Nevertheless, it is a story that ignores the broader historical and rhetorical implications of King's rise to prominence as the charismatic symbolizer of arguably the most important social and political movement of twentieth-century America.[2] "I Have a Dream" is clearly symptomatic of King's stewardship of the civil rights movement, but it does not by itself account for the power of either his leadership or the movement he led. For that account we need a fuller portrait of King's career as a public advocate from its beginnings in Montgomery, Alabama, in 1954 to its tragic ending in Memphis, Tennessee, in 1968.

This volume is animated by the belief that King's importance as a political and moral leader stemmed in some significant measure from the sermonic quality of his public discourse or rhetoric. King was first and foremost a preacher, a giver of sermons. Whether speaking before his congregation on Sunday morning, writing a public letter, or giving an interview to the representatives of the mass media, he was sermonizing, actively striving to craft what he called a "beloved community" from the key values of the Christian and democratic traditions of American society. Those who have written of King's beloved community have often treated it as a more or less static vision of an ideal, transcendent world, the end result of a philosopher's or theologian's utopian dream.[3] In practice, however, King was neither so much a philosopher nor a theologian as he was a public advocate, and while his dream of a beloved community was motivated by a spiritual transcendence of this-worldly, secular differences, it was never static. Rather, that dream revealed a dynamic vision of what American society could become, and it changed as King recognized and adapted to the social and political exigencies of time and place.

The nine essays in this volume offer critical studies of the range of King's public discourse as sermonic rhetoric. King was a prolific speaker and writer, and his collected papers will eventually fill a rather large multivolume work, literally thousands of pages in length.[4] The essays here focus attention on five different and relatively short works from that corpus: "Death of Evil on the Seashore," one of his earliest civil rights sermons, originally delivered in 1956 and subsequently repeated on numerous occasions throughout the nation; "Letter from Birmingham Jail" and "I Have a Dream," both presented at the zenith of the civil rights movement in the tumultuous summer of 1963; "A Time to Break Silence," his controversial critique of America's involvement in Vietnam, delivered from the pulpit of Harlem's Riverside Baptist Church in 1967; and finally "I've Been to the Mountaintop," his prophetic last speech delivered in 1968 at the Mason Temple in Memphis, Tennessee, only hours before an assassin's bullet ended his life. Taken collectively, these five works not only span the duration of King's career as a public advocate but also represent the scope and protean quality of his efforts to craft a compelling vision of a beloved community across time. In this introductory essay we elaborate on the rhetorical perspective that treats secular discourse as sermonic, offer a general overview of the sermonic function of King's beloved community by locating it in the context of the larger historical and symbolic environments in which it appeared, and preview the individual essays of the volume in terms of the power of sermonic discourse.

The Sermonic Function of Public Discourse

The word "sermon" refers generally to a form of religious exhortation in which a preacher admonishes a congregation *to understand* and *to act* in accord with a particular interpretation of the sacred values of their shared, religious community. It is thus both a hermeneutic and rhetorical enterprise. In the Judeo-Christian tradition sermons typically consist of three parts: the statement of scripture, the exegesis, and the application.[5] Sermonizing does not serve an exclusively ecclesiastical function, however, and in one form or another sermonic discourse has assumed a significant and powerful role in the civil and secular lives of Anglo- and African-American society since at least the seventeenth century.[6]

The focus in this book lies not on the purely religious form or structure of sermons as a discrete genre of discourse but on the implicit sermonic function of *all* public discourse. In characterizing the project as such we mean to highlight the sociorhetorical relationship between politics and religion or, more broadly, between collective power and public morality. As Richard M. Weaver notes, rhetoric is "an art of emphasis embodying an order of desire."[7] When addressing a public forum, the rhetor operates by depicting the most salient aspects of allegedly exigent circumstances with the purpose of crafting a collective response.[8] Rhetors thus play the role of "leader" arguing a "community" or order of collective being into existence.[9] The primary resources for such arguments are the key values that the members of an audience come to believe they share with one another and the speaker. The foundation of collective action is thus a pragmatic function of the rhetor's ability to "adjust ideas [an order of desire] to people [as a collective being], and people to ideas."[10]

Rhetors of both a secular and an ecclesiastical cast enact the sermonic function of discourse whenever they prescribe a relationship between communal values and collective action. This function entails three separate but related rhetorical processes: the identification and definition of core communal values, the structuring of a values hierarchy, and the performative display of communal existence.[11]

Identifying and Defining Core Communal Values

The first problem all public advocates confront is the need to establish common ground with an audience, literally to identify and define the basis upon which the communication or sharing of ideas and feelings can proceed. In a fundamental sense, language itself is the root of social identification. According to Kenneth Burke, "You persuade a man only insofar as you can talk his language by speech, gesture, tonality, order, image, attitude, idea, *identifying* your ways with his."[12] Of course, language is never neutral. In its usage it always expresses an order of desire, and it is the values or preferences signified through particular linguistic or social usages that serve as the motivation for both communal existence and collective action. The rhetor who would lead the individual members of an audience to believe that they constitute a community of interests must thus persuasively identify and define the core values of the community.

Signifying the core values of a community is the first step in the rhetorical process of establishing social identification. The values that define social unity are almost always little more than vague and idealized preferences that establish a general criterion for making selections from among competing alternatives in a world of contingencies and limited resources. When considered in the abstract, a community treats its core values as altogether compatible with one another, just as American democratic communities generally view the abstractions "liberty" and "equality" as wholly consistent and compatible with one another. In practice, however, the abstract consistency of such values can quickly evaporate as competing advocates choose to make one value more important or immediately relevant than another. So, for example, in trying to determine the desirability of "forced busing" as a means of achieving racially integrated schools, one finds advocates on opposing sides of the issue pitting "liberty" and "equality" against one another in ways that make them appear as incompatible value alternatives. Hence, the black parents living in the inner city who support forced busing to achieve a more equal education for their child—even though it restricts the alleged property rights of white parents living in the suburbs to have their child attend a school in their own neighborhood—imply that equality is a more important value than liberty when the issue of public education is at stake. The abstract nature of core values thus not only necessitates identifying and defining the range of meanings for such terms in a particular community but also requires a hierarchy to guide the order of preference among opposing values.[13]

Structuring a Hierarchy of Values

The structuring of a values hierarchy is the second function of sermonic discourse. As with core values, there is a tendency to locate values hierarchies in a sacred text, like the Declaration of Independence or the U.S. Constitution. Once sanctified, such texts are treated as authoritative, determinate foundations of the community. Of course, the public meaning and usage of values hierarchies are always open to interpretation. But more, they are actively crafted and constructed in the rhetorical interaction of speakers and audiences as they actively negotiate the grounds on which their sense of community rests.[14]

As a community begins to inscribe a history for itself, some interpretations of the hierarchical construction of core values begin to appear more foundational than others. Insofar as the prevalent meanings ascribed to these foundations serve the collective needs of the community, there is no problem. When they fail to meet the dynamic and often competing needs of the diverse members of a collectivity, however, they must be reinterpreted and recrafted so as to accommodate the larger interests of communal living. As a rhetorical process, the sermonic function of public discourse creates an opportunity for the members of a community to consider the range of creative possibilities available for collective action by calling attention to the prevailing order of values and by providing a public space in which rhetors can envision particular and plausible ways of affecting community's value hierarchy.

Performing Communal Existence

The third rhetorical process central to the sermonic dimension of public discourse is the performative display of communal existence. It is one thing to identify a set of values and to structure a hierarchy out of the shared language of a community; it is something else altogether to vivify a symbolic universe to the point of persuading an audience to adopt it as the very essence of its communal life. The performative display of communal existence is a rhetorical process in which speakers and audiences combine to enact their shared vision of a common unity through a public exhibition of presumably virtuous beliefs and behaviors.

We frequently think of the "performative" dimensions of the rhetorical process as solely concerning the speaker's expression of the message. Rhetorical performance is thus reduced to simplistic notions of style and delivery. This view ignores the fact that the effectiveness of any rhetorical process is by necessity a function of the vital interaction between speakers and audiences. The performative display of communal existence thus demands more than a stylized and practiced orator; it literally requires the speaker and audience to join together in consubstantial enactment of the community's values and values hierarchies. Quite obviously, a lone speaker cannot create a community without an audience. However, even the classical scenario of the individual speaker who shapes the beliefs and attitudes of a more or less passive audience risks reifying the rhetorical process beyond common experience, for audiences are seldom totally subject to the wishes and whims of speakers. Far more frequently, speakers and audiences bind together at a particular moment in time to interpret and negotiate a common vision of their shared community.[15] That negotiation is successful when speakers and audiences persuade one another to adopt and perform the respective roles of "leader" and "people" (or "minister" and "congregation"). When such enactment occurs, the sermonic function of public discourse calls attention to the phenomenological presence and power of community.[16]

As we suggested above, the sermonic function of public discourse is not necessarily religious in the sense of propagating a particular ecclesiastical faith. However, it is inherently religious in the more radical sense of *religio* as "to bind together" or "to yoke or gather meanings." As a result, we find the sermonic function operating in any discourse designed to "bind" a community into existence or action, regardless of its specifically ecclesiastical or secular foundations. When one has separated the ecclesiastical and the secular, it is nevertheless important to note that the interaction of the two can serve as a potent resource for effecting and authorizing the existence and power of a social and political community. Martin Luther King, Jr.'s beloved community is a case in point.

The Sermonic Function of the Reverend Dr. King's Beloved Community

When Martin Luther King, Jr., arrived in Montgomery, Alabama, in May 1954 to deliver his first sermon as the pastor of the Dexter Avenue Baptist Church, he came with the intention of preaching and ministering to the congregation for several years as a basis for eventually landing an academic position in a theological seminary.[17] He also came with a strong, though undeveloped, commitment to social activism, born both at the knees of "Daddy" King and in the theological seminaries at Crozer and Boston University.[18] Initially that social activism evinced itself in church-related activities designed largely to assist the needy, although it also included some participation in the local chapter of the National Association for the Advancement of Colored People (NAACP). By January 1957, fewer than three years later, King had led the Montgomery Improvement

Association (MIA) in its successful boycott of the Montgomery bus system and had founded the Southern Christian Leadership Conference (SCLC) in Atlanta, Georgia. What began as the desire to lead a relatively serene professional life thus quickly dissipated as King responded to the swirl of events and readily moved to the forefront of political leadership in the burgeoning civil rights movement.

As the essays in this volume attest, it is very difficult to identify King as either a religious or a political leader, for in practice he was both simultaneously. It is sometimes difficult for those schooled in the U.S. Constitution's doctrine of the separation of church and state to understand or countenance King's combination of these roles. What we must remember is that prior to the Civil War there were precious few opportunities for black leaders—freemen or slaves—to speak out publicly on political matters. The pulpit became one of the few places that black leaders could speak with their people in relative safety. It is thus not surprising that the black church became the center of African-American social and political organization and that black preachers and ministers served as both religious and political leaders.[19] Following the Civil War and Reconstruction, blacks continued to face all kinds of restrictions—legal and otherwise—against participating in the political system, and accordingly, the black church continued as the locus of black political action and the primary source from which black leaders emerged.[20]

In one sense, then, King's religious and political leadership of the civil rights movement simply enacted the traditional role of the black preacher in African-American history.[21] In a more important sense, however, his particular leadership was truly revolutionary. Prior to the Montgomery bus boycott the black church represented a relatively conservative political activism. Its foci and interests were generally and essentially privatized, the end result of which being to create a relatively silent black community operating within the boundaries set for it by the politically dominant white society. In E. Franklin Frazier's terms it created "a nation within a nation" functioning as an "invisible institution."[22] As long as the black church operated largely outside the public sphere, it served the social and political interests of the dominant white culture by promoting restrictive standards of passivity and civility. It thus achieved the support of the white church and white America at large. King's leadership in the black community abruptly altered the dynamics of that support by enacting an increasingly overt and public political activism designed to force a public confrontation with the inherently uncivilized relationship between blacks and whites promoted by segregation.[23]

Revolutions, of course, are never easy to effect, for on their very face they risk the total disruption of the values and hierarchies of the prevailing social order. They thus naturally engender resistance from a wide range of sources. The road that King traveled from his birth as the revolutionary leader of the civil rights movement in Montgomery to his death in Memphis fourteen years later was fraught with challenges at every turn and from a multitude of perspectives. He was constantly under attack, both physically and symbolically, by southern segregationists and those who dubbed him a communist sympathizer.[24] Additionally, he confronted battles within the various interests of the civil rights movement itself, as the NAACP and the Urban League treated the growing power base of his SCLC as a threat to their own political autonomy.[25] And just as he faced significant pressure from white liberals such as John and Robert Kennedy, Lyndon Johnson, and the mainstream white church hierarchy to become more moderate, so too he faced equal pressure from the increasingly radical Student Nonviolent Coordinating Committee (SNCC) and the growing black power movement to become more militant.[26]

Unlike most political revolutions that reject the core values of the politically dominant society, King's leadership of the civil rights movement demanded that the United States live up to the revolutionary potential implicit in its Declaration of Independence and Constitution. He sought to achieve his goal rhetorically by symbolically transcending the tension between America's avowed commitments to equality and liberty and its inherently racist social and political practices. He characterized his alternative as the beloved community, a Christian America embodying a "genuine intergroup and interpersonal living-integration."[27] This was no simple task, to be sure, but King's insistence on executing the core values of America's radical foundations made it difficult for his detractors in mainstream American politics to reject his demands out of hand.[28]

Enacting the beloved community served as the primary purpose of King's public discourse from at least the time that he founded the SCLC in 1957 through to his final 1968 speech. This is not to say that the phrase "beloved community" appeared in every speech he delivered, or letter, article, or book he wrote; neither is it to suggest that its meaning remained unchanged over time. It is to say that King's public discourse consistently signified an image of the beloved community as a flexible but potent depiction of what the American dream could become if black and white America sought to enact it in both their public and private interactions. The flexibility of its usages made it an image that could accommodate the needs and demands of black and white Americans simultaneously. For

African Americans it cast a forward gaze to a world in which Christian "love" mediated the secular tensions between racial equality and liberty, even as it provided them with an immediately renewed sense of self and pride as Americans by identifying the spiritual and secular grounds for personal action.[29] For white Americans it cast a gaze backwards to the nation's revolutionary roots as a usable past, even as it assured them that revolutions for justice could indeed be bloodless. Considered as a rhetoric, it served the sermonic function of binding the disparate elements of King's fragmented audience (the American people) into a unified whole by (1) identifying core communal values (love, justice, liberty, and equality); (2) structuring them as a values hierarchy (a transcendent liberal-Christian existentialism that sought to manage the tension between individual rights and communal duty rather than to sacrifice one to the other); and (3) publicly performing the beloved community's transitory existence (displaying the collectivized power of love, justice, liberty, and equality through nonviolent massive resistance).

The image of the beloved community enacted by King and his followers, and portrayed nationally by the media, was an extremely potent rhetoric.[30] It reached the zenith of its power at the March on Washington in August 1963, fewer than two months after the Birmingham riots, and it dominated the public discourse of the civil rights movement until the summer of 1965. When Watts erupted in violence in August 1965, and similar riots broke out in other major northern urban centers the following summer, the persuasive power of King's beloved community diminished, at least for a large portion of the black community who began to listen to the increasingly militant demands of the leaders of the SNCC to supplant nonviolent resistance with black power.

The turn of events in 1965 and 1966 has caused some to characterize King's beloved community as a political failure. To the extent that we treat it as an unrealizable, utopian image, one might be inclined to agree. But such a conclusion is altogether myopic. To treat the beloved community as a static and decontextualized ideal is to reify it as the stable product of King's sociohistorical background, or his religious training at Crozer, or his doctoral studies at Boston University, and so on. Of course, in one sense it was all these things, but more important, it was a rhetoric, a symbolic construction designed to argue a dynamic collective being into existence and to motivate social and political change at historically specific moments in time. King was the leader of a political movement, and he could ill afford the luxury of thoroughly intransigent meanings or stagnant ideals. To be continually effective, he needed to craft the meanings of his ideals to accommodate the changing demands placed on his leadership from one situation to the next. And craft them he did, as he actively engaged the American public in an effort to persuade it to interpret and enact the meaning of its constitutional creed. Thus King's beloved community did not disappear after 1966. Rather he adapted it to his increasingly radical critique of the relationship between racism and capitalism that began to emerge in the Chicago freedom movement.[31] And it continued to evolve over the next two years, slowly expanding its domain of inclusion until his last presidential address before the SCLC in 1967 where he identified the beloved community with a kind of democratic socialism that called for a "restructuring of the whole of American society."[32]

When we think of King's beloved community in these terms, as the embodiment of a dynamic, rhetorical process, questions of political success and failure become very difficult to address. Nevertheless, however we evaluate the specific changes that King's leadership motivated, there can be little question that it was rhetorically effective: It helped to create a national perception of a "moral crisis" that resulted in some of the most far-reaching civil rights legislation since the Civil War. At the same time, it crafted a public symbolic environment in which incremental change became a sign of national failure and thus inadvertently lent support to the demands for black power and all that followed from it.[33] It also effected significant change in the ways in which black Americans and other minority groups participate in the political process as well as the way in which politics itself has come to be practiced in the United States.[34]

What accounts for these rhetorical effects? This is not a question that can be answered either univocally or with ease. It requires careful and finely tuned analyses of the rhetorical process in situ. The essays that constitute the remainder of this volume all set out to answer this question in one way or another as they describe, explain, and evaluate the specifically rhetorical dimensions and sermonic quality of Martin Luther King, Jr.'s public discourse.

The Essays

The volume begins with one of several essays that bring an Afrocentric perspective to our understanding of King's public discourse. Afrocentrism operates from the point of view that the explanation and evaluation of African-American society and culture must be *centered* in African ideals, values, and behaviors.[35] Keith D. Miller argues that we can locate more readily the grounding of King's social gospel in the rhetorical world view of black religion that he experienced as a child growing up in Atlanta than in the rhetorical world view of white theology that he encountered in his graduate study of Rauschenbusch, Tillich, Niebuhr, and others at Crozer Seminary and Boston University. To this end, Miller describes the roots of black theology in three steps. First, he identifies the grounding of slave theology in Old Testament narratives, in particular in the book of Exodus where Moses battles Pharaoh for the freedom and souls of the Jews. Second, he demonstrates how the black pulpit traditions of "circulating sermons" and "embedding lyrics" helped to produce a sense of self for both the black folk preacher and the congregations he addressed. Finally, he elaborates the conception of "sacred time" animating black theology, which, unlike Western conceptions of progressive, linear time, allows one to transcend secular and spiritual considerations through the chronological fusion of "disparate characters and events." Against this backdrop, he indicates how the *thematic development* in King's formal sermons—he considers two in some detail, "Death of Evil on the Seashore" and "I've Been to the Mountaintop"—served to read the history of the Western world into the traditions of the black pulpit preacher by articulating them through the integration of form and content in the black religious tradition.

Miller's analysis thus invites the provocative possibility that, rather than having been passively influenced by white Christian theology, King actively appropriated white Christian theology as a means of adapting the tacit, lived experience of black religion to the rhetorical culture of white America. This claim is extremely controversial. It not only contradicts the prevailing assumption among King biographers, represented to some extent by John Patton's essay in this volume, that King's education in Christian theology had a profound, foundational influence on his development of the beloved community, but it also resonates with recent revelations concerning the plagiarism of portions of King's doctoral dissertation.[36] The issue of plagiarism in King's speaking and writing is a particularly difficult one to deal with given his canonization as an American cultural hero. What Miller's analysis helps us to understand is the sense in which King's public discourse, whether "borrowed" from other sources or not, served a significant rhetorical function in vividly and effectively portraying the possibilities for a beloved community within that culture. Thus, however either of these controversies eventually is resolved, Miller's rendering of King's sermons as culturally authentic rhetorics developed in light of the theology and typology of slave religion makes a compelling case for examining the black religious underpinnings of all King's public discourse.

The next two essays address what many consider to be King's most important rhetorical effort, his "Letter from Birmingham Jail." In the first of these essays E. Culpepper Clark identifies both the cultural authenticity of the letter and its justification of nonviolent massive resistance as rhetorical functions of the ideological context and historical circumstances in which it emerged. As Clark notes, there was relatively little new to the letter when it finally became public in June 1963, but time and circumstances were such that "like Voltaire's God, King's 'Letter from Birmingham Jail' would have had to be invented had it not existed." King and his civil rights movement confronted a perilous situation in Birmingham, Alabama. From 1944 to 1963 the movement had been fueled largely by the conservative assumptions underlying Gunnar Myrdal's optimistic prognosis in *An American Dilemma: The Negro Problem and Modern Democracy*, that "time equals progress." By the spring of 1963 the black community's faith in that commitment had begun to falter, and King recognized that the time for a peaceful solution to America's racial problems was quickly running out. Clark demonstrates how King employed the letter as an enthymematic appeal to the white, liberal conscience, at once implying the values consistent with the peaceful and progressive goals of Myrdal's optimism and simultaneously altering the underlying conservative assumptions upon which they rested. Thus, he concludes, 1963 marked a critical turning point in the civil rights movement, and it is evidence of King's rhetorical leadership of the movement that he recognized the winds of change and, at least for the time being, successfully molded them to his Judeo-Christian commitment to nonviolence.

While Clark locates the sermonic function of the letter in its ideological and historical context as a response to its situation, Judith D. Hoover argues that "Letter from Birmingham Jail" functioned to reconstruct the rhetorical situation confronting the civil rights movement. Rhetorical critics frequently treat the rhetorical situation as a set of exigencies, constraints, and audiences that objectively precede and invite public discourse. Hoover reverses that process by looking to the text of the letter in order to discern the rhetorical situation that it produced for those who would be affected by it. Her analysis demonstrates how King took advantage of the exigency posed by the public critique of the Birmingham campaign launched by eight white clergymen. As Hoover tells the story, rather than simply to respond to this attack on its own terms, King used it as the occasion to juxtapose and transcend the values hierarchies separating the advocates of moderation and gradualism from the advocates of nonviolent, massive resistance. As such, she notes, King's reconstruction of the rhetorical situation reunited the fundamental value commitments of American democracy and the Judeo-Christian tradition. In so doing, it served both to integrate many of the fragmented arguments for civil rights that had become disconnected over the years and to broaden King's audience's conception of itself as an American "people" (and, we might add, to unite the historical present with an imagined and hoped-for beloved community).

The portrait of that unity is nowhere more compelling in its representation than in King's "I Have a Dream." Next to Jesus' Sermon on the Mount, Patrick Henry's Liberty or Death speech, and Abraham Lincoln's Gettysburg Address, no other speech in American culture has been more often quoted or cited (or studied by schoolchildren). Indeed, it has become part and parcel of our national heritage, and it is addressed here by three different essays that explain its rhetorical significance, both as an artifact of 1963 and for its later cultural prominence.

Martha Solomon maintains that the power of the speech is a function of its vivid imagery, thematic unity, and philosophical substance, all of which King integrates through the metaphor of the "covenant." Solomon's reading of the speech illuminates the relationship between the ecclesiastical and secular functions of sermonic discourse as she illustrates how King integrated his religion and politics so that his commitment to Christianity subtly framed his conception of the American Dream. By organizing the speech around a covenant, metaphorically eliciting the sacred relationship between God and humanity, King set the stage for interpreting the relationship between America's revolutionary founders and its people in equally sacred terms. As such, he legitimized the incorporation and integration of sacred and secular allusions, archetypal metaphors, and aphorisms, all of which combined to lend cultural authority and authenticity to both the speech's vision of a beloved community and its demands for public moral action.

The issue of cultural authenticity is taken up in a slightly different context by John Louis Lucaites and Celeste Michelle Condit. These authors argue that King's legacy to future generations of Americans has less to do with his promotion or enactment of nonviolent, massive resistance per se than with the way in which his public discourse contributed to a sermonic (re)vision of America's ideological creed. According to Lucaites and Condit the battle for racial justice in America has been from the beginning a struggle to deal with the American paradox of equality, i.e., the desire to achieve social and political identity with the national character, without simultaneously sacrificing individual or cultural differences and autonomy. The African-American response to that paradox has produced what

Lucaites and Condit refer to as the "martyred black word," and it bears close comparison with what Henry Louis Gates identifies as the "double-voice" of African-American literature.[37] However, whereas Gates's concern is with the literary expression of this paradox in poetic discourse, Lucaites and Condit focus their attention on the practical, rhetorical effect it has had on the public discourse of black orators. They thus characterize the martyred black word as the whole body of black public discourse, consisting of both those who express a hopeful and conciliatory faith in the dominant cultural vision of equality and those who express disdain for the received vision, preferring instead to cast their lot with a militant and frequently separatist conception of equality. King, they argue, sat on the conciliatory end of this paradox, operating in a dialogical opposition to Malcolm X's far more threatening demands for a radical redefinition of equality. By locating King in this paradox, this essay demonstrates the larger rhetorical significance of his intertextualization of America's prevailing secular and spiritual narratives in "I Have a Dream" as a timely and culturally appropriate universalization of the commitment to equality.

"I Have a Dream" is of course an extremely powerful and emotional speech, and its power is in some important measure attributable to its orality. This point is reinforced every time we assign our students to study it in class. When they are asked to *read* the speech, students typically treat it with mild reserve; however, when they are asked to *listen* to a recording of it, their attention is transfixed, riveted to King's powerful and sonorous baritone voice and its rhythmic cadence. John H. Patton's essay argues that the special rhetorical power of King's "I Have a Dream" is the result of its integration of theology and orality.

In many ways, Patton's analysis bears important similarities to Solomon's discussion of the covenant metaphor as an integration of form and content. The difference is that whereas Solomon privileges the importance of the thematic unities in identifying the rhetorical action of the speech, Patton directs our attention to the formal unities of the speech contained in the integration of its orality with the structure of the New Testament kerygma. Structurally, the speech provides a framework for the formal integration of King's liberal commitments to Christianity and democracy. Orally, it contributes to the power of the speech in a variety of ways: It satisfies a mnemonic function for both the immediate audience hearing the speech and the nation's long-term cultural memory, it adds presence and vitality to the specific images in the speech employed to situate the polarities of good and evil in the lived world of the audience, and it helps to adapt the prescribed beliefs and values of the beloved community simultaneously to the expressive and rational expectations of the audience. In the end, Patton leaves us with the intriguing conclusion that the fusion of theology and orality in "I Have a Dream" represents a special type of public moral argument that functions to define and sharpen core communal values.

The issue of how core values are employed is made instructively problematic in Frederick Antczak's analysis of King's controversial Riverside Church speech, "A Time to Break Silence," delivered 4 April 1967. This is the speech in which King confirmed his unequivocal opposition to America's involvement in the Vietnam War, placing himself over and against both the Johnson administration and the mainstream advocates of civil rights who chose to be silent on the war lest they risk the success of the movement by affiliating themselves with an unrelated and divisive cause. King was quickly and viciously attacked from both sides. Those supporting America's involvement in Vietnam characterized him as a communist sympathizer. The more powerful and stinging accusation came from within the civil rights movement itself and from those who charged King with sacrificing the cause of civil rights in an attempt to bolster the waning power of the SCLC. The speech thus serves a serious and long-standing problem for the rhetorical and social critic concerning how to discern, distinguish, and account for the tension between the ethical and expediential motivations of public advocates.

Antczak argues that in this instance the solution to the problem can be addressed only by turning to the speech text itself, for those who would interpret King's motive on the basis of extrinsic or extratextual evidence miss the moral quality and tenor of King's ethical character. In examining the text, Antczak suggests that the speech embodies and enacts a complex revolution of values by shifting the meaning of the beloved community so as to transcend the false dichotomy between "us" and "them." In so doing, King empowers the revolutionary potential implicit in the nation's commitment to freedom and democracy by radically recharacterizing the audience being addressed and revising the discursive standards of decision making. This is not to deny that expedience is an important motivation for King. However, it is to suggest the significant degree to which expedience functions as King's larger commitment to enact a "moral stewardship of the living" by giving "a voice to the voiceless." Ultimately, Antczak's analysis of "A Time to Break Silence" offers an important insight into the general power of King's lifelong persuasion, for it demonstrates the sense in which King was a loving critic of America's social and political institutions as well as the way in which his leadership rhetorically performed the same critical demands that he would have the members of his beloved community enact, whatever the cost to himself.

Implicit in Antczak's analysis is an admonition to critics of all sorts to explore the intimate interaction between ethics and expedience in their discourse. The relationship between public discourse and academic criticism is addressed more fully in Michael Osborn's analysis of King's final speech, "I've Been to the Mountaintop." Osborn points out that the moral issues confronted by the public advocate and the critic are essentially the same, for each must ultimately justify his or her actions in terms of their effect on an "other" without regard to the personal risks involved. King engages the problem in his final speech by exhorting his audience to a "dangerous unselfishness" and recalling the parable of the Good Samaritan, who wonders not, What will happen to *me* if I assist those in need? but rather, What will happen to *them* if I fail to offer assistance? Analogously, Osborn addresses a key problem of academic criticism regarding the relationship between the critic and the object of criticism. The issue is not, What will happen to us as academic critics if we choose to ignore issues and events with which we are culturally and politically implicated? but What will happen to our cultural understanding of those issues and events if we choose not to address them as critical participants? By critically interpreting King's final speech from within the very texture of the event itself as a participant, Osborn offers the understanding of one who was there and experienced the speech as a living event, precisely at the moment at which, in his own words, "speakers, auditors, and events . . . come together in grand illumination . . . [and] time freezes [as] the meaning of its panorama stands revealed."

What is particularly engaging about Osborn's essay is the way in which his perspective as a critical participant in the rhetorical event testifies to the multiple tensions between being a preacher and politician, a revolutionary and a reformer, which characterize King's public life. The key to understanding King, Osborn maintains, is to recognize that in the final analysis he was *not* a political orator but a preacher, "a converter of souls." Thus, rather than to occupy ourselves with trying to understand how he achieved rhetorical power by simply integrating or transcending cultural values, we must focus much more careful attention on the specific crises of values that he caused his audiences to see and transform. As such, Osborn concludes, "what he was out to redeem was cultural sin, the way people treat each other as humans, the way they betray their own ideals." While we might therefore reasonably think of King as a more or less conservative political conciliator, one concerned to reform and revivify the underlying ideals of American democracy or the Judeo-

Christian ethic, he was also a radical revolutionary in the most fundamental sense of the word "radical," as one who identifies and characterizes the crises in our core values and commitments in an attempt to "save us from repudiating [our] own high principles."

The volume concludes with Robert D. Harrison and Linda K. Harrison's Afrocentric perspective on the performative dimensions of King's oratory and the sermonic function of call-response. Drawing specifically on Molefi Asante's analysis of the African foundations of *nommo* and the creative link it provides between speaker and audience, these authors show not only that the pattern of call-response is rooted in an African rhetorical tradition but also that its prominence in the black pulpit made it something with which both King and his black audiences would be familiar and comfortable. The larger point, of course, and it is one that Osborn supports when he recalls his own experience with the call-response phenomenon, is that to understand the creation of community and moral power attributed to King's public advocacy, one must look beyond the text of his words—whether written or spoken—to the very real and active interaction between speaker and audience that his performances enacted. The phenomenon of call-response is not the only source of this performative enactment, as a number of essays in this volume point out, but as Harrison and Harrison's analysis demonstrates, it is symptomatic of the core values of a community motivated by such interaction.

Taken as a group, the essays in this volume seek to identify and explain one of the sources of the power that Martin Luther King, Jr., wielded as a social and political leader. By describing that power through a rhetorical understanding of the spiritual and secular dimensions of sermonic discourse, we offer a perspective that helps to account for the relationship between the competing material and symbolic environments in which King operated. We hope what we have produced indicates the value in this perspective and will encourage others to join the endeavor, as a means both of enhancing our understanding of King as a political leader and cultural hero and of developing our knowledge of the role that individual agents can play in creatively crafting social and political change.

1

Alabama as Egypt: Martin Luther King, Jr., and the Religion of Slaves

Keith D. Miller

In his autobiographical essay "Pilgrimage to Nonviolence," Martin Luther King, Jr., explains his intellectual evolution as the result chiefly of his stint as a graduate student at Crozer Theological Seminary and at Boston University, where he read Hegel, Nietzsche, Marx, Walter Rauschenbusch, Paul Tillich, Reinhold Niebuhr, the Boston Personalists, and other Western philosophers and theologians. As if to emphasize his doctoral studies, King throughout his discourse sprinkles quotations of and references to many icons of Western culture, including Plato, Aristotle, Shakespeare, John Donne, Matthew Arnold, Carlyle, Tennyson, Emerson, Thoreau, Tillich, and Niebuhr.

Attracted to "Pilgrimage" and to King's quotations, scholars customarily ascribe his ideas and persuasiveness to what Stephen Oates calls "theological erudition" obtained in his graduate schools.[1] Harvard Sitkoff notes that King's "training in systematic theology had left him with an appetite for transcendent ideas, for theoretical constructs."[2] A whole book by Kenneth Smith and Ira Zepp traces the development of King's ideas and rhetoric to his course work at Crozer and Boston; another volume by John Ansbro provides an expanded but comparable examination. Smith and Zepp and Ansbro account for King's various positions by linking them one by one to the writings of Hegel, Marx, Rauschenbusch, Niebuhr, the Boston Personalists, Thoreau, Gandhi, and other thinkers whose tomes King investigated as part of his formal academic training. Paying scant attention to King's earlier environment in the black community, biographers and historians usually assume that white academia offered the future civil rights leader the intellectual climate that nurtured both his oratorical genius and his skill as a political strategist.[3]

This essay marches to the beat of a different drummer—an African-American drummer. The drumbeat is sounded by Eugene Genovese, Lawrence Levine, Molefi Asante, and Sterling Stuckey, who have greatly expanded our understanding of black life by challenging the common view that African-American culture and religion derive primarily from white America and ultimately from Europe. Building on the legacy of Melville Herskovits, these writers examine the African roots of black culture and later developments from those roots. Extending their general perspective to King, I claim that, while Crozer Seminary and Boston University did stimulate King's thought, black religion animated King's ideas and discourse much more than did his formal white schooling.

In a previous essay, "Composing Martin Luther King, Jr.," I opposed the standard interpretation of King's intellectual development, scrutinizing in detail each of the supposed Euro-American influences on King's intellectual maturation. This essay probes beyond that effort by exploring King's enormous, underlying debt to the black church. I maintain that the dominant theme of King's discourse and the typological epistemology undergirding it issue not from Hegelian dialectic or Niebuhrian social theory but from the world view of slaves. Assembling this argument requires an examination of slave theology and typology, theme and typology in the black pulpit, self-making in black folk sermons, King's relationship to the black church, and King's general theme and typology. I follow this analysis by investigating how all these elements shape two important addresses, King's sermon "Death of Evil on the Seashore" and his final speech, "I've Been to the Mountaintop."

Slave Theology and Typology

The theology of slaves featured both otherworldly and this-worldly salvation blended together to form what Eugene Genovese characterizes as "a pervasive theme of deliverance."[4] Frederick Douglass and others noted the double meaning of spirituals, which pointed both to heavenly redemption and to earthly freedom.[5]

One manifestation of the this-worldly side of slave religion was an intense and widespread identification with figures from the Hebrew Bible (or Christian Old Testament), especially the Hebrew people held captive in Egypt.[6] According to John Lovell, "nearly always, the slave chooses a revolutionary chapter from the Bible. Note that nearly all the Biblical personages the slave poet deals with were involved in upheaval and revolution (Moses, Daniel, David, the Hebrew children, Samson, Elijah, Gideon, Jesus, Paul)."[7] Identification with the Israelites is evident in many spirituals about Moses, the Pharaoh, the Red Sea, the wilderness, and/or the Promised Land. These songs include "My Army Cross Over," "O the Dying Lamb," "O It's Gonna Be a Mighty Day," "Wheel in a Wheel," "Didn't Ole Pharaoh Get Lost [in the Red Sea]," "I Am Bound for the Promised Land," "Leaning on the Lord," "Way Down in Egypt Land," "O Walk Together Children," "Turn Back Pharaoh's Army," "O Mary Don't You Weep," "Joshua Fit De Battle of Jericho," and "Go Down Moses."[8] Levine explains this identification as one that collapses history, replacing chronological time with a form of sacred time that allows biblical characters to become peers and contemporaries.[9] In Levine's words, "For the slaves, then, songs of God and the mythic heroes of their religion were not confined to a specific time or place, but were appropriate to almost every situation."[10]

How did typology inform the slaves' sense of sacred time? Typology essentially involves seeing Old Testament figures (e.g., Adam and Moses) as prototypes for New Testament figures (e.g., Jesus) or treating biblical characters as types that recur throughout history and that appear in the present as well. Typology patterns history according to knowable and repeatable forms of experience. It does not merely present a set of symbols, for believers view typological events as literally true. Nor does typology entail a set of analogies, for, unlike analogy, typology introduces and sustains an entire weltanschauung, fitting human experience into a system of interpretation both strong and flexible. While this system is theological, it is also epistemological, for it provides a means of self-recognition and social understanding: One understands one's self and others in a set of knowable and repetitive types of human experience as good and evil struggle in the recurring morality play of human existence.[11] Desmond Tutu provides an example of typological Christian thought: "Jesus is but the Greek form of Joshua who led the Israelites across the Jordan River into the Promised Land. . . . What was not fully realized in the Old Testament would find complete fulfillment in the New. Matthew sees Jesus as a second but greater Moses. . . . Luke, describing the transfiguration, tells us that the subject of the conversation between Jesus, Moses, and Elijah had to do with the destiny He was about to accomplish in Jerusalem. And Luke uses the Greek *Exodus* to describe that event. It can't have been merely coincidental."[12]

Slave religion functioned typologically when, as Genovese explains, slaves united Moses and Jesus "into the image of a single deliverer."[13] This conflation occurred, for example, in the lyrics of a spiritual:

> Jesus Christ, He died for me,
>   Way down in Egypt Land
> Jesus Christ, He set me free,
>   Way down in Egypt Land.[14]

In the experience of the ring shout, some slaves became, so to speak, their counterparts from the Bible.[15] Others saw Lincoln as Moses. In Asante's words, "the name Moses grew as important in Africans' minds as the person had been in Israel's eyes, and dominated the future of blacks as Moses had dominated the history of Jews."[16] The frequent and widespread nature of Moses/Pharaoh references in spirituals also testifies to an identification more profound and more sustaining than any offered by mere analogy, metaphor, or symbol. Expressing slaves' intense and persistent longing for freedom (from Moses/Pharaoh typology) provided hope in the form of a specific narrative equating blacks with an oppressed people whom God would eventually direct to the Promised Land.

Theme and Typology in the Black Pulpit

In black churches the theme of deliverance persisted long after slavery, as did the importance of scriptural heroes. Rev. Gardner Taylor, distinguished black preacher and longtime friend of the King family, observes that the sermonizing he heard as a boy presented "an indistinguishable mixture" of heavenly and earthly liberation, personal and social redemption.[17] Studying the black folk pulpit in rural Georgia in the late 1940s, William Pipes noticed strong identification with biblical figures.[18]

Often these characters were those involved in the Exodus. Just as David Walker, the fiery, nineteenth-century political radical, and Rev. Richard Allen, the first bishop of the African Methodist Episcopal Church, did not hesitate to identify slaves with the Chosen People chafing under the Egyptian yoke, black ministers in years subsequent to slavery continued to identify blacks typologically with the Israelites held captive by the Pharaoh. For example, five decades following the Emancipation Proclamation, Rev. L. J. Coppin used the Exodus to interpret the condition of American blacks: "Fifty years brings us to the border of the Promised Land. The

Canaan of our citizenship is just before us and is infested with enemies who deny our right to enter."[19] In 1926 Rev. J. M. Gates, a legend in the African-American folk pulpit, incorporated the lyrics of "Go Down Moses" into his recorded sermon "Moses in the Wilderness." Rev. C. L. Franklin, whom Tony Heilbut describes as "the most famous preacher in the gospel circuit," expounded the theme "Moses at the Red Sea."[20] During the 1940s and 1950s the highly visible, well-educated preacher and early civil rights activist Rev. William Holmes Borders delivered a number of sermons about the Israelites leaving Egypt.[21] Franklin's sermon "Dry Bones in the Valley" equates Hebrew slavery in Babylon with black slavery in America. Gates, prominent Baptist leader Rev. E. O. S. Cleveland, and other ministers also used "Dry Bones" to address the spiritual death and revival of the Israelites during their Babylonian captivity.

Sermonic repetition-with-variation on the typological theme of enslaved blacks/Hebrews never lost its usefulness for two reasons. First, the theme treated the condition of oppression blacks continued to experience under the system of segregation. How could preachers ignore the subject of slavery when blacks still suffered the semislavery of segregation? Second, the African-American religious community retained its sense of sacred time that acknowledged no boundaries of geography or chronology that could hamper the continued relevance of the biblical narratives of slavery and deliverance.

Self-Making in the Black Folk Pulpit

Preachers like Gates, Franklin, and Cleveland activate sacred time not only by invoking typological narratives but also by circulating sermons and embedding lyrics.[22]

Circulating Sermons

Forbidden by law from learning to read, slave preachers usually could not study the Bible and instead imbibed their faith from sermons and songs. Developing a profoundly oral pulpit tradition, these preachers at times reiterated each other's sermons—a practice that continued after the Civil War. One sermon enjoying widespread popularity was "Dry Bones in the Valley." Not only did Franklin, Gates, and Cleveland expound "Dry Bones," so also did numerous other homilists; at least five ministers recorded the ubiquitous sermon.[23] "Eagle Stirs Her Nest" ignited congregations at least as early as 1868 before appealing to Cleveland, Gates, Franklin, and others.[24]

Consider what happens when a pastor launches into "Dry Bones" or "Eagle Stirs Her Nest." Who is delivering the Word? Obviously, the individual homilist. But the preacher's voice is also the voice of earlier speakers. The voice and the identity of the preacher converge with those of sanctified predecessors who have previously articulated these popular homilies. Preachers create a voice and a self by merging their identities with other representatives of a well-known, authoritative tradition.

Embedding Lyrics

Anticipating the hymn of invitation that immediately follows the sermon, Franklin and many other Baptist ministers often incorporate the lyrics of spirituals and hymns into the last few sentences of their sermonizing. Cleveland frequently engages in this practice, capping one sermon with these words:

And with Jesus Our Leader, we shall Mount Up on Wings and Try the Air, and FLY-FLY-FLY-FLY-AWAY to Our Heavenly HOME. . . . Thank God I know How to Fly. Yes—I KNOW HOW TO FLY. . . .
Some glad morning when this life is over, I'll fly away To a home on God's celestial shore, I'll fly away. . . ."[25]

The final two lines and several succeeding lines serve as the lyrics of the familiar hymn "I'll Fly Away." But consider Cleveland's earlier declaration, "I KNOW HOW TO FLY," a statement that anticipates the lyrics. Who is the "I" of this sentence? The "I" is the person in the pulpit, but the "I" is also the narrative voice of the hymn, for the preacher interlaces the words of the hymn and the sermon, extending the hymn through the sermon and the sermon through the hymn. Following the sermon, each churchgoer joins the preacher in singing the hymn and, in the process of doing so, becomes the "I" of the lyrics. In addition, the "I" is everyone alive or dead who has ever vocalized "I'll Fly Away." All these identities converge in the preacher's extraordinary process of self-making.

Circulating sermons and embedding lyrics provide a means of self-making radically different from those offered by Euro-American print culture. Black folk preachers often do not create language from inside the self like a spider spinning a web by pulling material from its own body. Instead, they create an identity by subsuming themselves within the recognizable voices of a spiritual tradition. The procedures of self-making closely resemble the process of identifying with biblical figures: In both cases one discovers and defines a self according to a set of sanctioned, knowable, and recurring expressions of human personality. Both self-making and typology introduce sacred time by making the recognizable past (e.g., the Hebrews in captivity, a minister's sermon heard years before, a hymn sung by a parent or grandparent) immediately present. By activating sacred time, both self-making and typology provide a means for spiritual awareness and self-understanding and prevent history from deteriorating into a junkheap of cacophonous voices, unrelated experiences, and forgettable characters.

King's Relationship to the Black Pulpit

When Rev. Martin Luther King, Sr., moved to Atlanta, he apprenticed himself to Rev. A. D. Williams, who became his father-in-law. Williams whooped and moaned his folk sermons at Ebenezer Baptist Church. A political activist as well as a minister, Williams served as an NAACP fundraiser and agitated for the construction of the city's first black high school, which King, Jr., attended.[26] For his part the elder King, an able folk preacher, led a voting rights march in the 1930s and, in the words of his son, "this stern and courageous man . . . led the fight in Atlanta to equalize [black and white] teachers' salaries and has been instrumental in the elimination of Jim Crow elevators in the courthouse."[27]

Folk preachers Williams and the senior King attacked segregation from the Ebenezer pulpit, as did Borders from his pulpit one short block away. According to Borders, a young King often listened to his preaching in person and over an outdoor loudspeaker. King may also have heard the sermons of Gates, who pastored in Atlanta, and Franklin, who packed an Atlanta auditorium on several occasions and who once preached at Ebenezer Church. Furthermore, King could hardly have ignored Borders's highly successful social gospel ministry, his radio sermons, and his political visibility in the city.[28]

King scholars' claim that King learned the social gospel primarily by reading Rauschenbusch in seminary seems untenable when one considers the evangelical and political gospel expounded and practiced by the likes of Williams, the elder King, and Borders.[29] In reality, King's entire career expresses the liberatory theology of Ebenezer Church, the institution that nurtured him, and extends and intensifies the vision and commitment of his grandfather, father, and Borders. While King used his graduate studies to enlarge his self-understanding and his awareness of white society, he retained the theology of his community even though most of the elite thinkers he studied at Crozer and Boston rarely even mentioned the evils of segregation and racial inequality.

King's calm-to-storm, call-and-response delivery—especially evident in his addresses to black audiences—also reflects his training in the folk pulpit. So does his ability to lift an audience to a state of ecstasy and pandemonium at the conclusion of a speech or sermon. So does his recirculation of his own and other preachers' sermons.[30] So does his use of hymns and spirituals at the conclusion of most of his sermons and many speeches, including the most important ones—"I Have a Dream," "I've Been to the Mountaintop," "Remaining Awake Through a Great Revolution," "How Long?" and others.[31] In "I Have a Dream" he also enacts the self-making procedures of the folk pulpit by merging his voice with those of Amos, Isaiah, Jesus, Handel's *Messiah*, "America," and a spiritual.[32] Just as King scholars often effectively erase Williams and the elder King from any significant role in promoting King's intellectual development, and just as scholars almost entirely neglect Borders, they also overlook King's use of the themes, typology, and other resources for self-making provided by the black folk pulpit.[33]

King's General Theme and Typology

The slaves' pervasive, unequivocal theme of deliverance became the pervasive, unequivocal theme of the civil rights movement and of King's speeches, sermons, essays, columns, books, and politics. The theme reveals itself clearly in the movement's and King's application of the traditional Moses/Pharaoh typology. For example, civil rights songleaders updated "Go Down Moses" by taking the lyrics of the spiritual—

> Go down Moses, way down in Egypt land.
> Tell old Pharaoh to let my people go.

—and adapting them typologically to fit their own circumstance:

> Go down Kennedy, way down in Georgia land.
> Tell old [Sheriff] Pritchett to let my people go.[34]

King's lieutenant Wyatt Walker cites "Go Down Moses" and other spirituals as "the most suitable music" for the civil rights movement and regards "Go Down Moses" as offering "universal appeal for all oppressed people."[35] Agreeing with Walker, the leaders who organized the famous March on Washington distributed song sheets for "Go Down Moses" and other spirituals that served as anthems of protest. Spiritual and gospel singer Mahalia Jackson performed at the March and later described the proceedings in typological language: "here was a nation of people marching together. It was like the vision of Moses that the children of Israel would march into Canaan."[36] Such civil rights preachers as Kenneth Buford and Ralph Abernathy also equated segregated blacks with the Hebrews and powerful white rulers with the Pharaoh.[37]

Like song leaders and other preachers, King adjusted slave theology and typology to his situation. He often labeled racist opponents as Pharaohs, and many people—including white journalists—called him a black Moses. Outstanding civil rights organizer Septima Clark noted King's ability to mine the story of the Hebrews' escape from Egypt: "As he talked about Moses, and leading the people out, and getting the people into the place where the Red Sea would cover them, he would just make you see them. You believed it."[38] Andrew Young also observed King's and other activists' abilities to reinvigorate the familiar Old Testament and folk pulpit imagery of dry bones and the Exodus when straightforward political appeals had failed.[39] King repeatedly invoked the Exodus as an archetypal human experience—a narrative that spiraled through history—and, in unmistakably typological language, intertwined blacks' fate with that of the Hebrews: "The Bible tells the thrilling story of how Moses stood in Pharaoh's court and cried, 'Let my people go.' This was an opening chapter in a continuing story. The present struggle in the United States is a later chapter in the same story."[40]

"Death of Evil on the Seashore"

Delivered initially in 1956, "Death of Evil on the Seashore" is an early King sermon that the civil rights leader preached in several pulpits around the nation, including the Cathedral of Saint John the Divine in New York City, one of the nation's two or three most important liberal, white Protestant churches. Not content to reiterate the sermon orally, he included it in his homiletic collection, *Strength to Love;* he did so because he understood the immense power of the Exodus theme and its broad appeal to generations of blacks who sang songs of the Exodus and heard sermons proclaiming its message of liberation.

"Death of Evil" is especially important because it serves as the fullest and most extensive explanation of the biblical basis for the central theme of the civil rights movement—the escape from bondage to freedom. King's only sermon based entirely on the Exodus, "Death of Evil" provided him with an unparalleled opportunity to refute the complacency of white Christians who viewed dramatic social change as undesirable or impossible and objected to religious leadership of social movements. Intent on reducing Christianity to a personal fire insurance policy against the eternal flames of hell, southern whites could twist and constrict Jesus and—especially— Paul to suit their ends. The Exodus, however, militated against such a fundamentalist reduction because it undeniably involved massive, dramatic, social transformation as God placed his awesome power unequivocally on the side of an entire oppressed people, whom he led literally from slavery to freedom. More clearly than any other King pronouncement prior to his final speech, "Death of Evil" revitalizes the most noteworthy biblical precedent for radical social change and thus confounds fundamentalists' attempts to privatize religion. "Death of Evil" succeeds not simply because it reinterprets the Exodus but because it reawakens the slaves' theme of deliverance and their ability to telescope time and space. King begins his sermon by explicating the biblical Exodus, sketching the Hebrew march across the Red Sea and "the turbulence and momentum of the tidal waves" that drowned the mighty Egyptian forces.[41] Affirming the typological validity of the story, King remarks, "The truth of this text is revealed in the contemporary struggle between good in the form of freedom and justice and evil in the form of oppression and colonialism."[42] The Exodus reduplicates itself throughout the world, for, he declares, "In nearly every territory in Asia and Africa a courageous Moses pleaded passionately for the freedom of his people."[43] King organizes much of his sermon by way of a typological chain that extends the Moses/Pharaoh narrative into a variety of recent contexts. Relating how Gandhi and other Moses figures have rescued masses of Third World peoples "from the Egypt of colonialism," King explains that in the previous twenty-five years the number of independent countries in Africa had grown from three to thirty-two.[44]

Like Richard Allen, L. J. Coppin, J. M. Gates, C. L. Franklin, William Holmes Borders, and a multitude of other African-American preachers before him, King interprets the struggle of the slaves as a reenactment of the experience of the Israelites constrained within the Egyptian version of the peculiar institution. As King recounts the American chapter of the biblical story, Lincoln's signing of the Emancipation Proclamation brought the Negro "nearer to the Red Sea, but it did not guarantee his passage through parted waters."[45] Instead blacks suffered because "the pharaohs of the South" engineered an "Egypt of segregation."[46] Echoing the language of "Go Down Moses," King observes that southern oppressors "refused to let the Negro people go."[47] Then the Supreme Court split the Red Sea with its landmark decision of *Brown* v. *Board of Education of Topeka*, leaving the "forces of segregation" to face the fate of Egyptian soldiers left "gradually dying on the seashore."[48] Able to escape from Egypt, blacks through patient effort "shall reach the promised land."[49] Furthermore, any time God's people experience "the darkness of some oppressive Egypt," God can supply hope and redemption.[50]

In various places in the text King reinforces theological hope by reiterating a group of quotations from Shakespeare, Bryant, Carlyle, Lowell, Tennyson, Arnold, and Charles Beard. As I explain elsewhere, each of these quotations serves as a commonplace in liberal white homiletics, and each testifies to the ultimate triumph of good over evil.[51] One might ask: If good defeats evil and if God sent his ultimate revelation of himself two thousand years ago, why does evil return and even seem to prevail? The answer is that evil repeats itself typologically as, in King's words, "the death of one tyranny is followed by the emergence of another tyranny," which in turn dies on the seashore when the Egyptian narrative inevitably reasserts itself.[52]

"I've Been to the Mountaintop"

On the night before his assassination, King delivered his final speech, "I've Been to the Mountaintop," to a meeting of striking garbage workers and their supporters in Memphis.[53] In "Mountaintop" he revives the Moses/Pharaoh typology more effectively than he had ever dared before. The incandescent brilliance of the address derives mainly from his wholehearted and highly imaginative reconception and adaptation of the slaves' theme and typology of liberation.

In "Death of Evil" King and the civil rights movement remained largely outside the typological narrative as Lincoln guided blacks/ Hebrews toward the Red Sea and as the Supreme Court parted the waves with its epochal 1954 decision. By contrast, in "Mountaintop" King boldly inserts himself and the movement into the narrative and locates the new/old struggle of blacks/Hebrews in the expansive universe of the slaves—a universe that admits of no distinctions of space and time or of heavenly and earthly deliverance.

Calling Ralph Abernathy "the best friend that I have," King starts his speech with the "I" of his everyday self—a plain, straightforward "I" who is a close friend of Abernathy.[54] But he immediately enlarges the "I" when God enables him to undertake a grand tour of history. Adapting the slaves' sense of sacred time that erases all barriers of chronology and geography, King slips into a time machine to witness the Exodus and observes other profound events in ancient Greece, ancient Rome, and Renaissance Europe. Extending his magical travels through time and space, he gazes at Martin Luther ("the man for whom I'm named") as Luther nails his theses on the church door at Wittenberg; he next spies Lincoln signing the Emancipation Proclamation and listens as Franklin Roosevelt consoles a nation.[55] Several of these events—especially Luther's protest and Lincoln's declaration—were world-changing expressions of the broad, historical movement from oppression to freedom. These occurrences seem to serve as typological recapitulations of the Exodus.

Scanning all these majestic sights, however, would not satisfy King the time traveler, for he "wouldn't stop there" but would instead ask God to lead him into the present, where he could witness an enormous political awakening across Africa and the United States and learn that "the cry [of the oppressed] is always the same—'We want to be free.'"[56] Although the American awakening occurs in an atmosphere of crisis and confusion, it deserves to be cataloged among the greatest, most earth-shaking events in all Western history.

King next appeals for nonviolent solidarity, remarking that "whenever Pharaoh wanted to prolong the period of slavery in Egypt," he "kept the slaves fighting among themselves."[57] To frustrate this strategy, King urges mutual support: "When the slaves get together, that's the beginning of the end of slavery. Now let us maintain unity."[58] Who is the "us" of this sentence? The "us" are Egyptian slaves; the "us" are also King's listeners, the Memphis garbage workers, who chafe against the fetters of an American pharaoh.

After analyzing the struggle in Memphis, the civil rights leader reviews the movement's shining moment in Birmingham when demonstrators courageously faced police dogs and fire hoses as Police Commissioner Bull Connor failed to realize that protestors possessed "a certain kind of fire that no water could put out"—a sanctified, holy fire largely responsible for an enormous landmark in American race relations—the Civil Rights Act of 1964. Clearly the achievement of the Birmingham campaign seems to replicate the successful struggles King had cited before—the Exodus, the Reformation, the emancipation of American slaves, and Africa's emergence from European colonialism—and to exemplify the contemporary struggle he also noted.

After relating the experience of Birmingham, King declares, "Now we've got to go on to Memphis just like that."[59] Preachers should support the endeavor, King maintains, because "Somehow the preacher must be an Amos and say 'Let justice roll down like waters and righteousness like a mighty stream.' Somehow the preacher must say with Jesus, 'the Lord . . . hath anointed me to deal with the problems of the poor.'"[60] Undergirding this assertion is the typological assumption that religious leaders can and should leapfrog chronological time. A contemporary preacher can then be an Amos and can accept Jesus' mission to the poor. In this religious system, the needs of the poor are paramount and are essentially identical in the ages of Amos, Jesus, and twentieth-century America.

King next warns ministers not to focus on otherworldliness. He cites familiar black pulpit imagery of "long white robes over yonder" and heavenly "streets flowing with milk and honey," insisting that pastors who evoke "the new Jerusalem" must also outline "the new Memphis, Tennessee."[61] Like the clergy Gardner Taylor heard as a child—some of whom almost certainly were former slaves—King here blurs heavenly and earthly salvation, for the "new Memphis" is the "new Jerusalem" set down squarely on earth. After calling for local boycotts, King analyzes the Good Samaritan and tells his audience to treat sanitation workers as the Good Samaritan treated the innocent victim beaten along the roadside.

Then King remembers an attempt on his life in which a woman stabbed him in the chest; because he would have died had he merely sneezed, King reports his happiness over not sneezing. Sneezing would have prevented him from savoring watershed events in the agitation for civil rights. Extending the time-machine tour of history he used to open "Mountaintop," he enumerates examples of the American political awakening that he had hailed earlier: the 1960 lunch-counter sit-ins, the Albany movement, the Birmingham demonstrations, the delivery of "I Have a Dream," the Selma marches, and the Memphis garbage strike.

Here King arranges the undeniably noteworthy events of the crusade for civil rights within the context of several of the most important events of all time, including the Exodus, the Reformation, and the Emancipation Proclamation. The "I" who avoided sneezing also zoomed through time, pausing to witness epochal moments in the quest for freedom. King asserts that the meaning of the current struggle is quite comparable, if not identical, to the meaning of the Hebrews' triumph over Pharaoh, Luther's efforts to reform a corrupt church, and Lincoln's freeing of the slaves. Like previous episodes of the civil rights movement, the drama of Memphis allows for a successful reproduction of the Exodus because human identity remains stable in King's updated rendition of the inclusive, typological universe of the slaves, who invoked sacred time as they yearned for Moses to appear in the Egypt of Alabama and Mississippi.

King ends "Mountaintop" by describing his pilot's extra safety precautions, referring to recent threats on his life, and reflecting on the possibility of assassination. The ominous tone of these statements builds upon the atmosphere of crisis he had evoked immediately following his journey in the time machine. He had exclaimed: "The world is all messed up. The nation is sick. Trouble is in the land. Confusion all around."[62] Now his recounting of the nearly fatal stabbing incident and recent death threats intensifies the atmosphere of crisis and the looming possibility—or likelihood—of tragedy. All the dark imagery that King summons in "Mountaintop" reflects and modifies the vision of impending doom and Satanic hellfire common in the revivals led by traditional Baptist preachers, including those held in his home church. Here King simply applies a political, this-worldly twist to a stock theme of evangelical and fundamentalist sermonizing.

But King is not content to situate the movement within the narrative of crisis and typology and to locate himself as a performer in the drama. Perhaps because of his sense of the near-inevitability of his assassination, he ignores the risk of showboating and concludes "Mountaintop" by dramatically installing himself at the head of the typological procession. For the first time in his career, he boldly and explicitly equates himself with Moses, whom God had led to the top of a mountain where he could gaze upon a Promised Land he could not enter: "I just want to do God's will. And He's allowed me to go up to the mountain. And I've looked over. And I've seen the Promised Land. I may not get there with you. But I want you to know tonight that we as a people will get to the Promised Land. So I'm happy tonight. I'm not worried about anything, I'm not fearing any man. Mine eyes have seen the glory of the coming of the Lord!"[63]

King's final sentence is the first line of "Battle Hymn of the Republic." Union soldiers sang the lyrics as they marched into the Civil War, and churchgoers have often sung them as well. To whom does the personal, possessive pronoun "mine" of "mine eyes" refer? "Mine eyes" are the eyes of the narrator of the hymn. "Mine eyes" are also the eyes of Moses, the prototype in the Old Testament, who sees the glory of the coming of Christ the Lord, the fulfillment of the type in the New Testament. Moreover, "mine eyes" are the eyes of all people who have sung the anthem before, including soldiers and churchgoers. Of course, "mine eyes" are also the eyes of King, the speaker, the "I" of the speech—King the friend of Ralph Abernathy; King the interpreter of biblical typology who insists that the preacher "must be an Amos"; King the preacher who blurs this-worldly and otherworldly deliverance; King the activist who justifies his politics by aligning Memphis garbage workers with the recipient of compassion in Jesus' greatest parable; King the time traveler who observes the panorama of the Exodus, the Reformation, and the Emancipation Proclamation; King the sojourner who completes his historical odyssey by witnessing the sit-ins, the Birmingham crusade, the Selma protests, and the Memphis strike; and King the leader who repeatedly risks martyrdom. *All* these selves—the narrative voice of "Battle Hymn of the Republic," Moses, Union soldiers, earlier hymn-singing Christians, and King in his multiple, yet cohesive, identities—merge in King's extraordinary act of self-making.

Failing to adhere to a linear, European view of history, King involves himself and his audience in a single process of self-discovery and persuasion within a universe of sacred time that unites heaven and earth and fuses chronologically disparate characters and events. This process and this universe have little to do with the theories of the individual and history espoused by Rauschenbusch, Hegel, Marx, Niebuhr, the Boston Personalists, Tillich, Gandhi, and others whom King studied in graduate school. Instead, the typological theology and rhetorical process of self-definition manifested in "Death of Evil" and "Mountaintop" represent the consummate expression of the distinctive theology, epistemology, and rhetoric developed by slaves and sustained over many decades by humble, usually anonymous, and often illiterate African-American folk preachers.

Throughout his career and especially in "Mountaintop," King's oratory illuminates the American landscape because, like the slaves singing a certain spiritual, he essentially testifies that the road he and other blacks walked in Alabama and Georgia was the same "rough, rocky road what Moses done travel."[64]

2

The American Dilemma in King's "Letter from Birmingham Jail"

E. Culpepper Clark

Overture

"There is no chance for a political solution in South Africa unless there is a complete change of heart." This simple declaration, uttered by the bishop of the Dutch Reform Church in South Africa in response to a question from Morley Safer of CBS, seems so simple as hardly to need declaration at all. It sounds something like, "Yes, and if tomorrow morning we all wake up bright pink, the millennium will be at hand"—or so one might reason in reaction to such naive proclamations about the heart. And yet the same simple credulity drove the American human rights movement, with all its ups and downs, fits and starts, from the awakening of the American mind in the 1740s to the awakening of the American heart in the 1940s.

The formula for conversion of mind and heart seemed equally as simple: Fight a war, justify the sacrifice in terms of human freedom, then codify the justification. History confirmed the formula. The revolutionary war for independence, justified by a rhetoric of inalienable rights, gave rise to what Bernard Bailyn called a "contagion of liberty" that ended slavery in New England and infected neighboring middle states with the same progressive impulse. Trampling the grapes of wrath in a bloody Civil War created sufficient "moral capital" to yield the Thirteenth, Fourteenth, and Fifteenth amendments to the Constitution. Fighting the war to end all wars inspired the Eighteenth and Nineteenth amendments, while making the world safe for democracy launched America's Second Reconstruction.

In this sense history for America becomes a moral drama with time on the side of progress. Read Lincoln not as Gore Vidal would in the hackneyed, debunking spirit of the cynical New Left but as a schoolchild should read Lincoln: to learn lessons about time and progress and doing good. In this light the Great Emancipator *did* free the slaves *only* to save the Union, but he saved the Union because he believed it essential to the progressive improvement of the human condition. True, Lincoln *did not* believe blacks to be equal; but he could not conceive of a government dedicated to the proposition that they were not. Time, Lincoln thought, and the American Republic were on the side of equality, and when Stephen Douglas suggested that the founding fathers did not intend to include blacks in their declarations about equality, Lincoln ridiculed the little judge for his narrowness of vision.

Martin Luther King, Jr.'s "Letter from Birmingham Jail" is one of the great documents in this expanding tradition of human equality. It, too, is premised on the goodness of man. The letter is addressed to white clergymen who condemned King for adopting "direct action" tactics just at the moment when gradualism seemed to be working in Birmingham, Alabama. King chides these clergymen and seems to say that they and moderates like them are the principal obstacles to change. But at a deeper level King still holds to the view that the conscience of the white majority is essential to success. King may have regarded the "Letter from Birmingham Jail" as an appeal to Pharaoh, but the black Moses also believed that God hardened Pharaoh's heart so that in the end God's work and his signs might be made manifest.

The Letter as Invention

Most scholarly treatments of King's letter focus on its rhetorical form and its parallels to the epistolary tradition in Christianity.[1] These essays discuss at some length both the arguments King made and the intended audience. They all assume that King wrote the letter and that its success in large measure is owed to King's rhetorical genius. Though ultimately I subscribe to both assumptions, neither can be accepted without question. On the issue of authenticity, it is now commonplace that much of what King wrote and said was ghostwritten. Bayard Rustin, Stanley Levison, Nat Lamar, and Clarence Jones did a lot of work for King, and black author Al Duckett wrote most of the text for *Why We Can't Wait*, which chronicles the Birmingham campaign and includes an edited version of the original "Letter from Birmingham Jail."[2]

Adding to the suspicion about authenticity is the fact that no trace of King's original writing from the jail survives, nor does the typescript that was made from King's notes and allegedly shuttled to and from the jail for King's editing. Surely, one might reason, those who assisted King in the letter's production, and especially Wyatt T. Walker, a consummate media strategist, would have seen the historical value in such documents and would have preserved them for posterity. The first published copy of the letter did not appear for over a month after it had been written, and then as excerpts in the *New York Post*. The *Christian Century* published the first dependable copy on 12 June, two months after completion. A duplicated copy of the letter did circulate in Birmingham, but the date of its distribution is not known, and the American Friends Service Committee agreed to mass-produce the letter in booklet form. The only validation of King's authorship, external to those involved in its production, comes in a phone conversation, tapped by the FBI, between King and Stanley Levison. In this conversation, King talks about having written the letter and having excised at least fifteen thousand words.[3]

The letter, as eventually published, ran six thousand words, or about twenty book-sized pages. If King was right, then he wrote in three days approximately seventy pages of text, a prodigious effort under the best of circumstances.[4] The point, however, is not whether King wrote the letter. The point is that the letter had to be written. As we shall see, time and circumstance conspired to make it necessary, and like Voltaire's God, King's "Letter from Birmingham Jail" would have had to be invented had it not existed. His movement was under attack from the very people he needed for support: white moderates, the Kennedy administration, and black professionals in Birmingham. A document was needed, and in keeping with Christianity's higher law tradition, jail provided the ideal setting for its production. In fact, it so filled Christian expectations that black ministers in later years called for its inclusion as a chapter in the Bible. Also, it is noteworthy that King had been urged in the summer of 1962 to produce a similar letter from his jail cell in Albany, and for similar reasons, only to be persuaded by no less an authority on mass persuasion than Billy Graham's public relations specialist that the time was not right.[5]

The question of who wrote the letter or how it was written is important only because it underscores the interplay between rhetoric and audience, between the speaker and expectations. No matter how the document was written, there can be no doubt that both the inspiration and the style were King's. Nor can there be doubt that King wrote some or all of the letter while incarcerated. When later the scene is set, the imagination will be the story line of legend: King writing on the margins of the newspaper that contained the letter of the eight clergymen and, when that was exhausted, on toilet paper. In exercising this imagination, I also do not quarrel with those scholars who have patiently explored each line of the letter to reveal King's rhetorical genius. While I personally believe King to have spoken and to have written more eloquently on other occasions, on each reading of the letter I still hear the rolling thunder of his majestic voice as phrases and metaphors echo his Olympian oratorical power.

Thus I believe that the letter is authentic and moving, but I also believe that its authenticity and its appeal are the product of unfolding context. Perhaps only now has enough time elapsed to speak historically. Absent the historical perspective, the letter becomes a rhetorical event of and for 1963. Thirty years later, it can be viewed as a rhetorical document that served both to end one phase of the Second Reconstruction and to herald a new and, as of that time, unsettled beginning. To provide this perspective, I will describe the circumstances that brought the letter into being, the tradition of protest to which the letter belongs, and those features of the letter that pointed in a new direction. The first portion is by far the longest. In this section I set the scene and describe the multiple audiences for whom King wrote. In the second section I place King in the intellectual tradition articulated by Gunnar Myrdal, and in the final portion I discuss his break from the Myrdalian perspective. In some final thoughts, I return to the introductory notes about the rhetorical vision implicit in the American human rights tradition.

Scene 1

When King targeted Birmingham for the late winter and early spring of 1963, the SCLC and the movement were struggling. On 10 January, King and his chief lieutenants met in the little community of Dorchester, just outside Savannah, Georgia, to plan the Birmingham campaign. Dorchester had been a locus for black activity ever since Charles Colcock Jones, a slaveholder and accomplished defender of the regional faith, established a mission there in the 1840s to Christianize slaves. In 1963, through a grant from the National Council of Churches, the old Congregational mission operated as an SCLC citizenship training center under the direction of Septima

Clark. Above all, the Dorchester conferees did not want to repeat the Albany experience. In that southwest Georgia city the SCLC failed strategically by attacking segregation in general, rather than one of its particular manifestations such as busing or lunch counters, and it failed tactically by going after elected officials rather than the business community. Laurie Pritchett, the city's wily police chief, was not the typical tobacco-stained, sweat-soaked sheriff who emerges from the heat of the night. He proved to be a slippery target who knew how to flirt with the media. As a result Albany gave the movement some publicity but no symbols of brutal segregation and no tangible results. Failure in Albany meant that the SCLC risked losing its leadership to the students of SNCC or to CORE.[6] The time had come to pick the biggest apple of segregation.

Birmingham provided both opportunity and danger and for the same reasons. The city honestly earned its reputation as the most intransigent citadel of segregation. Dynamite became the weapon of choice, and the sobriquet "Bombingham" stuck. Locals named one middle-class black neighborhood "Dynamite Hill." Since 1957 there had been twenty-nine unsolved bombings in the city. In 1960 Harrison Salisbury wrote that "fear and hatred gripped Birmingham," and in turn the city sued the famous reporter for his temerity. Many blamed the city's problems on an industrial labor force, drawn from the farms and hill country of Alabama and governed by absentee owners from Pittsburgh. "The obvious thing about Birmingham," said one faculty member at the University of Alabama, "is that there's just a lot of goddamn white trash that's conglomerated there."[7]

More to the point was the absence of meaningful leadership from the business and legal community. Perhaps because Pittsburgh controlled the labor force, these merchants and lawyers acted with all the irresponsibility of those who are in fact powerless. Whatever the reason, they forfeited the city to Eugene "Bull" Connor. Since the 1930s Connor had made a career of busting both labor unions for his northern bosses and blacks for his hard-fisted followers. When in 1938 Birmingham hosted the Southern Conference on Human Welfare, considered the high-water mark of prewar southern liberalism, Connor and his private security force chafed outside while inside Eleanor Roosevelt and her southern friends presided over an interracial fete. By the 1950s Connor had become the commissioner of police and relentlessly set about enforcing the informal and formal sanctions of segregation. Because of Connor and the racially heated climate in Birmingham, King warned those gathered at the Dorchester meeting that some would die.

Scene 2

Bull Connor and possible death made Birmingham the most dramatic target for a movement in desperate need of a victory in the war to make the South safe for its black citizens. But Birmingham presented still another problem. The city was changing. A November plebiscite overturned the old commission form of government in favor of a mayor and council structure. Those who supported the new form of government were determined to get rid of Bull Connor, who was a candidate for mayor. With key mayoral elections set for 5 March, local black leaders and the Kennedy administration insisted that King put off demonstrations until 14 March. When the 5 March elections resulted in a runoff between Connor and the more soft-spoken segregationist, Albert Boutwell, moderates again importuned King to delay direct action tactics until after 2 April.

Connor's defeat at the polls raised hopes among white moderates and some black leaders that the pace of interracial progress would quicken. The day after the election, the new mayor proclaimed: "This, happily, is a new day for Birmingham. There's a new feeling in the air. There's a new spirit of optimism."[8] Bargains struck by black leaders with the white business community in the fall of 1962 had been set aside for fear of doing anything that would enhance Connor's fortunes. Now the prospects looked good for renewing those agreements. With Connor's demise, King faced the prospect not only of a lost symbol but of a divided black community as well.

Birmingham's blacks had long been among the South's most active in demanding human rights. In the thirties and forties they pushed aggressively for voting rights and for equity in salaries for black teachers. They supported the successful suit to desegregate the University of Alabama and raised money to aid the black applicants. In recognition of their enterprising spirit the NAACP located its southeastern regional office in Birmingham in 1952. Early leadership, however, meant old leadership by 1963, and many resented the black movement's new Moses. Moreover, King's man on the scene, Rev. Fred Lee Shuttlesworth, exacerbated tensions among Birmingham's black leaders. He possessed the courage of a lion and, some feared, the judgment of an enraged bull. When in 1956 a state court enjoined the NAACP from operating in Alabama, Shuttlesworth organized the Alabama Christian Movement for Human Rights and affiliated with the SCLC. He immediately undertook quixotic campaigns to desegregate Birmingham's buses and schools with predictably disastrous results.

Those who had been chiefs in the NAACP resented Shuttlesworth and his claims of divine guidance, which they considered, at best, brash. The same NAACP old guard considered King to be an inter-loper, and they wrote derisively of his late entry into their fray. As late as 1965, W. C. Patton, state president of the NAACP in the fifties, referred to King as "De Lawd," accused him of making "double jointed" speeches in Birmingham, and resented the "twenty-three staff members" who made up his entourage.[9] After visiting Birmingham in 1962, Paul Rilling of the interracial Southern Regional Council wrote a confidential interoffice memorandum. "One of the most depressing factors," he observed, "is the apathy and divisiveness of the Negro community. The Ware group, the Shuttlesworth group, the Gaston Circle, are working at cross-purposes and constantly at loggerheads. Emory Jackson of the local *World* [the black newspaper] serves the role of spoiler and tends to cut down potential leaders and movements with satire and other attacks."[10]

Still, it was a measure of King's preeminence and his persuasive power that by Easter of 1963 he could count on a united Negro leadership in his campaign to boycott white merchants and to fill the jails. He could count on their support because he too proved willing to pay the price. On the night of 11 April, King vowed to fulfill his pledge to the demonstrators by joining them in the Birmingham city jail. His father protested, but King knew that he had to maintain credibility with the demonstrators who already sat in jail. So on 12 April, Good Friday, he set off with a small band of followers to test Bull Connor's police. Wyatt T. Walker, his top lieutenant at SCLC, walked alongside the little parade, camera in hand. Within days Walker would have the symbols for which he schemed from the beginning: King in jail and dogs and fire hoses turned on the crowd. Walker knew the movement stood in critical need of symbols, and he counted correctly on Bull Connor's obliging the need. After all, Connor himself bragged that all he needed to solve the racial problem was "two policemen and a dog."[11]

The Audience

The threads of the story are now familiar. Eight white clergymen publish an open letter, coincidentally delivered to the *Birmingham News* on the day King enters jail for violating the ban on demonstrations and published the following day. (Ironically, the leading signatory and the man who delivered the letter to the newspaper was Bishop C. C. J. Carpenter, the great-grandson and namesake of Charles Colcock Jones, who founded the Dorchester mission near Savannah where King planned the Birmingham campaign.) These clergymen are the same men who, along with three others, in January published an open letter titled "Appeal for Law and Order and for Common Sense," a letter that took exception to George Wallace's ringing declaration for "segregation now, segregation tomorrow, and segregation forever." Their stand on that occasion drew threats and intimidation from diehard segregationists.[12] Now in April the clergymen condemn King as an outsider and counsel patience. They believe that local conditions favor mediation. King begins composing a response and shuttles the text in and out of jail by way of New York attorney and personal friend Clarence Jones and local attorneys Arthur Shores and Orzell Billingsley. Wyatt Walker goes over the copy each evening and has it typed by his secretary, Willie Pearl Mackey, before returning it to King for his editorial changes.

By 16 April the letter is finished. At some point, another of King's personal friends, Addine Drew, wife of one of Birmingham's most successful black businessmen (King stayed with the Drews while in Birmingham), claims to have gathered various manuscript fragments and to have had a copy typed by Rose White, a secretary at all-black Miles College. If Drew's recollection is correct, it appears that two copies of the letter were produced at the time: one by Walker and his secretary and one by Drew and her secretary.[13] Whatever the circumstances of its production, the letter is not delivered to its ostensible audience—a fact that rankled the clergymen who believed their motives and their courage to have been maligned in the interest of promoting King and his movement, not the betterment of Birmingham.[14] Nor do the Birmingham newspapers publish it. At the request of another movement leader, James Lawson, the American Friends Service Committee mass-produces the document under the title *Tears of Love,* and copies are circulated in Birmingham but create no public stir. The first known publication of the letter appears, unbeknownst to the author, in the *New York Post Magazine* on 19 May, more than a month after it is completed and then only as excerpts. Like other great rhetorical touchstones, the artifact is not recognized in its upsurge.

Also like other great rhetorical acts, it is not the product of the moment. In the FBI-tapped conversation with his friend Stanley Levison, King mentions having taken out over fifteen thousand words for fear that the letter was too long. Of course fifteen thousand is an exaggeration, something on the order of saying "a lot," but because there was nothing new in the letter, it is easy to imagine King having written much, if not all, of it in a short time. He had said or written it all before, often with the help of ghostwriters who faithfully reflected his thought. In late January, right after the Dorchester meeting that targeted Birmingham, King appeared at a symposium in Chicago and presented a paper titled "A Challenge to the Churches and Synagogues."[15] Many of the arguments and some of the phrasing in the Birmingham letter reflect the Chicago essay. Even the style is familiar. When King moves from argument to exhortation in the letter, he simply moves from the podium to the pulpit. King is not writing out of some epiphany, born of lonely confinement in a southern jail. His aim is more immediate and pragmatic. He is creating an argument in response to rifts between his movement and white moderates and to an equal extent between himself and Birmingham's own powerful and skeptical black clergymen who feared that direct action would compromise their hard-won negotiating position with the Birmingham power structure. King is also seeking to advance the fortunes of the SCLC against rival black organizations demanding more extreme tactics. It is a letter of justification.

By 1963 King believed federal authority to be the essential ingredient for change. In places like Little Rock, Ole Miss, and even in the Freedom Rides, though fraught with violence, the movement achieved positive results because the federal government had a clear reason to intervene, be it to enforce the *Brown* decision or fairness in interstate transportation. Birmingham was different. Demonstrators were being jailed for failure to obtain parade permits, and the Kennedy administration, in keeping with its general caution, was loathe to intervene on so local an issue. Moreover, unlike King's advisers, the administration believed Birmingham to be on the cusp of change. At the very moment the Dorchester decision was being made, Attorney General Robert Kennedy received a letter from a liberal white lawyer thanking him for agreeing not to come to Birmingham at that time because of the "delicate nature of our local situation."[16] Unlike the SCLC, the Kennedy administration proved sensitive to local imperatives.

Thus King felt compelled to justify both direct action and being in Birmingham at all. In fact King devoted the whole opening of the letter to a justification of his presence. He noted that the Alabama Christian Movement for Human Rights had affiliated with the SCLC and as such made his presence natural. Of greater moment, his citizenship as a Christian demanded his presence. Like Paul, he had the world for his parish. He was in Birmingham "because injustice exists here," and "just as Paul left his village of Tarsus and carried the gospel of Jesus Christ to the far corners of the Greco-Roman world, so am I compelled to carry the gospel of freedom beyond my own hometown. Like Paul, I must constantly respond to the Macedonian call for aid." No community was an island. "I cannot sit idly by in Atlanta and not be concerned about what happens in Birmingham. Injustice anywhere is a threat to justice everywhere. We are caught in an escapable network of mutuality, tied in a single garment of destiny. Whatever affects one directly, affects all indirectly. Never again can we afford to live with the narrow, provincial 'outside agitator' idea. Anyone who lives inside the United States can never be considered an outsider anywhere within its bounds."

Not only did King feel it necessary to justify why he was in Birmingham when the Kennedy administration thought it prudent to avoid confrontation, but he also felt it necessary to justify direct action at a moment when negotiation at last seemed to produce results. One can imagine King writing quickly at this point, for he had spent an entire week in February speaking to black business and professional leaders, not white moderates, to convince them that now was the time and Birmingham the place.[17] Here, the arguments for white clergymen and for black professionals became the same. "You may well ask," he acknowledged, "'Why direct action? Why sit-ins, marches, etc.? Isn't negotiation a better path?'" "You are quite right," King conceded, "in calling for negotiation. Indeed, this is the very purpose of direct action." Direct action created "tension," which King believed to be the necessary condition for negotiation. "I have earnestly opposed violent tension, but there is a type of constructive, nonviolent tension which is necessary for growth. Just as Socrates felt it necessary to create a tension in the mind so that individuals could shake off the bondage of myths and half-truths and rise to the realm of creative analysis and objective appraisal, so must we see the need for nonviolent gadflies to create the kind of tension in society that will help men rise from the dark depths of prejudice and racism to the majestic heights of understanding and brotherhood." The words tumbled from his pen and showed the marks of an uneasy combination of argument, historical allusion, and metaphor, but when one must combine and demonstrate wisdom, knowledge, and style in the teeth of implacable skepticism, elegance is often the first casualty.

The Myrdalian Enthymeme

King made a similar argument before a mass rally the day after Boutwell's euphoric victory in Birmingham's municipal elections. With Ralph Abernathy and Shuttlesworth at his side, he told the demonstrators, "If you create enough tension you attract attention to your cause" and "get to the conscience of the white man."[18] Of course, conventional wisdom is that the appeal to conscience formed the cornerstone of King's nonviolent philosophy. King's belief that the white man had a conscience susceptible to moral suasion constituted his leap of faith and shaped the movement he led. Ironically, to accept that notion, King had to accept the white man's personal assessment of his own soul, an assessment first conspicuously elaborated in Gunnar Myrdal's *An American Dilemma.*

It is not clear at what point King became familiar with the work of Myrdal, the Swedish economist who published *An American Dilemma* in 1944. Myrdal's massive two-volume treatment of race relations in America coincided happily with the moral fervor generated by World War II and later formed the sociological basis for the *Brown* decision. Myrdal argued that because the white man in the South had subscribed to the egalitarian creed of Thomas Jefferson, he could be persuaded by moral argument premised on that creed. The moral distance between creed (all men are created equal) and deed (segregation) created a dissonance, or what Martin Luther King, Jr., called "tension," that could be resolved only by progressively moving toward an extension of human rights. Thus time was on the side of those who advocated change. Southern intellectuals quickly adopted Myrdal's notion. In a justification for outside agitation that could easily have been written by King himself, a young historian, later to become a prominent scholar of the American South, denied "that 'outside' criticism weakens the forces of moderation in the South and generates nothing but intransigence. . . . It remains to be recognized," he concluded, "that criticism has other effects in a libertarian society, especially when the criticized share many of the assumptions [namely the American Creed] on which the criticism is based."[19]

Of course Myrdal did not fashion his argument from whole cloth. He simply compiled the best liberal thinking of the 1930s, particularly liberalism in the South. Myrdal focused this thought. By the time King finished his theological training at Boston University, he was conversant with Myrdal's ideas, and later King visited the Nobel Prize-winning Swede on several occasions.[20] Moreover, King used the idea of "tension" precisely as Myrdal intended it: Through nonviolent, civil disobedience, create a tension between the white man's deeds and his creed. The resulting guilt would place the white South on the intellectual defensive. Thus paralyzed, the white man's laws could be changed, and once changed, the heart would follow. It was a formula that offered hope and encouraged suffering and ultimately love of one's enemy.

It was also a naive formula. Even as King made it the cornerstone of his movement, his former mentors at Boston University were skeptical of its success.[21] Civil disobedience, they reasoned, might succeed in India where the oppressed constituted an actual and significant majority, but in the South, where blacks constituted the minority, it had little chance. Others joined the critique. In the late forties and fifties, sociologists and psychologists began an all-out assault on Myrdal's value-driven sociology and especially his pet notion about the role of tension and dissonance. Guilt did not lead necessarily to a rational resolution of feelings. Bigots, they found, were as susceptible to behaving destructively when confronted with their guilt as constructively. In *A Theory of Cognitive Dissonance*, Leon Festinger proved there were myriad ways of resolving dissonance without ever confronting, much less reconciling, moral dilemmas.[22]

Still, I am not sure that the studies would have moved King even had he acknowledged them. Social scientific truth about human behavior could not substitute for rhetorical possibilities of human behavior. When King complained to Levison about having to cut whole sections from his Birmingham letter, he noted particularly "a section—strong—[that the] whole idea [of the] struggle was not just something for the Negro but how it also frees the white man. . . . And it's to save the soul of America."[23] Moreover, he addressed the letter specifically to clergymen and generally to white moderates, not bigots. In one of the letter's most pointed sections, Kings says: "I must make two honest confessions to you, my Christian and Jewish brothers. First, I must confess that over the past few years I have been gravely disappointed with the white moderate. I have almost reached the regrettable conclusion that the Negro's great stumbling block in his stride toward freedom is not the White Citizen's Councilor or the Ku Klux Klanner but the white moderate who is more devoted to 'order' than to justice; who prefers a negative peace *which is the absence of tension* to a positive peace which is the presence of justice; who constantly says, 'I agree with you in the goal you seek, but I cannot agree with your methods'; who paternalistically believes he can set the timetable for another man's freedom; who lives by mythical concepts of time and who constantly advises the Negro to wait for a 'more convenient season.' Shallow understanding from people of goodwill is more frustrating than absolute misunderstanding from people of ill will. Lukewarm acceptance is much more bewildering than outright rejection."[24]

King clearly despaired of the white moderates, but he was not about to abandon them. He saw strategic value in the Myrdalian approach even if it did not win outright converts to the cause. In summing up the Birmingham campaign, King noted a paralysis that swept the white community in 1963. "Strangely enough," he observed, "the masses of white citizens in Birmingham were not fighting us." Only a year before "Bull Connor would have had his job done for him by murderously angry white citizens," but in 1963 they stayed away. King was not foolish enough to believe "that they were in sympathy with our cause. . . . I simply suggest," he concluded, "that it is powerfully symbolic of shifting attitudes in the South that the majority of white citizens in Birmingham remained neutral through our campaign."[25]

The whole "Letter from Birmingham Jail" is an appeal to conscience along the same lines that Myrdal thought would work. Toward the end of the letter King proclaimed, "We will reach the goal of freedom in Birmingham and all over the nation, because the goal of America is freedom." To reach the goal, moderates in the white community were essential, a handful as allies, the vast majority as neutral noncombatants. Either way they contributed. And if appeals to conscience alone were not sufficient, King warned white moderates of dire consequences should they reject the hand of brotherhood offered through a common creed. "I stand," he wrote, "in the middle of two opposing forces in the Negro community. One is a force of complacency made up of Negroes who, as a result of long years of oppression, are so completely drained of self-respect and a sense of 'somebodiness' that they have adjusted to segregation. . . . The other force is one of bitterness and hatred, and it comes perilously close to advocating violence." The message was clear. Reject nonviolent, civil disobedience, grounded as it was in an appeal to conscience, and reap the whirlwind.

Transformation: 1963 and Beyond

King was a master of political theater. A Christian minister, jailed in a righteous cause and criticized by eight Pharisees, presented King an opportunity he could not pass, a confluence of time and circumstance from which flowed a mighty stream of rhetoric. In its floodplain, local conditions and imperatives slipped from sight. The clergymen, who after all had been among the first to speak for racial change even as they urged moderation to let the forces for change work, were ever after branded bigots, at best old tree stumps along the banks of this mighty stream, impeding but not influencing its progress.[26] On the other side, Fred Shuttlesworth, who invited King to Birmingham, came to believe that King had bargained away the hard-earned gains of Birmingham's black community in an effort to placate the Kennedy administration. Shuttlesworth saw the letter itself as one more evidence of King's willingness to sacrifice the movement for his own personal ends. His mixed feelings still showed a decade later. "My feeling," he said, "was that the letter should have been signed jointly by all of us . . . simply because we had agreed to do things together, you know. It wouldn't have taken anything for him to let me, but I guess as I look at it now . . . I think King deserves all the credit. . . . He was the spokesman, and he was the one that God chose to be the charismatic person for that age, and you can't argue against what God does, you know."[27]

But King's legacy was not to be measured in the pain of misunderstood intentions or frustrated egos. More than anyone else, King expressed the philosophy of the movement for racial justice because he understood it better than anyone else. Shuttlesworth may have known its confrontational edge better, but King knew its transforming rhetorical potential. Writing from the Birmingham city jail in 1963, King saw that the movement was on the precipice of great change. In a foreword to a 1963 book on the Negro leadership class, King repeated Ghandi's oft-quoted remark: "There go my people, I must catch them, for I am their leader."[28] The Myrdalian view that dominated the movement for almost twenty years was nearing the end of its rhetorical usefulness. The assassination of Kennedy and the Johnson legislative successes gave the vision life through 1964, but violence in the movement brimmed on the horizon and indeed flared momentarily during the 1963 Birmingham campaign.

King's awareness of this changing temper led him to alter one of the cardinal tenets of the Myrdalian perspective: that time equaled progress. This presumption about time and progress, into which Myrdal breathed new life, had been the linchpin of the American human rights movement from its inception in the Great Awakening. But two hundred years had passed, and America's blacks had very little to show for all that time. "Time itself," King now wrote in his famous letter, "was neutral." There would be no "convenient seasons." Moderates must act now or forfeit the future to extremists. The whole Birmingham struggle was about time. King had "hoped that the white moderate would reject the myth concerning time in relation to the struggle for freedom. . . . More and more," he continued, "I feel that the people of ill will have used time much more effectively than have the people of good will." Then, breaking sharply with the Myrdalian ideal, King concluded, "Human progress never rolls in on wheels of inevitability." As if to punctuate King's thought, the executive director of the Alabama Council on Human Relations, a white man, observed, "Birmingham has made it crystal clear to the country that gradualism is no longer a possible approach to our racial problem."[29]

When King wrote the letter, he had five years to live. In those last years he seemed to grope for the right words and the right formula to catch up with his people. Those of us forty-five and over, especially the whites among us, were the children of King's movement. We now lament the passing of that first phase, 1944 to 1964, when the issues were matters of conscience, guilt, and the prospect of ushering in a century of Christian progress. Sooner than we should have, we transmogrified into young adults of the late sixties and seventies, still passionate but also angry and suspicious. The enemy was no longer our own souls to reclaim, but the establishment and all symbols of authority from which racism and war emanated. We could not distinguish between love and hate, nor did we find it useful. We could not differentiate between compassion for the common soldier and flowers in a gun barrel. Appeals to conscience were no longer chic, and we welcomed in its place an angry rhetoric designed to lacerate the feelings of white America while cloaked in a mantle of cultural pluralism. In all this we were eminently right.

But our new-found rectitude came at the expense of our youth and our naiveté. In his "Challenge to the Churches and Synagogues," the speech that foreshadowed his "Letter from Birmingham Jail," King spoke of love not as "emotional bosh" or "spineless sentimentality. . . . It would be nonsense," he said, "to urge men to love their oppressors in an affectionate sense." Instead, he spoke of love as "treating fellowmen as persons, understanding them with all their good and bad qualities, and treating them as potential saints." Love, he said, would "cause us to enter the new age which is emerging without the fatigue and poisonous drain of bitterness." Love would not tolerate the substitution of one supremacy for another; "black supremacy is as injurious as a philosophy of white supremacy." "God is not interested," he concluded, "merely in the freedom of black men, and brown men, and yellow men; God is interested in the freedom of the whole human race." The forgiveness of love, he declared, was "necessary for both the oppressor and oppressed alike."[30]

Retrospectively, King's letter seems like hopeless sentimentality, something on the order of changing the hearts of white South Africans. But we cannot doubt his success. In 1960, Harrison Salisbury compared Birmingham to Stalin's Moscow and Hitler's Germany, reigns of terror he knew from experience. His editors at the *Times* deleted those two references, but even at that, Salisbury thinks he understated the ugly temper of Alabama's "Magic City."[31] Not long ago on NBC's *Today Show*, Salisbury declared Birmingham, more than any city he knew, to be living the American dream. The declaration may have been hyperbolic, but it is clear that in Birmingham Martin Luther King, Jr., at the very least lifted the crushing weight of segregation from the city's white community, if he did not remove completely the shackles of racism from its black community.

King's own words smile back from the past. "I like to believe," he wrote, "that Birmingham will one day become a model in southern race relations. I like to believe that the negative extremes of Birmingham's past will resolve into the positive and utopian extreme of her future; that the sins of a dark yesterday will be redeemed in the achievements of a bright tomorrow. I have this hope because, once on a summer day, a dream came true. The city of Birmingham discovered a conscience."[32] It was for Fred Shuttlesworth, King's ally, gadfly, and occasional nemesis, to put Birmingham into perspective. "Birmingham," he observed, "really made SCLC. In fact, when we [later] went to the White House, Kennedy . . . used these words: 'But for Birmingham, we would not be here today.' 'But for Birmingham'; I think that oughta be remembered."[33]

Coda

My purpose has not been solely to lament the passing of the first phase of America's Second Reconstruction into the realpolitik of the second—nor to assert that one vision was superior to the other. Indeed we know enough about tides in human affairs to know that they ebb and flow out of some inability to sustain for more than a generation any single mode of thought. Each way of thinking in its own season is right. King and Myrdal were right to believe that tension arising from the creative primacy of the American Creed would yield progress. The social psychologists and the black power advocates were right to conclude that such hopes were more optimistic than realistic.

One should read the letter not only for its pivotal argument about time and progress but also because it stands in synecdochical relationship to the movement King inspired. One cannot now imagine documentary anthologies including King's earlier "Challenge to the Churches and Synagogues," though his arguments are the same and his style equally appealing. The letter becomes essential reading because the circumstances of its creation fulfilled Judeo-Christian expectations, cultural expectations that King transformed into the controlling metaphor for interpreting nonviolent civil disobedience. The letter could have been shorter or longer, arranged differently, or fashioned from other stylistic material. It is not like the Gettysburg

Address, elegant beyond other imaginings. Still, it is a moving letter, as eloquent as most of King's pleadings. What gets the letter into the anthologies is a jail cell in the land of the Philistines and a prophet calling to his people. It resonates with the Judeo-Christian struggle against human bondage.

Reconstruction of the Rhetorical Situation in "Letter from Birmingham Jail"

Judith D. Hoover

Although not literally a speech, "Letter from Birmingham Jail" has been shown by Malinda Snow to be a sermon, not in a "limited, modern sense" but in a functional sense.[1] The letter itself, whether a sermon or an essay, has been reprinted by a variety of biographers, editors, and organizations and is considered an "eloquent expression of the philosophy of the American civil rights movement."[2] Martin Luther King, Jr., wrote the letter on scraps of paper while in jail for walking through the streets of Birmingham protesting a court injunction against demonstrations.[3] In his letter he responded to a letter published in the *Birmingham Post Herald* and *Birmingham News* on 13 April 1963, which consisted of "criticisms . . . voiced by local white religious leaders."[4]

These leaders urged that court orders be "peacefully obeyed," since "responsible citizens" had begun to work on the causes of "racial friction and unrest." Now, they charged, "unwise and untimely" demonstrations are being "directed and led . . . by outsiders," even though the "facing of issues" could be handled by "citizens of our own metropolitan area." The white ministers' letter denounced even peaceful protest as incitement to "hatred and violence" as well as "extreme measures." It commended the local Birmingham community, the news media, and "law enforcement officials in particular" for their "calm manner" and urged "restraint." Finally, it concluded by suggesting that the "Negro community . . . withdraw support" from "demonstrations" and press its cause in "the courts." In so doing, it appealed to the principles of "law and order and common sense."[5]

King's arrest and his letter in response came at a time when both he and the civil rights movement labored under the weight of court orders and financial difficulties. Bail for hundreds of marchers in a variety of cities had had to be raised and then raised again. An injunction issued by a state court, ostensibly to preclude violence, stopped peaceful marchers in their tracks. The phrase "law and order" became synonymous with white supremacy, and thus the innocent and even righteous-sounding appeal disguised the segregationist intent.

That the assertion of "law and order" came from white clergy, one of the few groups in the South King hoped would support his nonviolent campaign, complicated his "rhetorical problem" in Birmingham. Both King and the civil rights movement faced multiple needs and thus addressed multiple audiences. The various groups within the movement competed for scarce resources and leadership opportunities. After all, the Kennedy administration moved cautiously on civil rights when it moved at all.[6]

To confound King's problems, the "NAACP had lost members when the Rev. King seized the initiative in the South," and "King had lost prestige when he stayed only two days in jail in Albany, Georgia," the result of an earlier march. Other "spokesmen and action groups were competing for leadership, for followers, and necessarily for headlines." A "crisis" would give them greater "bargaining power" and exert more "creative pressure" on the president.[7]

Solitary confinement in Birmingham provided King an opportunity to construct an essay that accomplished multiple functions: to answer his immediate critics, to show the legitimacy of nonviolent resistance, to counter the claim that law enforcement officials were showing restraint, and to repair and build his ethos that had been damaged by charges that the movement's anonymous leadership consisted of unwise outsiders who had no sense of proper timing and no respect for the law.

An analysis of King's letter provides a window on the connections between a rhetorical artifact and its context. Lloyd Bitzer refers to this context as the rhetorical situation and outlines three constituents of this context: an "exigence" or need that can be modified by rhetoric, an "audience" consisting not of mere hearers but of "mediators of change," and "constraints" that are part of the situation and can modify the exigence. Of course, the context also includes the speaker and the message. To Bitzer the rhetorical situation calls forth and thus creates the rhetorical response.[8]

Richard Vatz disagrees with Bitzer by claiming that rhetoric creates situations by focusing attention on salient features chosen by the rhetor and creates meaning by interpreting and translating the features' significance through the use of "value-laden" language. Rather than giving "situation" the power to "dictate" rhetoric, Vatz shows that a rhetor controls both the characterization of the situation and the response to it.[9]

In this essay I argue that King's "Letter from Birmingham Jail" is neither only a response to the rhetorical situation created by others nor only a means to dramatize the situation and regain his damaged credibility by strategies of political apologia. Additionally, the letter gave King a means of appealing to a wider audience than Birmingham's white clergy by a significantly broader interpretation of the situation than they had described in their public letter. He could attract the notice of both President Kennedy and the leaders of other segments of the civil rights movement by enacting what he called "creative extremism." In the letter King moved beyond a defensive posture toward the creation of a new rhetorical situation crafted through his careful layering of values to build contrasting hierarchical structures. King took ethos-building strategies beyond response, beyond defense, into the realm of constructive argument through which he created a new rhetorical situation to which others would then be forced to respond.

Apologetic Response to Existing Rhetorical Situation

Good debaters respond to the charges or claims of their opponents, and King clearly followed this imperative. A preliminary summary of his strategies by way of B. L. Ware and Wil A. Linkugel's concept of political apologia is helpful in this regard, for it highlights how King countered these claims and then moved past them to unite his appeal with an overarching system of values. The model of apologia through which a speaker attempts to defend him- or herself after an attack consists of four different but related strategies: denial, bolstering, differentiation, and transcendence. If the speaker either cannot or does not choose simply to deny the charges, then the three other options remain available. Bolstering involves connecting the rhetor with some thing or concept approved by the audience, while differentiation separates the rhetor from the existing audience reality, and transcendence places the rhetor above that reality. A speaker or writer may combine these factors in order to achieve absolution, vindication, explanation, or justification for either self or actions.[10]

King refuted the claim that he was an "outsider" first by denial.

He referred to his presidency of the Southern Christian Leadership Conference (SCLC) and showed that his office provided his "organizational ties" in Alabama. If this were not enough, he used "bolstering" to connect himself with the eighth-century prophets and Saint Paul, all of whom left their homes when they heard a call for help.[11]

King made at least sixteen such references to ethos in the letter, either for himself or for the civil rights movement, all of which may be considered a part of his apologetic strategies because they helped provide a "fitting response" to the rhetorical situation. First, because the letter to which he was responding failed to mention him by name, he not only identified himself, but he also very neatly defined himself as a leader (president of the SCLC) who both administered (had secretaries) and accomplished goals ("constructive work"), all in the first two paragraphs.[12]

He then turned to biblical and historical sources, tying himself and the civil rights movement to the prophets and the saints, to Socrates, to Jesus, and to those identifiable to his readers as "creative extremists." He quoted Reinhold Niebuhr and Martin Buber, Paul Tillich and T. S. Eliot. He claimed brotherhood with his critics and looked forward to meeting them, not as an "integrationist" but as a "fellow clergyman."[13]

To counter the charge of precipitating violence, King used logical denial, showing that such reasoning blames the victim. He compared himself to the "robbed man" whose money caused the "evil act of robbery." He spoke of Socrates and Jesus and then concluded that "it is immoral to urge an individual to withdraw his efforts to gain his basic constitutional rights because the quest precipitates violence."[14] To counter the charge of extremism, King bolstered his public character by connecting his activities with "good extremists" such as Saint Paul, Martin Luther, Abraham Lincoln, and Thomas Jefferson. He concluded that "the South, the nation, and the world are in dire need of creative extremists."[15]

King sought vindication from the charge that his activities were "untimely" by combining a list of Birmingham's "history of wrongs," such as police brutality and unsolved bombings, with a list of his own group's virtues, such as the goal of self-purification. He further sought justification by showing that the existing power structure was "dedicated to the task of maintaining the status quo" and by asserting that no direct action movement had ever been seen as "well-timed" by those who had not suffered from the "disease of segregation." He concluded that " 'Wait' has almost always meant 'Never' " and that they had already "waited for more than 340 years."[16]

To counter the charge that extremist demonstrators were causing violent disturbances and breaking laws, King sought moral justification by showing that the "white power structure" left them "no other alternative."[17] In his references to early Christian "agitators" who also broke laws but "pressed on, in the conviction that they were called to obey God rather than man," King employed the strategies of bolstering and transcendence to gain vindication and justification.[18] He also sought absolution from the charge of breaking the law by carefully particularizing the charge, dividing the laws into just and unjust categories, and then defining and exemplifying both kinds.[19] It is precisely in this differentiation that the heart of King's argument rested.

King devoted more time and space to refutation of the "law and order" argument than to any other. He distinguished between just and unjust laws by looking for a "harmony with the moral law," to see if the "human law" were "rooted in eternal and natural law." He looked for laws that "uplift" rather than "degrade" the "human personality." He condemned segregation because it "distorts the soul and damages the personality" and results in false senses of superiority and inferiority. He said that segregation was "politically, economically, and socially unsound" as well as "morally wrong and sinful."[20]

King further defined an unjust law as "a code that a . . . majority group compels a minority group to obey but does not make binding on itself" and likewise a "code . . . which that minority had no part in enacting or creating because they did not have the unhampered right to vote." A law may be "just on its face and unjust in its application," such as that for which he was arrested that denied "citizens the First Amendment privilege of peaceful assembly and protest."[21]

King portrayed those who broke unjust laws "openly and lovingly" as "expressing the highest respect for the law." His examples included both early Christians facing the lions and Socrates, whose "civil disobedience" led to the development of "academic freedom." He turned from ancient to modern examples in invoking those who disobeyed Hitler's "laws" against giving "aid and comfort" to Jews. He vowed he would "openly advocate disobeying . . . anti-religious laws" if he "lived in a Communist country . . . where . . . principles dear to the Christian faith are suppressed." He condemned most severely the "white moderate who is more devoted to 'order' than to 'justice,'" and he asserted that "law and order exist for the purpose of establishing justice."[22] Finally, he expressed disappointment that ministers had asked their congregations to "comply with a desegregation decision because it is the law." He preferred, instead, that they say, " 'Follow this decree because integration is morally right and because the Negro is your brother.' "[23]

Creation of a New Rhetorical Situation

While we may be able to analyze the rhetorical context for King's letter by looking at his response to the public letter from the white clergy, is it possible to describe the "rhetorical situation" in Birmingham, in the South, or in the nation in April 1963? Taylor Branch requires over a thousand pages to describe it in *America in the King Years*.[24] Kenneth O'Reilly spends nearly half that number in *The FBI's Secret File on Black America*.[25] The archives of the Birmingham Public Library contain thousands of pages of police surveillance reports, meticulous descriptions written by white police officers observing the Alabama Christian Movement for Human Rights (ACMHR) in its mass meetings that had been going on for seven years by 1963.[26] In these three sources the reader is repelled by but engrossed in violence—in beatings and shootings, in lynchings and bombings, in senseless pain inflicted on those demanding rights by those righteously sure of their superiority. The reader also sees the Federal Bureau of Investigation passively and silently fulfilling its intelligence-gathering mission while freedom riders, sit-in protesters, nonviolent marchers, and children are pistol-whipped, barricaded inside burning busses, kicked and urinated on, bitten by police dogs, and flung down city streets by high-pressure water cannons.

In the police reports we find nightly pleas for volunteers who will "march to jail for freedom" and for contributors who will pay to bail them out. We are moved by descriptions of the reassurances given by preachers to parents of jailed children that their sons and daughters will safely get out of jail, even though those descriptions were written by members of the Ku Klux Klan, who "supplied ad hoc personnel for the police department's surveillance squad."[27] We read direct quotes from speeches, one from King after Birmingham's worst night of violence, 10 May 1963, in which he said, "There may be more blood to flow on the streets of Birmingham before we get our freedom, but let it be our blood instead of the blood of our white brother." According to Officer B. A. Allison, King "cautioned them to hold their heads high and be nonviolent."[28]

Other than calls for boycott and nonviolence, the most common theme running through the speeches of men like James Bevel, Ed Gardner, A. D. King, Abraham Woods, Ralph Abernathy, and Fred

Shuttlesworth was "going to jail." On 6 March, Shuttlesworth, president of the ACMHR, asked the audience of six hundred assembled at the Saint James Baptist Church if any were willing to go to jail "to further the cause of the movement." The police report noted that the answer was "unanimous including the white people" at the meeting.[29] On 3 April, Shuttlesworth announced that twenty-five people had come to him that morning and said, "Here's my body." He replied that if they were not ready to "go to jail and give your body and your soul to our movement then go home." They chose jail. At that same meeting, Shuttlesworth introduced King, who had just arrived from Atlanta, and advised his hearers to "Follow him to jail. In the end he will lead us to freedom."[30]

In his own speech that night King explained the steps in nonviolent action: collection of facts, negotiation with your opponent, direct action, and nonviolent action. Direct action, he said, "may mean going to jail but we are ready." Nonviolent action could result in jail, but, he said, "Suffering has a way of getting to our opponent's conscience."[31] Abernathy, SCLC treasurer, spoke next declaring that he had come to Birmingham "because Martin Luther King is here and I have gone through hot and cold with him. We have been in jail together." When asked for volunteers to follow King to jail, "approximately 75 or 80 people from the congregation came forward."[32] These speeches from Shuttlesworth, King, and Abernathy set the tone for the Birmingham campaign. Nearly every night one speaker or another would announce the number in jail, ask for testimony from those who had been in jail, call for more volunteers, and ask for bail to get them out.

Variations on the theme included references to King's trips to Africa and India where "the leaders . . . had been to jail several times for freedom before freedom was granted."[33] Those who could not go to jail were urged to participate in the boycott, to "keep our money in our pockets and out of the downtown merchants' pockets." King and others began wearing overalls and other old clothes on 6 April to tie together the ideas of the boycott and going to jail. King urged "our friends all over the country to wear old clothes to church on Easter Sunday." He announced that Shuttlesworth was in jail and that he, too, would soon go. He boasted, "I have been in jail twelve times, and this time in Birmingham will make thirteen." All the other speakers that night proclaimed their intentions to go to jail, including John Porter, M. H. Smith, A. D. King, and Andrew Young.[34] Two nights later Al Hibler sang for the crowd and announced that he had "come down to Birmingham to go to jail for freedom." Abernathy claimed that he and King were going to jail and challenged the audience to go with them because "If you go with me President Kennedy will be looking in, Lyndon Johnson will be looking in and 'Old Bull' will be shaking in his boots."[35] Hibler was "refused the honor of going to jail . . . [because] they didn't have anything at the City Jail that he could do." Hibler quoted the city's public safety commissioner, Bull Connor, as saying. "You are blind and can't work."[36]

With this emphasis on the imagery of jail, King's journey to the Birmingham jail seemed almost inevitable. However, there was nothing inevitable about it, for King both chose the emphasis and chose when and under what circumstances to be arrested. On Wednesday, 10 April, King and Abernathy announced their plan to march on Good Friday, 12 April.[37] On Thursday, 11 April, they spoke in defiance of the new state injunction that forbade marching. On Friday, 12 April, they marched. After being taken into custody, "King disappeared into solitary confinement, 'the hole,' sealed off from his fellow prisoners and the outside world alike." According to Branch, "Silence made the tumult of his arrest fade into memory, and a man accustomed to an intense bombardment of news and emotion passed over into a vacuum where day and night were indistinct."[38]

Into this vacuum, this interlude in chaos, flowed time. King said in a speech three weeks later in Birmingham, "every time I go [to jail] it's a new spiritual experience. You can get a lot of things done that you need to do and you can't get done in the hurly-burly of everyday life. Jail helps you to rise above the miasma of everyday life. You can think about things. You can meditate a little."[39] His thoughts and meditations during this trip to jail enabled him to rise above the miasma of Birmingham, to redefine the "problem," to interpret reality for himself, and then, most important, to superimpose that interpretation over the arguments of his opponents. He needed to transcend law and order, to replace paternalism with brotherhood, to assert that human oppression among citizens had no place in American society. The need that could be satisfied by discourse consisted not only of defense but also of restructuring, in this case and at this time in American cultural life, restructuring of attitudes about human beings.

Chaim Perelman and L. Olbrechts-Tyteca claim that "argumentation is an action which always tends to modify a pre-existing state of affairs." Their view of argumentation as an alternative to violence blends well with King's philosophy of nonviolence. To Perelman and Olbrecht-Tyteca the "presence" of argumentation "assumes the establishment of a community of minds, which, while it lasts, excludes the use of violence."[40]

In order to lay a foundation for his new rhetorical situation, King phrased his letter in the form of an affirmative argument, and to the "community of minds" he stated his case: "I am in Birmingham because injustice is here." He identified "just" and "unjust" laws, "extremism," and "negative" and "positive peace" as his key terms, and then he laid out the following contentions:

- "We are . . . tied in a single garment of destiny."
- " . . . freedom is never voluntarily given by the oppressor; it must be demanded by the oppressed."
- "One who breaks an unjust law must do it openly, lovingly . . . , and with a willingness to accept the penalty."
- "We must use time creatively, and forever realize that the time is always ripe to do right."
- "Oppressed people cannot remain oppressed forever."
- " . . . the question is not whether we will be extremist, but what kind of extremist we will be."
- " . . . the judgment of God is upon the church as never before."
- "We will reach the goal of freedom in Birmingham and all over the nation, because the goal of America is freedom."
- " . . . it is wrong to use immoral means to attain moral ends."
- " . . . it is just as wrong, or even more so, to use moral means to preserve immoral ends."[41]

King tied each contention into his case with evidence from example, from testimony of renowned philosophers and political heroes such as Jefferson, and from the Bible and the Constitution. He reasoned from analogy. He threatened that if nonviolence failed, "millions of Negroes . . . will seek solace and security in black nationalist ideologies, a development that will lead inevitably to a frightening racial nightmare."[42] He argued a question of value by weighing one set of values against another and justifying his hierarchical placement through a combination of reason and threat.

Audience

The eight ministers to whom King responded composed only his immediate audience. They could not function as the audience capable of effecting change of the magnitude needed for reconstructing a world view. King's juxtaposition of positive and negative values in the letter reveals that certainly the "fellow clergymen" made up but a small segment of his intended audience. They were neither responsible for all the harms he deplored nor capable of accomplishing all the goals he desired.

David Lewis asserts that King's message was aimed at "professional theologians" and "meant to have the special impact redolent of the divinity-school seminar." King, Lewis says, wanted to raise memories among these clergy of their young dreams of "truly Christian service," of "emulating the conduct of the early saints."[43] Snow asserts that "white American churchgoers" were the "major audience of the 'Letter.'"[44] She finds this focus in King's indictment of those who have "remained silent behind the anesthetizing security of stained-glass windows."[45]

On a national level President John F. Kennedy and his attorney general, Robert Kennedy, were, of course, bound by the values of "law and order," and the president had used the phrase in numerous speeches.[46] Still, they were not tied into the segregationist values of the local and state political establishments of Alabama. Sorensen says that black leaders were "angry at the Kennedys for requesting a moratorium on demonstrations while an agreement was worked out and the [Birmingham] city government settled." Indeed, he goes on to claim that although they "knew they had a President willing to listen and learn," they were impatient for him to "do something."[47]

Those attending the mass meetings in Birmingham heard constant references to the Kennedys, who in turn heard a great deal about the civil rights movement, particularly from J. Edgar Hoover and the FBI. As early as the 1920s and 1930s, the FBI connected the movement with communism and later "noted the efforts of such black comrades as Hosea Hudson of Birmingham to 'conduct classes in cooperation with the NATIONAL NEGRO CONGRESS for the purpose of teaching negroes how to become qualified voters.'"[48] The bureau compared the Communist Party's views on lynching with those of "journals like *The Nation* and the *New Republic*" and concluded that "only communists supported racial justice in America." To Hoover, "the advocacy of racial justice was itself a subversive act."[49] Although its agents in the role of information gatherers witnessed all the major events of the civil rights era, "not even the most disturbing incidents of brutality unduly troubled the FBI."[50]

With notable exceptions, the Justice Department's representatives were no more "activist" than were the FBI agents. Robert Kennedy preferred fewer sit-ins and freedom rides and more emphasis on the "more manageable and less confrontational voting litigation campaign."[51] The attorney general, according to Branch, had spoken in opposition to the Birmingham demonstrations as an "ill-timed ambush on a reform city government that was not yet in office."[52]

Neither Kennedy could afford to "ignore political reality as they saw it," and as a result, they chose not to "alienate the white South."[53] Neither could they force the FBI to change its no-arrest policy nor "take an aggressive stand on the protection issue themselves."[54] In a phone conversation from Robert Kennedy's office in early 1963, King "pleaded with [the president] to include civil rights legislation in his State of the Union address." The president replied that "he could do more for civil rights by appointment and executive order than by the futile, costly gesture of sending impassable bills to Congress."[55]

Constraints: Values

If King wished to speak to religious leaders and churchgoers, as well as to law and order advocates such as the president and the attorney general, and to competing factions and leaders in the civil rights movement itself, he had to find a method of tying their diversities together. The unifying threads running through both the letter and the ministers' criticisms consist of woven strands of values. Richard L. Johannesen defines values as "conceptions of the Good or The Desirable that motivate human behavior and that function as criteria in our making of choices and judgments."[56] Perelman and Olbrechts-Tyteca show that "values enter, at some stage or other, into every argument" and that values appeals are made "in order to induce the hearer to make certain choices rather than others."[57]

Both King's letter and the ministers' letter contrast positive values either with their opposites or with outcomes that result from failure to adopt the values. Figure 1 illustrates these message elements in the letter from the clergy in the order in which they were written. King's letter is much lengthier than the ministers' letter, and he expands upon and gives many examples of some of his values and outcomes. Figure 2 illustrates these message elements generally in his order of presentation.

Figure 1

Values	Negative Values/Outcomes
law and order/common sense	racial friction and unrest
obedience to court decisions	natural impatience
honest/open negotiation	unwise/untimely activities
calm manner of police	hatred and violence
public restraint	actions that incite violence
protection of city	extreme measures[58]

Figure 2

Values	Negative Values/Outcomes
justice	injustice
beloved Southland	segregation laws
dialogue	monologue
eternal/natural law	unjust law = no law
protection of the "robbed"	blame of the victim
brotherhood/democracy	paternalism
human dignity	complacence
obedience to God	obedience to law
discipline/courage of marchers	brutality of police[59]

King's own words bring passion, beauty, and clarity to these abstractions. In his denial of outsider status and his defense of nonviolent demonstrations, he says, "I am in Birmingham because injustice is here." He describes the injustice that "engulfs this community," such as the "ugly record of brutality," the "unjust treatment [of Negroes] in the courts," the "unsolved bombings of Negro homes and churches," and the "humiliating racial signs." Through "nonviolent direct action," he shows, "creative tension" will "help men to rise from the dark depths of prejudice and racism to the majestic heights of understanding and brotherhood."[60]

In answer to the charge regarding the timeliness of the protest, he asserts that the rights for which they have waited so long are "constitutional and God given." He explains that "there comes a time when the cup of endurance runs over, and men are no longer willing to be plunged into the abyss of despair."[61]

In terms of the law-breaking charge, he places one law above another and claims that "a just law is a man-made code that squares with the moral law or the law of God." Thus "segregation is not only politically, economically, and sociologically unsound, but it is morally wrong and sinful." The same is true of laws against marches, since they "deny citizens the First Amendment privilege of peaceful assembly and protest." In all cases the "higher moral law" ought to take precedence.[62]

King deplores the "paternalism" of the "white moderate" who "believes that he can set the timetable for another man's freedom." He wishes such persons "would understand that law and order exist for the purpose of establishing justice." He asserts that "now is the time" to achieve democracy and brotherhood and to "lift our national policy from the quicksand of racial injustice to the solid rock of human dignity."[63] He seeks to motivate the white "religious community largely adjusted to the status quo, a taillight behind other community agencies" that could instead become a "headlight leading men to higher levels of justice."[64]

In his conclusion King links his appeals and groups the values clusters that he wishes to leave in the thoughts of his readers. He hopes that "one day the South will know" that the "disinherited children of God" who "sat down at lunch counters" were really "standing up for what is best in the American dream and for the most sacred values in our Judaeo-Christian heritage." Those same children took the "nation back to those great wells of democracy which were dug deep by the founding fathers in the formulation of the Constitution and the Declaration of Independence."[65]

Constraints: Values Hierarchies

Rhetoricians have long explored the relationship of values to persuasion and, further, the arrangement of values into hierarchies.[66] Richard Weaver describes such a hierarchy which leads "up to the ultimate good" and which gives "intelligibility to the whole discourse." Weaver's simile for the hierarchy of values is "links in a chain stretching up to some master link which transmits its influence down through the linkages."[67] Kenneth Burke also has written extensively on the concept of hierarchy or "ultimate terms." He contrasts the "dialectical" with the "ultimate" treatment of conflict and shows that while dialectic "would leave the competing voices in a jangling relation with one another," an ultimate order "would place these competing voices themselves in a hierarchy, or sequence, or evaluative series. . . ." Burke explains that the ultimate order differs from the dialectical "in that there would be a 'guiding idea' or 'unitary principle' behind the diversity of voices." The voices in conflict would be "arranged developmentally with relation to one another." The conflict itself would be thus "endowed with design."[68]

Perelman and Olbrechts-Tyteca explain that "argumentation relies not only on values . . . but also on hierarchies," and they illustrate by pointing out that "values relating to persons are superior to those relating to things." They claim, further, that "value hierarchies are, no doubt, more important to the structure of an argument than the actual values." They conclude that the "simultaneous pursuit of these [hierarchical] values leads to incompatibilities, obliges one to make choices" and that the structure itself "will indicate which value will be sacrificed."[69]

King used reasoning about just and unjust laws in combination

Figure 3

OBEDIENCE TO GOD

JUSTICE, MORAL AND NATURAL LAW

HUMAN DIGNITY, BROTHERHOOD, DEMOCRACY

OBEDIENCE TO THE LAW, ORDER, AND COMMON SENSE

---

with denial of the values found in the letter from the ministers to create contrasting values hierarchies. At the bottom lie legitimate values, but above stand concerns for both God and human beings. Figure 3 provides a structure that illustrates the positive hierarchy.

A companion hierarchy of negative values or outcomes completes the concept. At the bottom of the structure in figure 4 lie legitimate problems, but unjust laws allowed by complacent public opinion and paternalistic attitudes stand above as worse wrongs.

Figure 4

INJUSTICE/ESTRANGEMENT

PATERNALISM, COMPLACENCY, STATUS QUO

RACIAL FRICTION, UNREST, VIOLENCE, EXTREME MEASURES

Through King's creation of positive and negative hierarchies we can see an illustration of Burke's "ultimate order" with the "jangling voices" of racial conflict in Birmingham placed in a developmental relation to one another in an "evaluative sequence." From Perelman's view we see that "things" such as "law and order" must be sacrificed to "persons." To use Weaver's terminology, King's "master link" is obedience to God.

Implications

Branch asserts that the "Letter from Birmingham Jail," "so exquisite a blend of New Testament grace and Old Testament wrath," did not "spring quickly to acclaim" because it failed to appear in the "white or Negro news media for a month." King had not "rescued the beleaguered Birmingham movement with his pen." Rather, "unexpected miracles of the Birmingham movement later transformed King's letter from a silent cry of desperate hope to a famous pronouncement of moral triumph."[70] Branch summarizes, "Having submitted his prestige and his body to jail, and having hurled his innermost passions against the aloof respectability of white American clergymen, all without noticeable effect, King committed his cause to the witness of schoolchildren."[71]

Of course, these events may not fit quite so neatly into a cause and effect relationship. Perhaps the process of thinking through his philosophy and articulating it in the "Letter" gave King the courage to send the black children of Birmingham into the streets. National and international news coverage of line after line of children confronting dogs, fire hoses, and state and city police officers turned opinion toward civil rights more than any words could do. However, King's words, published finally in the national media, clarified why it was wrong to treat black adults in ways that were so obviously barbaric when applied to children.[72] In his letter King chose carefully the points to emphasize through "value-laden language."

Any judgment of the effects of a single rhetorical artifact is hazardous if not impossible. The momentous events of 1963 have yet to be sorted out. This letter may have resulted in no major breakthrough in the struggle for equal rights, but its phrases stand up twenty-five years later as models in movement rhetoric. For King and all the others seeking civil rights, the letter may have crystallized many formerly disconnected arguments. In the space of approximately thirteen pages, King managed to counter the major criticisms of the entire movement, i.e., that "outside agitators" led it, that the nonviolent campaigns themselves caused violence, that those who marched or sat-in broke laws and thus were criminals, that there could be a time that was better for protests than other times, that those not involved in the protests could best determine when that time occurred, that negotiation alone could bring forth change, and that the police were nonviolent.

The March on Washington in August 1963 indicated King's interest in showing the Congress, the president, and, through the help of television coverage, the American people that nonviolent mass protest could also be peaceful protest. On that occasion, of course, King took the opportunity to return to an even more eloquent pronouncement of his values in the "I Have a Dream" speech. His ideal audience for both occasions would certainly have included white liberals and nonracist Christians whose values he never challenged, but reinforced. Idealist though he was, King undoubtedly knew that the purest of persuasive messages could not sway those who stood in schoolhouse doors or practiced the cruel uses of fire hoses and vicious dogs.

Martin Luther King, Jr., would never have chosen to apologize either for his beliefs or for his actions. However, he chose actions that led to his arrest. The critical letter from the Birmingham clergy provided concrete charges to which to respond, and his choice of Judeo-Christian "religious truth" as text broadened his audience to include those who had criticized King himself or the movement's members or methods.

It is acceptable and even expected in American society to respond to an attack whether the assault is verbal or physical. The criticism King received provided him the opportunity to take advantage of the rhetorical form of political apologia to meet multiple audiences. His use of apologetic strategies enabled King to repair his ethos in order to become a credible source for the assertion of the values hierarchy. Instead of a radical outside agitator, he became a sincere, reasonable, and responsible "Christian brother."

A study of this "Letter from Birmingham Jail" provides us with a means through which not only to view the cultural practice of apologia but also to observe the usefulness of values to the process of persuasion in general. More particularly, it helps us to investigate the tension between those who argue that situations produce rhetoric and those who claim that rhetoric produces situations. King's skillful use of apologia provided a positive response to the immediate situation, but his craftsmanship extended to the creation of a new rhetorical situation. He captured the high ground with his contrasting hierarchies of values, and he restored harmony by means of a unifying value system derived from a mutual Judeo-Christian and American democratic heritage.

4

Covenanted Rights: The Metaphoric Matrix of "I Have a Dream"

Martha Solomon

> I say to you today, my friends, so even though we face the
> difficulties of today and tomorrow, I still have a dream. It is a
> dream deeply rooted in the American Dream. . . . I have a dream
> today.
>
> —Martin Luther King, Jr.

Few speeches have so excited the public and moved so quickly into
our national consciousness as Martin Luther King, Jr.'s "I Have a
Dream." Delivered at a civil rights march on Washington on 28
August 1963, King's speech was one of many on the program, but it
quickly eclipsed the others. Despite its immediate effectiveness, its
clear significance as a cultural artifact, and its key position in King's
oeuvre, King's speech has received little attention from rhetorical
scholars.[1]

Although various approaches can yield insights into the speech,
its imagistic richness suggests one promising avenue. The vivid
images in the speech emerge largely from King's extensive use of
disparate metaphors. This essay will examine the speech's metaphoric elements to discover their role in shaping the address. In
particular, I will argue that (1) an implicit matrix metaphor, most
clearly and fully expressed in the passage depicting black demands
as a check, underlies the speech and generates many of the diverse
elements in it; (2) the use of this metaphor provides imagistic
richness and thematic unity to the speech; (3) this matrix metaphor

used key symbols to encourage both the synthesis and elaboration of the audience's experiences; and (4) King's wise choice and skillful manipulation of this metaphorical matrix was a key factor in the speech's impact.

The Concept of a Matrix Metaphor

Since Aristotle, metaphors and their influence on thought have fascinated scholars in our field. Recent critics have examined archetypal metaphors,[2] their rhetorical function,[3] the psychological processes underlying them,[4] and the significance of particular metaphorical patterns in individual orators.[5] Blankenship's survey of the metaphors embedded in political discourse suggested the tremendous influence this "stylistic flourish" has on our perceptions and actions.[6]

One area scholars have not explored fully is the relationship among and function of disparate metaphors in a single work or text. The question arises as to whether some thematic or substantive element may unite the varied metaphors in a text and, if so, what the significance or function of that commonality may be.[7] Drawing from the terminology of structural linguistics, we may consider whether the diverse "surface" metaphors reflect some "deeper," "embedded" formulation. For King's speech in particular, we can ask whether some theme or concept, perhaps inherent in his political philosophy, underlies his diverse metaphors and coalesces them in a unified, effective rhetorical appeal.[8]

Michael Riffaterre's explorations into the semiotics of poetry suggest how a matrix metaphor may function in a piece of discourse. Riffaterre has been fascinated with the elements that provide unity to a poem while simultaneously generating a text filled with rich and varied references.[9] Assuming that a poem is a unity, Riffaterre argues that a poem "results from a transformation of the matrix, a minimal and literal sentence, into a longer, complex, and nonliteral periphrasis."[10] A poem has underlying it, then, a core statement or concept, which the poet expands and manipulates to produce the text. "The poem . . . results from the transformation of a word or sentence into a text."[11] To accomplish this transformation of a straightforward core statement into a richly evocative poem, the writer must use words or phrases which function as poetic signs to refer to preexistent word groups, called "hypograms." A hypogram may be "a cliché, a quotation, or a group of conventional associations . . . or a thematic complex."[12] The "hypogram," thus, corresponds roughly to what Sherry Ortner would label "key symbols,"[13] to what Michael McGee has termed "ideographs,"[14] and to what Doris Graber designates condensation symbols.[15] In other words, Riffaterre argues that the core statement underlying a poem may generate disparate images and elements that form a coherent pattern when interpreted in the context of the matrix or core statement underlying them. The poet exploits the poetic signs to take advantage of their correlated "hypograms" (key symbols, ideographs, condensation symbols).

If we assume, as Riffaterre does about a poem, that a piece of rhetoric is a unity, we can seek the matrix or core element that generates its surface diversity.[16] Such a matrix need not be conterminous with nor equivalent to the thesis of a piece. While my analysis of King's speech will demonstrate this point, the distinction is implicit in much rhetorical criticism and seems to me central in Burkeian theory.[17] While Riffaterre avers that the matrix of a poem is a statement, this limitation does not seem necessary for a piece of rhetoric. For example, Burke's representative anecdote may embody the matrix of a piece of discourse.[18]

This essay will suggest that the matrix of King's speech is a metaphor. For purposes of this discussion, I shall define a matrix metaphor as a comparison of two concepts or objects that at a minimum stimulates or generates other metaphors and, consequently, provides a unifying bond among those diverse figures. In a sense, a matrix metaphor is like the trunk of a tree. A tree's branches, limbs, and twigs rely on and derive from the trunk, although they differ from the trunk and each other. In the same way, the disparate surface metaphors in a text stem from the core comparison or matrix metaphor. While this terminology may be somewhat novel, the concept seems implicit in various discussions of metaphor. For example, Lakoff and Johnson's analysis of our view of argument as warfare reflects this perception of a matrix metaphor realized in many surface metaphors.[19]

As I hope to demonstrate later, matrix metaphors can exert varying degrees of influence from mildly esemplastic to controlling. Moreover, I shall contend that the power of a particular matrix metaphor is linked to the evocative richness of its constituent elements (its tenor and vehicle) and the philosophy, if any, it encapsulates. Because King's matrix metaphor was both richly evocative and philosophically compelling, it was, I believe, one important source of his rhetorical power in this text.

Metaphors and Images: The Constitution and Declaration as Covenant

One key to identifying the matrix of King's speech is to examine the prominent images and their interrelationships. Within the speech King develops three extensive images: (1) the Constitution as a promissory note (about 170 words), (2) the dream of achieved racial justice (about 290 words), and (3) the "ringing out" of freedom through the country (about 220 words). These images constitute a substantial portion of an address of about 1,600 words. Moreover, the three images are closely interrelated: the Constitution and the Declaration of Independence constitute for all citizens a metaphorical "promissory note" that embodies the creed of this nation. Rising up and living out the "true meaning" of this creed (honoring the check) will lead to the realization of King's dream and will let freedom ring throughout the land. Uniting the three images is the contrast between promises made by the government to all citizens and the government's failure to fulfill those promises for blacks.

The three images, taken together, suggest the philosophical viewpoint underlying King's speech: full civil rights for blacks are inherent in these documents' (Declaration of Independence and Constitution) establishment of the United States as a legitimate government. One can conceptualize this political philosophy relatively unmetaphorically as I have just done. However, within the speech, King's surface metaphors suggest a metaphorical statement closer to the spirit of his analysis: that the instruments establishing the American state are a *covenant* between the state and all citizens.[20] This implicit matrix metaphor, the Declaration of Independence and the Constitution as a covenant (with the Emancipation Proclamation as a reaffirmation of them), provides both a unifying center and a generative framework for the address.

If one grants that the speech evolves out of the covenant matrix, the check-bank image assumes a critical position. Since it is the most direct expression of the speech's metaphoric matrix, King develops it carefully and at great length. First, after asserting that the demonstration is "to dramatize a shameful condition," King continues:

In a sense we've come to our nation's Capitol to cash a check. When the architects of our republic wrote the magnificent words of the Constitution and the Declaration of Independence, they were signing a promissory note to which every American was to fall heir. This note was a promise that all men—yes, black men as well as white men—would be guaranteed the unalienable rights of life, liberty, and the pursuit of happiness. It is obvious today that America has defaulted on this promissory note insofar as her citizens of color are concerned. Instead of honoring this sacred obligation, America has given the Negro people a bad check, a check which has come back marked "insufficient funds." We refuse to believe that there are insufficient funds in the great vaults of opportunity of this nation. So we've come to cash this check—a check that will give us upon demand the riches of freedom and the security of justice.

Thus King develops an extended metaphor that suggests the deeper matrix metaphor. Among the elements in the extended image are the following:

Tenor	Vehicle
(1) Constitution, Declaration of Independence	promissory note
(2) contemporary American policy	defaulter, passer of bad checks
(3) Black demands	check
(4) nation	vault of opportunity
(5) justice	bank

Analysis of the Cluster

Four observations are particularly salient about this extended metaphor and its underlying matrix: (1) the implicit political philosophy, (2) the moral perspective, (3) the generation of other images, and (4) their status as an organizational principle.

King's implicit political philosophy in this metaphor is axiomatic in American public rhetoric but controversial in its implications. In depicting the constitutive documents of our government as a covenant, King highlights the perspective of the individual citizen. As the nineteenth-century debates over abolition and woman's rights had demonstrated, Americans did not agree fully about the implications of being deemed a citizen and what rights the Constitution intended as essential for citizenship. Thus one amendment was necessary to free the slaves and another to grant freed men the right to vote. Much later, the Nineteenth Amendment enfranchised women, who had always been "citizens," at least for tax purposes. Before the Civil War, women believed that the Constitution already provided them the right to vote, and after the war some persons opposed the amendments relating to ex-slaves on the grounds that becoming freed citizens entailed enfranchisement. But many other Americans viewed the national government as a compact between and among the states. They argued that the rights of citizens within each state were the province not of the federal government but of the governors and state legislatures. Thus these actions were necessary, if somewhat redundant.

During the period in which King was speaking, southern governors were still urging that states had the rights of interposition and nullification: They could refuse to obey the mandate of the federal government and could, in effect, control the access of their citizens to such civil rights as the ballot. That view of the republic privileged states' rights over individual rights. King's metaphor undercut that perspective. Thus, for some Americans, King's view that the framers of the Constitution had entered a covenant directly with all citizens hinted at difficult issues in regard to states' rights. In essence, King's depiction was bypassing such state claims and even contemporary political policies to find the roots of black demands in the founding fathers' expressed will. The American government was, as Lincoln had said, of, by, and for the people; their rights, not the claims of the states, were primary.

Interestingly, the amendments to the Constitution mentioned above had facilitated King's interpretation. They had reemphasized that citizenship and civil rights were natural rights guaranteed to all persons. Those rights could be restricted on the basis of reasonable standards (age, for example), but they could not be denied categorically. In this sense, then, all Americans believed that their rights were guaranteed by the key documents of the nation. To deny that view was to jeopardize their own access to civil liberties. King's metaphor played to that political sensitivity, not to state legislatures' and officials' claims to their right as elected representatives to interpose themselves between the central government and their residents.

King's metaphor highlighted another aspect of his political philosophy: Rights curtailed by any circumstance were, in effect, rights denied. If Negroes had been granted freedom by the Emancipation Proclamation, they were still "sadly crippled by the manacles of segregation and the chains of discrimination." Such factors forced the Negro to live "on a lonely island of poverty in the midst of a vast ocean of material prosperity," to languish "in the corners of American society," and to find himself "an exile in *his own* land." The time had come, as King had announced in his first speech on civil rights in Montgomery and as he echoed here, "to make real the promises of democracy." Americans must decide, King implied, whether theirs was to be a "real" democracy or was to masquerade as one hypocritically. As Anna Howard Shaw had argued in regard to the vote for women, either the United States was a republic, in which case all persons subject to its laws should have the right to vote, or it was falsely calling itself one.[21] Rights abridged were rights denied, and rights denied were abrogations of national values. More directly to the point, without additional federal action, blacks because of discriminatory practices could not enjoy "life, liberty, and the pursuit of happiness." The marvelous portion of the speech which repeats "we cannot be satisfied until . . ." eloquently expresses the consequences of this view.

While King's political view could be termed "liberal" rather than "conservative" in its call for government intervention to solve social problems and protect individual rights, it is tinged with a moral and religious fervor not always found in liberal rhetoric. A modern counterpart may prove illustrative. Jesse Jackson's call for a "rainbow coalition" united religious and political values in contrast to Mario Cuomo's less moralistic view of the American body politic as family.[22] What separates Cuomo from Jackson is the latter's insistence on and effectiveness in viewing political questions through a religious lens. In the same way, King drew on religious values and attitudes to substantiate his political views.

This political philosophy of rights as guaranteed directly to individual citizens through a covenant also provided part of the moral force of King's imagery. From the beginning, the civil rights struggle had its foundation in black churches and had drawn many of its leaders from the ministry. King's ethos as a minister had, in fact, been one reason he was chosen to lead the Montgomery bus boycott. And from the beginning, King had refused to separate political actions from moral and religious values. In this case, to consent to denial or abrogation of a sacred covenant was, in effect, to participate in civil sacrilege. Government was not a contract or compact— legal instruments—but a binding covenant. American citizens were the chosen people of the founding fathers; all men were to "fall heir to" the pledges contained in the Constitution and Declaration of Independence. Refusal to assert one's ordained rights was acquiescence to oppression and political hypocrisy. In contradistinction, insisting on the rights to which one was entitled would force America to "rise up and live out its creed." Thus participation in the struggle for civil rights was both a moral duty because of the covenant to which one was heir and an exercise of moral leadership in forcing all Americans to honor the founding fathers' wishes. Significantly, blacks, in demanding their rights, were serving as the moral conscience of the body politic. King's metaphor assumed it was possible and appropriate to apply strong moral standards in the political arena. Arguments based on pleas for "gradualism" were intolerable not simply because they delayed progress; more significantly, they were betrayals of a sacred trust, and that value, King implied, was far more important than pragmatic politics.

Third, this metaphoric cluster generates the two other principal images in the speech, the dream and the "let freedom ring" sequences. To begin his dream sequence, King says "I have a dream that one day this nation will rise up and live out the true meaning of its creed: 'We hold these truths to be self-evident; that all men are created equal.'" Fulfilling the covenant will "open up" this nation's "vault of opportunity" for blacks and enable them to enjoy the "riches of freedom and the security of justice." King's quotation from "America" underscores the covenantal relationship between citizens and the government, as it provides the thematic focus of the dramatic closing: "*My* country 'tis of thee, sweet land of liberty, of thee I sing. *Land where my fathers died,* land of the pilgrim's pride, from every mountainside, let freedom ring." The language of the song assumes "new meaning" because it highlights blacks' participation in the government ("my country") and the good faith sacrifices they have made to sustain their part of the covenant ("land where my fathers died").

As the speech plays out the implications and ramifications of the denunciation and future affirmation of this covenant, clusters of images and metaphors coalesce around the two alternatives. A host of images and archetypal metaphors cluster around the affirmation of the covenant. For example, the Emancipation Proclamation affirming the covenant was "a great beacon light of hope" and "a joyous daybreak to end the long night of their captivity." Its reaffirmation now will allow the nation "to rise from the dark and desolate valley of segregation to the sunlit path of racial justice" and will "lift our nation from the quicksands of racial injustice to the solid rock of brotherhood." Acknowledging the covenant will replace "this sweltering summer of the Negro's legitimate discontent" with "an invigorating autumn of freedom and equality." At the same time, "Mississippi, a state sweltering with the heat of injustice, sweltering from the heat of oppression, will be transformed into an oasis of freedom and justice." Finally, freedom will be allowed to ring out even from Stone Mountain in Georgia, Lookout Mountain in Tennessee, and "every hill and molehill of Mississippi." Faith in this covenant will help adherents "hew out of the mountain of despair a stone of hope . . . [and] transform the jangling discords of our nation into a beautiful symphony of brotherhood."

Denial of the covenant, in contrast, "seared" blacks "in the flame of withering injustice." Further, denied covenanted rights, "the Negro lives on a lonely island of poverty in the midst of a vast ocean of material prosperity" and "is still languished in the corners of American society and finds himself an exile in his own land." Black children "are stripped of their selfhood and robbed of their dignity" by the denial of the covenant. "There will be neither rest nor tranquility in America until the Negro is granted his citizenship rights. The whirlwinds of revolt will continue to shake the foundations of our nation until the bright day of justice emerges." Blacks insist on reminding the nation of "the fierce urgency of now" and warn against taking "the tranquilizing drug of gradualism."

These metaphoric clusters around the principal themes of affirmation and denial of the covenant are noteworthy for their diversity, their archetypal dimension, and their religious allusions. For example, the cluster surrounding affirmation used light, heat, height, and structure metaphors. But these are united through their relationship to the covenant's affirmation. Denial of the covenant evokes metaphors of flame, slavery, and alienation. But these, too, revolve around a philosophical core. Thus the archetypal metaphors develop the implications of the matrix metaphor.

Religious allusions are also abundant in the images. For example, "the desolate valley of segregation" echoes biblical references to the "valley of death"; "the captivity" and enslavement of blacks parallels that of the chosen people; and "justice . . . like waters and righteousness like a mighty stream" is drawn from Amos 5:24. The covenant theme itself parallels the agreement between God and the Jewish people chronicled in the Bible. The use of such biblical allusions and themes not only underscores the sacredness of the covenant but also stirs powerful emotional reverberations in King's audience. Implicitly they suggest the image of King as Moses leading his people to the promised land.

Finally, the implicit matrix metaphor provides the organizational basis for the speech.[23] Although its organization is quite clear, the speech does not reflect the classical pattern Fulkerson observed in "Letter from Birmingham Jail."[24] King includes a brief introduction with a reference to setting and occasion. Then using the literal place, the Lincoln Memorial, and Lincoln's Emancipation Proclamation as transitions, King declares the purpose of the demonstration: "So we have come here today to dramatize a shameful condition." The bulk of the speech falls into two main divisions: an explanation of that "shameful condition" (denial of the covenant) and a vision of the nation when the situation is remedied (affirmation of the covenant). King concludes with an inspiring challenge.

The explanation of the "shameful condition" is also clearly organized. First, King establishes the basis of blacks' demands as the promissory note of the founding fathers. Having identified this foundation, King explains the urgency of answering blacks' demands, which will not fade after the demonstration. He then reaffirms the importance of nonviolence as a tool in achieving social change: "We must forever conduct our struggle on the high plane of dignity and discipline. We must not allow our creative protest to degenerate into physical violence." Finally, he suggests that blacks will be satisfied only when the abuses and injustices are eradicated.

In a transitional passage King acknowledges their past sacrifices, but he urges their continued efforts to eradicate injustice. Reminding them that their "creative" and "unearned suffering" will be redemptive, King exhorts them to return to their struggles.

The last portion of the speech, over a third of its total length, is an inspiring visualization of America when the shameful conditions are eradicated. The vision of America living out her creed gives King the hope and courage to continue the struggle. Echoing the words of "America" in the peroration, King challenges his audience to "let freedom ring" throughout the land until all people can exclaim, "Free at last! Thank God Almighty we are free at last."

Clearly, the touchstone for King's organization is the contrast between the denial of the covenant and its affirmation. In the first section King describes the implication of the current abrogation of the sacred agreement, and in the second he envisions its fulfillment. The primary organizational principle, thus, reflects King's concern with the covenant he perceives.

Implicit in this organization is the motif of a journey or quest. For example, King uses various movement images and references to suggest that blacks should pursue freedom:

We cannot walk alone. And as we walk we must make the pledge we shall always march ahead. We cannot turn back.

Go back to Mississippi, go back to Alabama, go back to South Carolina, go back to Georgia, go back to Louisiana, go back to the slums and ghetto of our Northern cities knowing that somehow this situation can and will be changed. Let us not wallow in the valley of despair.

Moreover, the dream sequence envisions a future state that can be realized if blacks continue their efforts. The rough chronological structure of the speech—past promises, present problems, and future goals—reflects the pattern typical of a romantic quest in which a hero because of some difficulty undertakes a perilous journey to gain an important goal.[25]

Rhetorical Analysis

To understand the significance of King's use of a matrix metaphor, one must consider it from two perspectives: King's and his audience's. The key question from both perspectives is, How did the metaphor function rhetorically?

King's Perspective

King's rhetorical situation at the march was difficult. The acknowledged leader of the civil rights movement, he was only one of many speakers on that warm August day. But as the final speaker he was in a position to bring the demonstration to a dramatic close. Allotted only eight minutes, King, according to biographer Stephen B. Oates, "wanted to say something meaningful, something Americans would not soon forget. . . . his remarks would be the highlight and the benediction, not only for the crowd at the Lincoln Memorial, but for millions of people who would be watching on television or listening by radio."[26] But how to say "something meaningful" in so short a time was problematic. Moreover, King was very hesitant to overstep his time limit.

On a larger scale King's rhetorical challenge was equally formidable. The march was in part an attempt to force congressional action on civil rights legislation. Although President Kennedy had somewhat reluctantly urged congressional action on civil rights in a televised address on 11 June, the congressional and public debate still raged. King's task was both to pressure Congress into legislation and to coalesce public support for his position. Moreover, segments of the black community were criticizing King for his "Uncle Tom" stance.[27] Thus he needed to reassure his supporters of his adamancy and dedication. To be conciliatory for the disparate factions and yet confrontational toward the recalcitrant legislators, to insist on action yet reassure those fearing social turmoil were some of the conflicting exigencies facing King.

Finally, King's desire to say "something meaningful" was impeded by the diversity of his audience, including not only those present at the march but also those listening and watching the broadcast media and those who would learn of the march through snippets in the press. What message could inspire such varied listeners without fading into the bland? In addition, while the widespread media coverage of the Birmingham demonstration had garnered support for the demonstrators as victims of police brutality, King sought to transcend that image of powerlessness and convey the moral superiority of the movement over its opponents. He wished to convince all Americans of the stake they had in the movement's outcome.

From King's perspective, then, the situation mandated a simple, direct, inspiring, conciliatory, yet assertive speech. He needed to dramatize the moment while he transcended it. His statement needed to be consonant with his often-expressed philosophy of non-violence and to elicit a strong emotional response from the various audiences.

Since King had urged Kennedy to commemorate the centennial of the Emancipation Proclamation in 1963 with a forceful affirmation of his support for the civil rights movement, and since the demonstration was at the Lincoln Memorial, it is not surprising that King was drawn to Lincoln's words for inspiration.[28] The check metaphor was a simple, unusual image to dramatize the contrast he saw between Lincoln's proclamation and the status of blacks. That this contrast was already familiar to the crowd is evident from some of the banners at the march: "Seek the Freedom in 1963 promised in 1863!" "A Century-Old Debt to Pay."[29] So King chose the check metaphor to express his theme, also determining to echo Lincoln's words in his depiction.[30]

For King's purposes the check metaphor was an ideal vehicle to convey his deeper philosophical view. It was a concrete depiction of the blacks' situation, but the metaphor behind it expressed a political philosophy acceptable to most Americans. The check metaphor was readily understandable by his audience, and its colloquialism contrasted effectively with his theme and the opening words echoing Lincoln. Apparently, King intended to focus the presentation solely on the thematic device. But inspired by the situation, he departed from his text and appended the dream sequence, which he had used in a previous speech in Detroit.[31] In fact the dream sequence was a natural extension of the past (Declaration, Constitution, Emancipation Proclamation)-present (shameful condition) contrast King had developed.

With the check metaphor as a focus, King was able to satisfy many of the various exigencies he faced. Its image of black demands as legitimate and even morally necessary helped the audience perceive the march as a firm demand for covenanted rights, not as a petulant insistence on privileges. The inspired addition of the dream sequence redeemed the speech from its pessimistic assessment, offering an appealing rhetorical vision without sacrificing thematic unity or coherence. Moreover, since King was recalling a passage he had used before, he was comfortable with the material and was able to capitalize on the audience's powerful emotional response.

Audience Perceptions

The covenant metaphor that was the underlying matrix of King's speech had two great strengths as a rhetorical device for his audience. First, its most direct expression in the speech, the check metaphor, was well suited for the immediate audience. Second, its utilization of key symbols gave it powerful rhetorical force for all listeners.

Not only was the check metaphor easy to interpret, but also, as noted above, the banners at the march suggest that seeds for it were already present in the audience's perceptions. The metaphor was a concrete, even mundane expression of the political philosophy undergirding blacks' demands. As such it vivified a rather abstract political view. For the audience, then, this explicit, colloquial image crystallized the philosophy underlying their position in a readily understandable way.

Moreover, the tenor of the metaphor ("the check," "a promissory note") alluded to blacks' experiences of economic inequities. Living "on a lonely island of poverty in the midst of a vast ocean of material prosperity," blacks knew economic problems first hand. The metaphor called up those associations as it highlighted the injustices that had often underlain the deprivations. Since the metaphor also conveyed a view of government as a covenant, it stimulated blacks and those sympathetic to them to connect the actual economic problems they had experienced with government's immoral abrogation of a commitment. In short, the metaphor provided a scapegoat for blacks' experiences of economic frustration.

On a deeper level the matrix metaphor of the governmental covenant effectively uses what anthropologists term "key symbols" in our society. Having identified key symbols as elements that are crucial to a culture's organization and that help members formulate meanings within it, Sherry B. Ortner classifies and describes two varieties:

Summarizing symbols are primarily objects of attention and cultural respect; they synthesize or "collapse" complex experience and relate the respondent to the grounds of the system as a whole. . . . Elaborating symbols . . . are . . . valued for their contribution to the ordering or "sorting out" of experience. Within this are symbols valued primarily for the ordering of conceptual experience, i.e., for providing cultural "orientations," and those valued primarily for the ordering of action, i.e., for providing cultural "strategies." The former includes what Pepper calls "root metaphors," the latter includes key scenarios. . . .[32]

For example, in American culture the flag would be a synthesizing symbol for the "American experience," the machine might be one conceptually elaborating symbol for cultural progress, and the Horatio Alger story would be a key scenario.

King's matrix metaphor of the governmental covenant integrates examples of each type of symbol in a powerful rhetorical appeal. The Declaration of Independence and Constitution are clearly synthesizing symbols for all Americans, while the Emancipation Proclamation has especially powerful associations for blacks. In using these as the tenor of his matrix metaphor, King sets up powerful emotional reverberations in his audience. Since these documents embody and represent the essence of our government, they are virtually sacred writ to Americans. They synthesize quite powerfully disparate aspects of the American experience. Moreover, the covenant, which serves as the vehicle in the matrix metaphor, has rich associations in Judeo-Christian culture. Not only does it convey the moral imperative underlying black demands, but also it suggests both the "chosenness" of the participants in the covenant and their ultimate triumph. The coalescence of the religious and political associations surrounding the two terms in King's metaphor provides both patriotic and moral sanction for his view. The joining of these key symbols also helps the audience "collapse" the complex arguments surrounding demands for civil rights legislation into a single element: such legislation is simply a fulfillment of moral and political commitments. The protestors' path is the Christian *and* American way.

King's matrix also generates powerful elaborating symbols. The implicit journey motif encourages sustained effort ("go back to . . .") toward a clearly defined goal ("the dream"). Blacks are encouraged not only to persevere in pressing their demands but to persist with their nonviolent strategies. The suffering they experience will, King assures them, be "redemptive." The parallel to any Christian's life as a journey toward a heavenly reward is clear. King even alludes to the problems which have beset them on their "quest for freedom" and which may recur: "narrow jail cells . . . storms of persecution . . . winds of police brutality." King's handling of this motif is masterful. By depicting the struggle as a "quest for freedom," he stimulates his followers to view their past experiences as meaningful steps in a long journey. Their efforts, which may have produced no immediate progress and which may have incurred real physical suffering, are "creative" and "redemptive" because they are part of a larger, sacred effort. Moreover, the journey motif helps followers rationalize and accept their suffering as part of a painful but productive process. No journey is without troubles, but they are vital because the destination makes the transient suffering worthwhile.

Moreover, King's use of the covenant allows his followers to conceptualize their roles as simultaneously preserver-guardians and perfecters of the social order. As Duncan explains: "guardians speak as protectors of the great principles of social order which sustain the community. In this guise, the guardians are the voice of tradition and custom or of the utopias which lie ahead for all who do their duty. . . . the guardians warn . . . of the doom that awaits those who violate the sacred principles of social order which uphold their community."[33] This perspective transforms King's followers into community leaders, bestowing a sense of power and importance on many who had felt powerless and alienated.

Furthermore, they are demanding rights already promised in American sacred writ; they are not repudiating the hierarchy. They are instead "truer" to it than are their opponents. Yet they also perceive the imperfections in the implementation of the government's promises and insist on their correction. Their efforts thus embody the American values of justice and progress and reflect our national optimism. King's followers are dreamers of the American dream who insist that it can be realized. They are pointing the way for America to "rise up and live out the true meaning of its creed." They appreciate far more fully than their opponents the beauty, breadth, and potential of the American creed. In essence, the journey motif provides a key scenario for King's followers which outlines the motives for their quest and the strategies they should pursue. This motif "implies clear-cut modes of action appropriate to correct and successful living in the culture."[34] Blacks, for example, are not inferiors supplicating a master who can bestow special gifts. The relationship is an agreement between equals, one of whom has faltered in fulfilling commitments.

In addition, the barriers and persecution blacks have experienced are both unmerited and unjust because of the nature of the relationship. The personal experiences of violence and discrimination assume new meaning from this perspective. Translated from the realm of personal injustice, these episodes become violations of a sacred order. Those who endure them for the sake of a principle are heroes. Their suffering is "redemptive" in the sense of the Beatitudes and in the sense that it demands payment for a pledge. Further, the suffering is "creative" because, by drawing attention to blacks' rights, it helps develop a new social order.

In short, King manipulated his rhetorical resources to take advantage of his audience's experiences, emotions, and cultural heritage.

The result was a remarkably simple yet marvelously subtle speech. King's ability to marshal his means of persuasion so effectively for his audience is a tribute to his intellect and his rhetorical skill.

Conclusion

In probing for the source of the rhetorical power in King's dream speech, this essay has argued that an implicit matrix metaphor both generates the imagistic richness and creates the structural, thematic, and philosophical unity of the text. These functions are crucial to the speech's impact because they allow figurative diversity while assuring substantive unity. Any conclusions based on a single case study such as this must be tentative, but some observations about the nature and function of a matrix metaphor and its impact in rhetorical invention seem warranted.

First, this study has suggested that a matrix metaphor may exert varying degrees of rhetorical force on a text, from mildly esemplastic to controlling. This range of power is tied to the levels on which the metaphor functions, the evocative force of its constituent tenor and vehicle, and the dynamic interaction of these two factors.

A matrix metaphor may work on three levels: It can provide stylistic variety by generating diverse images; it can enhance thematic unity; and it can offer a philosophical underpinning. The first two of these are closely related; several images that cluster around a particular metaphor would inevitably produce some thematic unity. One can envision a speech in which a central metaphor simply produced a series of related, though diverse, images that create a unifying theme. For example, David Henry has argued convincingly that Mario Cuomo's keynote address to the 1984 Democratic National Convention revolved around the metaphor of the American body politic as family.[35]

While metaphors that serve as a stylistic and thematic matrix are interesting and important, they are less powerful rhetorically than those that also reflect a philosophical perspective. King's speech demonstrates this point effectively. King could, and on occasion did, turn to close, careful argument to explain his position and defend his position. His "Letter from Birmingham Jail," for example, is a model of cogent reasoning and stinging refutation. But he also understood the power of images and symbols to persuade and motivate. However, rhetoric using vivid images and symbols can degenerate into demagoguery and bombast. What distinguishes this speech is King's use of evocative images unified and dignified by the philosophy which underlies them. The speech's substantive foundation, encapsulated in its matrix metaphor, redeems it from charges of being only a series of emotional appeals and lends it argumentative force. The metaphorical matrix allows King to stir his immediate audience and to speak eloquently to the future.

The matrix metaphor in this case also involves both a tenor (the various documents) and vehicle (covenant) that stimulate rich emotional reactions. While such elements enhance the rhetorical power of a matrix, they are not crucial. Again, Henry's analysis of Cuomo's speech is illustrative. While the matrix metaphor of the American body politic as family is appealing, neither the tenor (body politic) nor the vehicle (family) is a powerful condensation symbol. Although the concept of family is appealing to many Americans, neither element in Cuomo's metaphor has the rhetorical status of those in King's speech. The richer each element in a matrix as a condensation symbol, the more rhetorically powerful and effective the metaphor as a whole.

Moreover, the philosophical nature of this particular matrix and the individual power of its components interacted to increase its rhetorical force. Probably this impact is not simply additive. Rather the impact of the whole may well exceed the sum of the parts. What occurred in King's speech was the mutual reinforcement of image and implicit argument. The particular evocative force of the metaphoric elements complemented and supplemented the argument implicit in the philosophy expressed. Because the argument (government is covenantal) is almost axiomatic to many Americans, the combined force of image and political truism became unusually powerful.

Finally, it is important to observe that the matrix metaphor is not necessarily equivalent in function or substance to the thesis of a text. In this case, for example, while King's point is clear, his thesis is not. If critics can extract a thesis from the work, any such post hoc formulation would not only ignore how the speech functioned rhetorically for the audience but also would direct attention away from the text's essentially imagistic quality. Because of the way the matrix metaphor works in this speech, King's text provides an interesting example of how a rhetor can meet the demands for rational public discourse and, simultaneously, speak primarily to the emotions of his audience. Although this speech is clearly not argumentative and thus lacks an explicit thesis, it cannot be dismissed as irrational or judged substantively deficient. The speech remains compelling for Americans because it warrants its discussion in the matrix metaphor of government as covenant.

On a second front, the existence and function of the matrix metaphor in King's speech also elucidates the close connection between the rhetor's philosophical outlook and the process of rhetorical invention. In King's case, his political philosophy and religious beliefs led him to perceive American government as a covenant between citizens and the state. This perception is evident in his earliest speech on the Montgomery bus boycott, in which he averred, "We're here in a general sense because first and foremost, we are American citizens, and we are determined to acquire our citizenship to the fullness of its meaning."[36] This interpretation became, in turn, a perceptual frame, what Burke has labeled a "terministic screen."[37] Confronted with the problems of blacks in American society, King both interpreted and depicted their situation in light of his political philosophy and religious beliefs. As he sought to express his outlook graphically and concretely in this speech in vivid images and metaphors, his controlling perceptual frame (government as covenant) served as a storehouse of rhetorical resources on three levels. On the first level, the covenant was more concretely described as a "promissory note," a depiction that combined the contractual element with sensitivity to economic concerns. This image, in turn, stimulated a series of financial metaphors, which not only spoke to real economic inequities but also emphasized blacks' demands as legitimate claims. Third, archetypal images with negative associations (darkness, enslavement, extreme heat) were natural expressions for the contemporary plight of blacks in a society that had ignored its covenantal obligations. In contrast, positive images (invigorating coolness, sunlight, an elevated path) conveyed the promise of a future in which the covenant was honored. In a sense, King moved from philosophical abstraction in two related metaphorical directions: toward greater concreteness of images expressing that philosophy (the check metaphor) and toward greater emotional intensity through archetypes. But the concrete, fresh metaphor was connected to the archetypal images by their common source in the matrix.

Other scholars have probed the function of recurrent metaphors across texts. While this study has focused on the intratextual function of King's metaphors, evidence also suggests that this metaphor was implicit in his much earlier works. As mentioned above, his first speech on the Montgomery bus boycott revealed this outlook. Biographer Stephen Oates mentions this same concept in other works by King and in his public rhetoric.[38] Thus the metaphor that provided the matrix in this speech was a recurrent feature of King's rhetoric and a bedrock of his thinking. Because of his status and prominence as a leader of the civil rights movement, most of his followers were familiar with his views and arguments. He did not need, therefore, to reiterate his position. As a result, he used his matrix metaphor as part of an enthymematic process without having to spell out his arguments fully. The matrix metaphor was, in a sense, both a topos for rhetorical invention and a recurrent enthymeme. Because not all matrix metaphors will enjoy that status in a rhetor's repertoire, this unusual situation helps explain the particular force of this matrix and, in turn, the rhetorical power of King's speech.

This essay has produced few clear conclusions about the nature and function of matrix metaphors, but it has, I hope, suggested the value of such an approach. The role of metaphors in rhetorical invention and their functions for audiences merit much greater scrutiny. While few texts have the power of King's speech, and no critic can fully explain its force, perhaps this analysis has at least heightened appreciation for this remarkable work.

Universalizing "Equality": The Public Legacy of Martin Luther King, Jr.

John Louis Lucaites
Celeste Michelle Condit

> [N]ot long ago, I toured in eight communities of the state of
> Mississippi. And I have carried with me ever since a visual image of
> the penniless and the unlettered, and of the expressions on their
> faces—of deep and courageous determination to cast off the imprint
> of the past and become free people. I welcome the opportunity to
> be a part of this great drama, for it is a drama that will determine
> America's destiny. If the problem is not solved, America will be on
> the road to its self-destruction. But if it *is* solved, America will just
> as surely be on the high road to the fulfillment of the Founding
> Fathers' dream, when they wrote "We hold these truths to be self-
> evident. . . ."
>
> —Martin Luther King, Jr.[1]

Many view nonviolent massive resistance as Martin Luther King,
Jr.'s most important public legacy to America.[2] It is, after all, what
King considered to be the most effective means for influencing
reform in the face of intransigent cultural and institutional oppression.[3] And there can hardly be any question that his strategic use of
it in the civil rights movement of the 1950s and 1960s was masterful.
It would thus certainly be an error of major proportions to underestimate the significance of King's development of civil disobedience as
a legitimate agency of mass social and political change. It would
be equally erroneous, however, to imagine that the agency of change
he employed can be divorced in our judgments from the specific
changes it enabled. As we argue in this essay, King's larger public

legacy has less to do with his use of nonviolent massive resistance per se than with the arguments such protest publicized and the influence they had—and continue to have—on how Americans talk about themselves as a unified "people." Put more specifically, King's public legacy is contained by his universalization of America's vision of "equality" as a necessary and fundamental commitment of the national community.[4]

The word "equality" serves as a rhetorical foundation of America's liberal-democratic political tradition.[5] As all American schoolchildren are taught early in their civic education, Thomas Jefferson began the Declaration of Independence by pronouncing "all men are created equal," and in so doing he institutionalized one of the most important traditions in Western political philosophy. Of course, for Jefferson the Declaration functioned more as revolutionary rhetoric than political theory, his particular usage of the word "equality" serving more as a strategically ambiguous wedge against British colonialism than as an attempt to establish an inexorable, constitutional commitment.[6] Jefferson's particular motivation for using the word "equality" in 1776 notwithstanding, by 1944 the economist Gunnar Myrdal could indicate without serious opposition that the ideal foundation of the "American creed" resided in the commitment to equality.[7] A mere ten years later, the U.S. Supreme Court cited Myrdal's analysis favorably in *Brown* v. *Board of Education of Topeka*, the landmark decision that subsequent courts and legislatures translated as establishing the doctrine that "separate is inherently unequal."[8] As we approach the turn to the twenty-first century, the word "equality" functions as one of the primary political commitments of American society.[9]

Social and political philosophers, historians, jurists, and social scientists have all demonstrated an increasing interest in the topic of equality in recent years. Most of those who study sociopolitical equality treat it in more or less realist terms as either a transcendent ideal or a quantitatively measurable condition of existence. Moreover, in virtually every instance, those who write about equality ignore its historically specific, *rhetorical* presence in public discourse designed to affect the beliefs and behaviors of particular audiences.[10] We find this last fact particularly curious, because it has been precisely in the domain of public discourse that the culturally relevant meaning of "equality" as a commitment of American community initially emerged and, over time, changed. Such changes have almost always been linked to a range of public controversies, most notably concerning racial and sexual relations, in which strategic interpretations of the meaning of "equality" have been employed as a powerful rhetoric of control functioning to alter the criteria of inclusion and exclusion in the social and political life of the nation.

In order to understand how such cultural ideals gain practical *meaning-in-use*, we must examine the rhetorical processes through which advocates employ such ideals in public discourse designed to accommodate and/or reconfigure the relationship between ideological commitments and the material conditions of collective being.[11] This task is rather large, requiring a detailed rhetorical history that charts the shifts in meaning in the key units of a public vocabulary from their point of origin to their present usages. The rhetorical etymology for a protean word like "equality" cannot be completed in a short essay. What we offer here, then, is an analysis of a relatively late episode in the rhetorical history of the word "equality" in American public discourse, focusing in particular on the role that Martin Luther King, Jr., played in crafting its public usage through his leadership of the civil rights movement in the 1960s. We proceed by (1) briefly discussing the long-standing problem the word "equality" has posed for African-American rhetors, (2) characterizing the rhetorical context of "equality" in which King sought to constitute the "beloved community" of racial integration and harmony, and (3) examining how he employed the rhetorical process of *universalization* to effect a compelling (re)vision of America's commitment to "equality" as a means of mobilizing biracial, national support for his program of civil rights.[12] Along the way, we hope to demonstrate insight into the rhetorical dimensions of King's public legacy as well as into the role that public discourse plays in influencing mass social and political change.

"Equality" as the Martyred Black Word

The history of African-American rhetoric may be fruitfully told as a story of two competing public voices striving to negotiate the Anglo-American commitment to "equality."[13] These voices correspond to what scholars and politicians alike have long identified as the two strands in the martyred black vision of social, political, and economic progress.[14] The first strand of this vision is a conciliatory rhetoric that retains faith in the possibilities and promises of the traditional American dream and simply asks that America make that dream real for its African-American citizens. Eloquent public advocates of this voice have included Benjamin Banneker, Frederick Douglass, Mary Church Terrell, Booker T. Washington, and more recently Barbara Jordan, Jesse Jackson, and Andrew Young. The second strand of this vision is a more revolutionary and frequently separatist voice that despairs of the possibility of persuading white America to grant its black citizens full and equal place in the American dream. Advocates of this vision urge African Americans to improve their social, political, and economic lot by staking an independent cultural and ideological position outside the traditional dream. The leading and forceful public advocates of this voice have included Henry Highland Garnet, Marcus Garvey, W. E. B. Du Bois, Stokely Carmichael, Eldridge Cleaver, and most recently Louis Farakhan.

The problem confronting the black advocates of African-American interests is and has long been the paradox of Anglo-American equality. Although ultimately vital to the colonists' battle for independence, the commitment to "equality" did not initially dominate American public discourse, a discourse largely organized around the rallying cry for "liberty and property."[15] In point of fact, the word "equality" did not appear as a central political commitment in American public discourse until the early years of the nineteenth century, and even then its public usage referred typically to individual and group identification, not the equal potentialities or powers of individuals and groups.[16] Since that time, of course, the public usage of "equality" has expanded so that in contemporary times it has become the basis for the full range of affirmative action programs instituted by the federal government.

Much has been written about the multiple meanings of "equality" in American political discourse, but such treatments typically miss the paradox implicit in the commitment to equality for those who would achieve equal status with the socially, politically, and economically dominant group. As long as the dominant group in a society requires *identity* as the essence of equality, to be equal necessitates a sacrifice on the part of those who are *different* and would yet choose to reap the benefits of such a social or political arrangement. So, for example, European immigrants who came to the United States in the late nineteenth and early twentieth centuries had to adopt the history and conventions of their new nation, often at the expense of their own ethnic histories and cultures. Many immigrants voluntarily chose the United States as their new nation, and so they did not frequently express a sense of national loss. Perhaps more to the point, whatever sense of cultural or ethnic loss that did exist for such immigrants diminished quickly as each new generation came of age in the language community of a presumably homogenized culture vividly characterized as "the melting pot." As the desire to become equal participants in the American dream flourished, ethnic accents disappeared, and with them disappeared the ethnic cultural practices that would make an immigrant appear different or alien. The social and political commitment to "equality" thus served as a rhetoric of control, encouraging, if indeed not requiring, assimilation to the beliefs and values of the dominant culture.

America's European immigrants shared a considerable number of racial characteristics with the dominant, white, Anglo-American culture, and this bond eased the problem of assimilation. Once immigrants from Ireland, Italy, Germany, Poland, Greece, and other countries assimilated culturally with their new nation, the problem of physical difference became a relatively minor consideration in achieving social and political equality. America's black citizens faced a more complex problem, for even if they could assimilate the cultural conventions and history of Anglo-America—a history that from the outset not only violently separated them from their own cultural roots but also designated them as more or less inferior and insignificant—they could not assimilate the Anglo-European racial characteristics of the dominant culture. No matter what they did, they bore the physical sign of their difference as alien, cultural others.[17] Advocates for racial justice therefore found themselves doomed to fight the most frustrating of battles: to achieve recognition and status as significant social, political, and economic individuals without sacrificing the difference that made them inherently unique and individual.

"Equality" thus became the martyred black word in American history, a term whose constitutive, public meaning has paradoxically demanded the assimilation of even the unassimilable. More than any other commitment in Anglo-American political life, "equality" offered African Americans the possibility of achieving a modicum of progress in the new nation. Indeed, it was a term that black advocates were virtually forced to employ in public arguments designed to assure their own cultural legitimacy. Ironically, however, as a restrictive commitment of community it required African Americans to repress their difference as cultural others, a difference that ultimately they could neither eliminate nor hide from public view. The result, noted W. E. B. Du Bois, was a "double-consciousness" that haunted the "souls of black folks," an apparently unreconcilable desire to be simultaneously both "American" and "Negro."[18] The commitment to "equality" has been the pivot point of that double consciousness in American political discourse. To gain a clearer purchase on its power as a rhetoric of control, we need to examine how it operates in public usage as a historically specific rhetorical context for social and political action.

The Rhetorical Context of "Equality" in the 1960s

The most forceful and creative engagement of the paradox of equality occurred in the 1960s in the public discourse of two of the most prominent African-American spokespersons of the post–World War II era: Malcolm X and Martin Luther King, Jr. Both Malcolm X and King sought to adapt a conception of what it means to be "equal" to the immediate needs of African Americans as a way of improving their social, political, and economic conditions. But each did so in remarkably different ways.[19] Indeed, so different were their rhetorical efforts that most white Americans have enshrined King in the nation's cultural memory as the primary leader of the civil rights movement and the savior of racial justice, placing him on par with George Washington and Abraham Lincoln, while they have reviled Malcolm X as the radical advocate of black supremacy and racial violence. The immediate concern in this essay is to understand the grounds for King's universalization of "equality" in a manner that appealed to the public consciousness of white America, but in order to do that it is necessary first to identify the rhetorical context in which it emerged as a dialectical opposition to Malcolm X's radical redefinition of "equality."

From the perspective of the 1990s, the 1960s mark a key stage in the two-hundred-year-long battle for civil rights and racial equality. It is nevertheless important to remember that as the 1960s began, African Americans confronted an extremely precarious situation. The Supreme Court had indicated in 1954 that the institutionalization of racial discrimination through Jim Crow legislation violated the Fourteenth Amendment of the Constitution. The efforts of the Court to enforce its decision notwithstanding, segregation and racial discrimination persisted throughout the nation well into the next decade. The problem was especially bad in the Deep South, where White Citizens' Councils and powerful public advocates like Senators Herman Talmadge and Richard Russell and governors like Alabama's George Wallace committed the region to the policies of de jure segregation. At the same time, vigilante groups like the Ku Klux Klan terrorized the southern black community. But the situation was only marginally better in the North, where de facto segregation in the form of social and economic discrimination produced predominantly black ghettoes in every major city. Thus while the federal government seemed to stand firmly behind a public commitment to "equality" for all citizens, the materialization of that commitment eluded most African Americans in both the North and the South.

The black leaders of the 1960s thus confronted the problem of finding a way to combat the two centuries of racial discrimination that produced white America's seemingly intractable attitudes and behaviors toward racial equality. That problem became all the more complex by virtue of the fact that this intransigence persisted throughout the nation, even after the federal government publicly acknowledged the necessity of guaranteeing the equality of *all* American citizens. It should come as no surprise, then, that the national commitment to "equality" played an especially central role as an argumentative warrant in the public discourse of African-American advocates striving to ensure racial justice.[20] And indeed, it is not difficult to find it at the core of the public discourse of both Malcolm X and Martin Luther King, Jr.

Malcolm X emphasized the significance of "equality" to the struggle for civil rights in representative fashion as he spoke before the largely white Militant Labor Forum in 1964: "All our people have the same goals, the same objective. The objective is freedom, justice, *equality*. . . . We don't want to be integrationists. Nor do we want to be separationists. Integration is only a method that is used by some groups to obtain freedom, justice, *equality* and respect as human beings. Separation is only a method that is used by other groups to obtain freedom, *equality* or human dignity."[21]

The centrality of the commitment to "equality" was no less manifest in King's public discourse, though here we find it so subtly woven within the fabric of his texts that it often emerges as a figurative image of the American dream without being explicitly invoked.[22] King's "I Have a Dream" serves as a representative example. In this speech King vividly portrays an enslaved Negro population sitting in the literal and figurative shadows of Abraham Lincoln, the Great Emancipator, metonymically manacled by the constraints of "segregation and discrimination."[23] At the outset of the speech the word "equality" does not appear, but its image is clearly present as the motivating term of the narrative that King articulates. We do not mean to suggest that the word never appears in this speech, but its sparing and strategic usage heightens its value as it serves to motivate the action of the text at critical junctures. Thus the word appears quite strikingly as the point of contrast between the African Americans' past as a "sweltering summer of . . . legitimate discontent" and their inevitable future as an "invigorating autumn of freedom and equality." And of course King features it in the preamble of the "dream" sequence as the organizing principle of the entire last third of the address: "So I say to you, my friends, that even though we must face the difficulties of today and tomorrow, I still have a dream. It is deeply rooted in the American dream that one day this nation will rise up and live out the true meaning of its creed, 'we hold these truths to be self-evident, that all men are created equal. . . .'"

We should not be surprised that Malcolm X and King both employed "equality" as an argumentative warrant or that it held a privileged place in their public discourse. After all, as we have already suggested, the public terms for the national debate over racial justice had been established in the United States long before either entered the scene. Given the course that the public debate over racial relations had taken, it is altogether unlikely that any public advocate could have even imagined making a persuasive case for social and political change without rooting their argument in some particular expression of "equality."[24] What we do find notable about their public use of "equality," however, is that in seeking to manage the paradox of equality in relationship to the specific problems of African Americans in the 1960s, each took such different paths in recharacterizing what "equality" could mean. While Malcolm X sought to eliminate the paradox by radically recasting the underlying test or principle of equality in terms of what he phrased "the ballot or the bullet," King sought to co-opt the paradox by transcending the terms of racial difference that informed it. The result was a crudely formed but clearly recognizable public dialogue in which two separate and competing visions of what equality could mean served as a rhetorical context for how each might be interpreted and understood. The implicit rhetorical effect of this dialectic was twofold: First, it directed attention to the way in which the word "equality" resonated in the rhetorical history of American public discourse as a potent and paradoxical argumentative warrant for social and political behavior. Second, and no less important, it heightened the public presence of what was at stake for white America in negotiating—or failing to negotiate—one or another interpretation of its meaning in the national dialogue on race relations.

For Malcolm X, "equality" represented a commitment to a relationship of equivalence between two or more clearly separate entities, each of which possessed its own independent identity but was similarly powerful. From this perspective, one might have said that the United States of America and the Union of Soviet Socialist Republics were *equally* strong nations. In his *Autobiography*, Malcolm X characterized the commitment to "equality" voiced by northern, white liberals as an empty deceit: "he [the white liberal] grins with his teeth, and his mouth has always been full of tricks and lies of 'equality' and 'integration.' When one day all over America, a black hand touched the white man's shoulder, and the white man turned, and there stood the Negro saying 'Me too . . .' why, that Northern liberal shrank from that black man with as much guilt and dread as any Southern white man."[25] This characterization implicitly rejects the dominant, Anglo-American commitment to "equality" as identity or individual interchangeability. A few pages later Malcolm X replaces this conception of equality with one ground in the functional equivalency of power enacted through separation and opposition:

The American black man should be focusing his every effort toward building his *own* business, and decent homes for himself. As other ethnic groups have done, let the black people, wherever possible, however possible, patronize their *own* kind, hire their *own* kind, and start in those ways to build up the black race's ability to do for itself. That's the only way the American black man is ever going to get respect. One thing the white man never can give the black man is self-respect. *The black man never can become independent and recognized as a human being who is truly equal with other human beings until he has what they have, and until he is doing for himself what others are doing for themselves.*[26]

For Malcolm X, then, the commitment to "equality" invoked a condition of respectful reciprocity between two equals in power. The separateness of such equals becomes vividly apparent in his definition: "we believe in equality, and equality means you have to put the same thing over here that you put over there."[27] When it became clear to Malcolm X that such a conception of equality was inconsistent with the orthodox, Anglo-American conception of "equality under the law," he sought to alter its meaning by urging black Americans to assert their "equal power" under the banner of "the ballot or the bullet!"[28]

This perspective is at direct odds with King's projection of "equality" as a formal and identical sameness between two entities. In King's world, two individuals achieve equality when each is ultimately indistinguishable from and interchangeable with the other, much as we might say that "two plus two *equals* four." As we indicate below, when one studies King's public discourse it becomes increasingly clear that the commitment to "equality" that he expressed presumed what he called the "beloved community," a world defined in terms of the total assimilation and integration of all races and creeds.[29]

The link between power and the commitment to "equality" as a condition of community concerned both Malcolm X and Martin Luther King, Jr., but again, manifest differences in their respective visions separated the two from one another. Whereas Malcolm X saw "equality" as the empowerment of the self or group, present only in the active condition of opposition and separation, King had a Christian concept of moral power, attainable only through the consolidation of the self with a transcendental, collective force that eschewed separation and disunity. It is thus that King argued in his "Letter from Birmingham Jail" that the failure to achieve assimilation and integration counted as a "sin" in the eyes of God.[30]

The differences between Malcolm X and King are instructive. When faced with the conditions of sociopolitical and economic oppression, a cultural history that characterized the identity of African Americans as insignificant or inferior, and a paradoxical commitment to "equality" that denied the possibility for any complete cultural assimilation, Malcolm X chose to reject white America's authority to define "equality" and offered an entirely new definition that gave African Americans a more distinct and powerful cultural presence. To redefine completely one of the central and foundational commitments of a political ideology, as Malcolm X sought to do, is tantamount to revolution. In the eyes of the prevailing, white political culture, it automatically identified him as a dangerous outlaw and relegated him to the peripheries of legitimate and reasonable public discourse.

By contrast to Malcolm X, King challenged 1960s white America to enact the role of a transhistorical American "people" guided in its contemporary social, political, and economic practices by the founding commitment to "equality" as the motivating term for its national constitution. Rather than to reject and redefine the Anglo-American commitment to "equality," King crafted a verbal tapestry that invited a public (re)visioning of the term's usage in the Declaration of Independence and the Emancipation Proclamation, two of the political nation's most sacred documents. In so doing he contextualized the word "equality" in a discursive structure that literally intertextualized white America's faith in the promises of the American dream, with its faith in the Christian guarantees of redemptive justice and salvation. The American dream and Christianity serve here as culturally authorized narratives functioning to emphasize the transcendent, ideological, and moral imperatives of cultural identity, unity, and sameness. Thus instead of rejecting the prevailing narratives of American political culture, King amplified and redirected them so as to lead white America to envision their commitment to "equality" in a more fulgent light. At the same time, he enthymematicly intertextualized his (re)vision of the American dream with the implicit threats posed by those like Malcolm X, whom he characterized as the advocates of a "marvelous new militancy." Eventually, his efforts compelled a relatively large number of white Americans to act in obeisance to the unique and radical potential implicit in the meaning of "equality" as a universal, Christianized, liberal-democratic commitment rather than to the long-standing, particular, and partisan interests of a white power structure.

A fairly strong case can be made that Malcolm X and Martin Luther King, Jr., addressed two different audiences and that each carefully calculated his approach to the commitment to "equality" with a rhetorical sensitivity to the different needs and interests of his respective listeners. To quit our analysis at this point, however, would be to ignore the important sense in which the public influence of the vision of "equality" each advocate offered presumed in part the historically specific rhetorical context created by the other. The implicit rhetorical effect of this dialetic was twofold: First, it directed attention to the way in which the word "equality" resonated in the rhetorical history of American public discourse as a potent and paradoxical argumentative warrant for social and political behavior. Second, and no less important, it heightened public awareness of what was at stake for white America in negotiating—or failing to negotiate—one or another interpretation of "equality" in the national dialogue on race relations. Elsewhere, we consider the sense in which King's discourse served as an important element of the rhetorical context for Malcolm X's revolutionary critique and radical redefinition of "equality."[31] Here we examine King's efforts to (re)envision America's egalitarian heritage by universalizing the cultural resources of the dominant white, Christian-American ideology in the rhetorical context of Malcolm X's vivid threat to achieve radical change "by all means necessary."

Universalizing "Equality" in Christian America

Martin Luther King, Jr., was an extremely prolific public speaker, delivering over three thousand speeches between the time he took over as the minister of the Dexter Avenue Baptist Church in Montgomery in 1954 and his untimely death in 1968. Of all these speeches, none stands out in sharper relief than "I Have a Dream." On the day following its delivery, James Reston observed in the *New York Times* that "it will be a long time before Washington [or the nation] forgets the melodious or melancholy voice of Reverend Dr. Martin Luther King crying out his dreams to the multitudes."[32] Reston's judgment proved prophetic, for in the time since its delivery it has become an American cultural icon, a symbolic touchstone for anyone who would try to interpret the meaning of the American character. Central to the speech's cultural power and longevity is its universalization of the commitment to "equality" as the motivating term linking America's political and religious foundations.

"Universalization" refers to the inherently rhetorical process of public argumentation whereby advocates strive to constitute and legitimize the most universal audience necessary to frame and manage the often heterogeneous, particular audiences relevant to a specific rhetorical interaction.[33] Public argumentation is always an effort on the part of advocates to pose their listeners as a community invested in some sort of collective, public interest. The success of such an endeavor relies on the advocates' ability to persuade listeners to sublimate their individual differences in favor of some set of collective similarities. Once the physically and often culturally heterogeneous members of a particular audience begin to think of themselves as constituted by their homogeneous, organic interests as a community or "people," they come to embody the beliefs, values, and commitments of a historically specific universal audience.[34]

The phrase "historically specific universal audience" in the preceding sentence is *not* an oxymoron, for in the domain of public argumentation rhetorical processes are always concerned with the immediate, lived conditions of speakers and audiences, and those conditions are always contingent and particular, always subject to change. The universal audience is not truly universal, then, in the idealist sense of a transcendent reality. Rather it is the intersubjective imagination of a particular speaker and a particular audience in a particular historical moment. It is thus rhetorically constituted, and it owes its continued existence to the power and presence of the rhetorical moment of its conception. If a specific instantiation of the universal audience continues to exist beyond that moment in time—whether for a few short weeks or for millennia—it is because the speaker and the audience are capable of persuasively disseminating their characterization of it to larger, particular audiences. But even in such circumstances it is unlikely that the specific prevailing conception of the universal audience remains unchanged over time. By its very nature, therefore, the rhetorical process of public argumentation inclines advocates who would motivate and legitimize collective action to seek to appeal to or to craft audience-specific, universal representations of communal values.

The commitment to "equality" as a universalizing value emerges as the central and organizing image of "I Have a Dream" through the stylistic intertextualization of two prevailing cultural narratives: the American dream, with its promise for material progress, and the Christian faith in the cycle of guilt, purification, and redemption.[35] We have already noted the symbolic significance of the physical scene of the speech and how King employs it in his opening paragraphs to evoke the audience's cultural memory of Abraham Lincoln as the Great Emancipator. Lincoln's place in American history as a political messiah literally sets the stage for (re)visioning "equality" within the texture of America's secular and spiritual tapestry. The first step in evoking this weave occurs immediately in the following paragraphs as King invokes a check metaphor, with its commonly accepted, capitalistic commitment to contracts, i.e., the relationship between "promises" and "performances," to call attention to the very real obligations and failings of American "equality":

So we have come here today to dramatize a shameful condition. In a sense we have come to our nation's capital to cash a check. When the architects of our republic wrote the magnificent words of the Constitution and the Declaration of Independence, they were signing a promissory note to which every American was to fall heir. This note was the promise that all men, yes, black men as well as white men, would be guaranteed the unalienable rights of life, liberty, and the pursuit of happiness.

It is obvious today that America has defaulted on this promissory note in so far as her citizens of color are concerned. Instead of honoring this sacred obligation, America has given the Negro people a bad check, which has come back marked "insufficient funds." We refuse to believe that the bank of justice is bankrupt. We refuse to believe that there are insufficient funds in the great vaults of opportunity of this nation. So we have come to cash this check—a check that will give upon demand the riches of freedom and the security of justice.

Specific mention of the word "equality" is missing here, of course, but King's earlier references to the Emancipation Proclamation combine with his depiction of the "sacred obligation" inherent to the Declaration of Independence and Constitution to make it conceptually present as the common, fundamental term uniting these documents. By implication, then, King identifies "equality" as the ultimate term necessary to the enactment of freedom and justice. Additionally, in signifying "equality" through an economic metaphor, he contextualizes its usage within a cultural narrative that presumably universalizes the guarantee of *equal* opportunities for material success to *all* citizens.

Following the introduction, King invites a slight shift in the focus of his audience's attention by reframing the narrative of the American dream through archetypal, metaphorical representations that invoke and legitimize a Christian conception of justice.[36] In creating a discursive frame that allows a Christian/American audience to integrate its secular beliefs with its spiritual faith, King characterizes the commitment to equality in terms that transcend political or partisan interpretation: "We have also come to this hallowed spot to remind America of the fierce urgency of now. This is no time to engage in the luxury of cooling off or to take the tranquilizing drug of gradualism. Now is the time to make real the promises of democracy. *Now is the time to rise from the dark and desolate valley of segregation to the sunlit path of racial justice. Now is the time to lift our nation from the quicksands of racial injustice to the solid rock of brotherhood.* Now is the time to make justice a reality for all God's children" (Emphasis added). The symbolic transformations linking ideological promises with a transcendental Christian "justice" in this passage are too obvious to require specific elaboration here. What is important to note, however, is that the same universalizing transformations take place under a variety of different guises throughout the speech. Consider, for example, the studied placement of the words "hope," "dream," and "faith" throughout the speech. In the first third of the speech, where King discusses America's failure to perform its promise, he displays and portrays his fervent "hope" that this problem can be resolved. By the second third of the speech, that hope disappears, replaced by the dream that King links with the American dream. But notice that the American dream is specifically *not* a dream in the sense of a hope or wish for a better world, but rather a vision of the guarantee of every American's birthright to "equality." By the last third of the speech, however, the hope of the first part of the speech transcends even the ideological guarantees of the American dream and becomes precisely a transcendental "faith" in a Christian-American future. That faith closely approximates what King would later refer to as the "beloved community," and in so doing it simultaneously recalls and universalizes the prevailing white American commitment to "equality" as individual sameness and identity.

Taken in its totality, "I Have a Dream" is a textual distillation of what King had said on numerous occasions since the Montgomery bus boycott nine years earlier. As a rhetorical process, however, universalization entails more than simply creating an interpretive framework for transcending otherwise separate or disparate narratives. In order to engage an audience's active interest or commitment, universalized values need to vivify the moral power of those narratives. It is not enough simply to be reminded of one's collective past in order to be motivated to act on its behalf, particularly when there are significant individual risks at stake. Rather, for such universalization to be effective, it must entice its audience literally to experience their *past* as the members of a collectivity at a critical moment in *time present* with a clear image of the degree to which their collective *future* is at stake. It is thus necessary that a speaker find ways to vitalize the often timeworn symbols that give presence to the narratives that contribute to the universalization process.

King gave vital presence to his image of a Christian/American equality through the projection of powerful aural and visual images. To begin with, he employed the relatively simple stylistic techniques he had mastered as a Baptist minister speaking from the pulpit, including repetition, subtle alliteration, and the use of broad and resonant vowel sounds. Though one must actually listen to "I Have a Dream" in order fully to appreciate the eloquent integration of style and content that it fosters, the sense of its power emerges in his use of repetition as a framework for responding to those who criticized the civil rights movement for demanding too much, too soon:

There are those who are asking the devotees of civil rights "When will you be satisfied?" *We can never be satisfied* as long as the Negro is the victim of unspeakable horrors of police brutality. *We can never be satisfied* so long as our bodies, heavy with the fatigue of travel, cannot gain lodging in the motels of the highways and the hotels of the cities. *We cannot be satisfied* as long as the Negro's basic mobility is from a smaller ghetto to a larger one. *We can never be satisfied* as long as our children are stripped of their selfhood and robbed of their dignity by signs stating "for whites only." *We cannot be satisfied* as long as a Negro in Mississippi cannot vote and a Negro in New York believes he has nothing for which to vote. *No, we are not satisfied, and we will not be satisfied* until justice rolls down like waters and righteousness like a mighty stream. [Emphasis added.]

In this passage King artistically secularizes the sonorous tones of the black preacher to vitalize a series of material conditions that effectively nullify and deny even the appearance of equality as a lived condition in the lives of African Americans. In so doing, he vividly articulates a cultural resonance that seeks, in its incessant repetition and negations, to enlist the prior commitment to "equality" of his presumably Christian/American audience as the argumentative warrant that imagistically highlights, and thus undermines, the irony of the original question, "When will you be satisfied?"

The commitment to "equality" is likewise animated in King's usage of rhetorical figuration. Having intertextualized the structures of a more or less materialistic American dream with a spiritual, redemptive Christianity as the sociopolitical, rhetorical foundations for the nation, he seeks to visualize the moral authority of these founding narratives by linking them with archetypal metaphors. A particularly important source of such metaphors for the rhetorical audience King was trying to constitute was the Bible. Evoking biblical imagery, he thus invited his listeners to experience the "solid rock of human dignity" as the moral cornerstone to the commitment to "equality." Relying on the cyclical quality of the day/night pair of archetypal metaphors, he assured his listeners of the moral guarantees of their cause in inviting them to visualize the inevitability of the "daybreak of freedom and justice" as it emerged from "the bleak and desolate midnight of man's inhumanity to man into the bright and glittering daybreak of freedom and justice." Alternately, he implored their sacred, moral conviction to move vertically toward the "majestic heights of understanding and brotherhood." Such simple, archetypal images lend a clear and simple, universalizing authorization to otherwise political and partisan commitments like "equality," for they attach the meaning of such commitments to the presumably fundamental, primitive, and transcultural experiences of the human community. They thus offer a vivid frame of reference from within which to motivate a particular audience, such as King's, to overcome the immediate and particular resistance to racial justice that the perverted forces of history and economics had momentarily subverted.

In order to be successful in calling a universalized audience into existence, the narratives woven together must rely upon the particular audience's recognition and acceptance of specific and concrete rhetorical characterizations of the various acts, scenes, agents, and agencies employed to make the narrative coherent.[37] It is here that King's usage of biblical imagery did the most to vitalize the commitment to "equality" as a commitment that demanded the active participation of the audience. Throughout his career King characterized blacks and whites as identical, ignoring the physical differences separating them from one another and thus implicitly ignoring the paradox of equality. To effect this characterization he relied heavily on his faith in a generic or universal "person" as created *by God* in his own image. The Christian belief in the similarity of "all men" is most evident in King's definition of love as the necessary path to human salvation. As he noted in his address to the Fellowship of the Concerned in 1961, "when one rises to love on this level [agape], he loves men not because he likes them, not because their ways appeal to him, but he loves every man because God loves him."[38]

In "I Have a Dream" the underlying commitment to a transcendental love of God gets translated as a rhetorical characterization of "creative suffering," the agency of nonviolent massive resistance through which the integration of an empowering Christian/American unity would effectively perform its purpose. As King freely noted on numerous other occasions, such unity could not be achieved by means that required or allowed division, violence, or separation. Only the broad sense of Christian love, enacted through non-

violence and the willingness to suffer for the oppressor, would ultimately achieve the universal condition of "equality" for all men.
Thus, he notes:

> You have been the veterans of creative suffering. Continue to work with
> the faith that unearned suffering is redemptive.
> Go back to Mississippi; go back to Alabama; go back to South Carolina;
> go back to Georgia; go back to Louisiana; go back to the slums and ghettos
> of the northern cities, knowing that somehow this situation can, and will be
> changed. Let us not wallow in the valley of despair.
> So, I say to you, my friends, that even though we must face the difficulties
> of today and tomorrow, I still have a dream. It is a dream deeply rooted in the
> American dream that one day this nation will rise up and live out the *true
> meaning* of its creed—we hold these truths to be self-evident, that all men
> are created equal. [Emphasis added.]

It is significant that the link between the Christian faith that
"unearned suffering is redemptive" and the "true meaning" of the
American creed occurs precisely at the point in the speech that King
shifts his attention from acknowledging the absence of equality as a
material condition of society to representing the dream of the at-
tainment of "equality" as a universalizing commitment to brotherhood, freedom, and justice. Consequently, it garners its rhetorical
power by, once again, simultaneously unifying and vivifying America's fundamental religious and political commitments to community in the context of the particular sociopolitical crisis confronting
the audience, i.e., the choice posed by the tension between the
rhetorical constructions of "equality" one finds in King's vision of a
universalized American dream, or Malcolm X's vision of the "ballot
or the bullet."

King's Legacy

At the outset we maintained that Martin Luther King, Jr.'s legacy
to America had more to do with his universalizing (re)vision of
the dominant and prevailing commitment to American "equality"
than with his use of nonviolent massive resistance as an agency of
change. In the end it is of course impossible to separate the two, for
as we have shown above, King's dream for America and his specific
means of enacting it were stylistically and ideologically unified
with one another. This is not to undermine the importance of his
program for nonviolent resistance, but only to suggest that such a
program must be measured and understood in the context of the

pragmatic, sociopolitical consciousness it enabled in the life of the community in which it was rhetorically enacted.

The design of King's program for social and political reform suggests that his primary concern was to empower those he finally described as America's "voiceless" citizens, the men and women who lacked rhetorical access to the powerful cultural and symbolic resources of the nation.[39] For King, the most important resource denied the voiceless was the commitment to "equality," in his (re)vision, a sacred and universalizing promise made by the nation's founding fathers that *all* Americans would have identical opportunities to exercise their inalienable rights to "life, liberty, and the pursuit of happiness." In adopting the historically dominant, Anglo-American commitment to "equality," King risked locating himself squarely within the paradox of equality that has been a problem for African-American advocates since the time of America's revolutionary war.

The argument here is that King's most significant legacy to America rests in the public consciousness of "equality" that his rhetorical management of this paradox made possible. Rather than to allow his listeners to envision the nonviolent civil rights movement as *the* primary opposition to the preservation of a segregationist America in which the commitment to "equality" represented a rather narrow and restrictive set of meanings, he triangulated the choices available to the nation. Americans were thus faced with choosing to live uncomfortably with the knowledge of a massive contradiction between their national creed and deeds, to risk a potentially violent and revolutionary rejection of American "equality" by the growing numbers of African Americans seduced by the "marvelous new militancy" being articulated by the likes of Malcolm X, or to universalize the radical potential in America's history and thus to constitute the nation in terms of a fundamental commitment to "equality." Those in a position to interpret and enact the U.S. Constitution in the mid-1960s chose the last alternative. And in so doing, they thus lent authority to King's (re)vision of American "equality" as a viable cultural resource for future generations of public advocates.

Martin Luther King, Jr.'s dream for America is of course not yet a material reality. But that failure is more ours as a nation than it was King's as a moral and political leader. By crafting the public meaning of "equality" in terms of both America's liberal-democratic commitment to progress and the Christian faith in a redemptive destiny, King produced the vision for a compelling possibility, a community which, if enacted, would decrease the likelihood that any members of American society would be forced to sacrifice the dream of "equality" to the pains and frustrations of achieving its promise. It is the rhetorical consciousness of the future possibility of such a "guarantee," rooted in our national, collective past, that stands as King's most compelling legacy for America.

6

"I Have a Dream": The Performance of Theology Fused with the Power of Orality

John H. Patton

Martin Luther King, Jr.'s most acclaimed speech, "I Have a Dream,"[1] has been frequently cited but not always carefully studied from a rhetorical perspective. The speech is noteworthy not simply because of the phrase from which its name arises nor because of its social significance and reception at the time of delivery alone. Rather it stands as an enduring emblem of oral discourse at its best, performing the powerful, cohesive functions of oral traditions over many historical and social periods. The power of this speech not only pays tribute to King but equally underscores the significance of the oral dimensions of discourse in crucial historical situations. The speech deserves examination as a distinctive rhetorical text because it provides an enduring set of ideas centered on the normative concepts of justice and unity, along with the presentation of those ideas in a powerful narrative pattern. As such it not only illuminates the thought of King and the events of our culture at a critical moment but also contributes to our understanding of rhetoric as an oral form. My purpose in what follows is to examine "I Have a Dream" as a significant example of theo-political rhetoric distinguished by substantive elements of the concept of proclamation in the Judeo-Christian tradition and by formal elements reflecting essential features of orality. The rhetorical and permanent social importance of "I Have a Dream" results, I maintain, from its creative blending of theological and oral dimensions in the context of a major rhetorical situation.

"I Have a Dream" as Theological Proclamation

The substance of King's argument throughout the speech is developed in the fashion of a theological proclamation. By this I mean that King invokes a pattern consistent with the major dimensions of the kerygma or essential argument forms utilized in New Testament apostolic preaching. Interestingly, this sets King's preaching somewhat apart from the pattern associated with Old Testament prophecy, a pattern frequently evidenced in earlier forms of American religious rhetoric, notably in Puritan preaching. This observation is important because it allows us to see the manner in which King develops the archetype of the suffering servant as the moral base for the fulfillment of the dream of equality. It also directs us to King's use of what some theologians term "realized eschatology," the idea that the kingdom of God has already begun and is in the process of being fulfilled, to portray the vision of a just society coming into being. The concept of eschatology is rooted in the Greek New Testament *eschatos* indicating "something which is last either materially or in space" and came to represent the doctrine of the end of time: "the end began with the coming of Jesus" coupled with the "expectation of the coming last day," which brings judgment and triumph of the eternal realm of God over the temporal world.[2] Eschatology as a governing theological doctrine has been significantly traced, for example, by Rudolph Bultmann who noted that eschatology gave the Church an original understanding of itself involving a sense of otherness and transcendence that gradually became modified as the end of time became less apparent. He observed that "while the consciousness of being a non-worldly society belonging to the other world and filled with its powers does not actually get lost, it nevertheless suffers a peculiar transformation. In consequence of the delay of the expected *parousia* the transcendent character of the Church gradually comes to be seen not so much in its reference to the future as in its present possession of institutions which are already mediating transcendent powers in the present: a sacramental cultus and finally a priestly office."[3] The decline of eschatology as a force in the life of the church and an effort to renew it as the center of Christian theology was more recently developed in the work of Jürgen Moltmann. He identifies hope as the authentic legacy of early eschatology and argues that a theology of hope restores the eschatological power of believers by creatively connecting the present with the future. Moltmann writes: "That is why faith, whenever it develops into hope, causes not rest but unrest, not patience but impatience. It does not calm the unquiet heart, but is itself this unquiet heart in man. Those who hope in Christ can no longer put up with reality as it is, but begin to suffer under it, to contradict it. Peace with God means conflict with the world, for the goad of the promised future stabs inexorably into the flesh of every unfulfilled present."[4] Precisely this dynamic of hope is powerfully expressed in "I Have a Dream" as King portrays the oppression of the unfulfilled present in response to what Moltmann called the vision of a promised future.

In almost every instance Martin Luther King, Jr., described himself simply and directly as "a preacher." One gets the sense that this was a singularly significant term for King, reflecting a central theological impulse which informed his life and thought, that knowledge of God was instrumental in nature and that it led directly to action in the world. Indeed, preaching was the performance of theology for King, the actualization of the concepts he held. We see this impulse from his earliest days as pastor of Dexter Avenue Church in Montgomery. David Garrow observed that in that period King "threw himself into his preaching. Each week he would devote hours to writing out and memorizing the complete text of his Sunday sermon. His young pulpit assistant, John Thomas Porter, was always impressed by how King would bring that text with him, but would leave it in his chair and ascend to the pulpit without any notes. The results impressed almost all."[5] One of those most impressed was a visitor to Dexter Avenue Church, James Baldwin. His biographer reports that "sitting in the congregation, Baldwin sensed a feeling 'which quite transcended anything I have ever felt in a church before.' He had heard all kinds of preachers and was no mean preacher himself, but he considered King 'a great speaker.' He thought King's secret lay in his intimate knowledge of his audience, black or white, and in the forthrightness with which he spoke of those things that hurt and baffled them."[6] Baldwin's acute sensitivity to intimacy and forthrightness in expression are especially notable. His commentary provides a sense of the implicit and explicit bonding King's use of language made possible, particularly for audiences who shared a common base of oppression. The language of the speech, the sound of his voice, and the quality of King's physical presence combined as he articulated the hurts and hopes of blacks, at the same time extending the symbolic canopy of oppression and redemption to all those in the larger public who have experienced the pain of unjust discrimination. King's language of the dream was both an account of the historic oppression of African Americans and an announcement of the theology of redemption grounded in an eschatology of hope.

The theology King performed in his sermons drew deeply from dual, quite different yet interrelated, sources: his background and experience in the African-American church tradition and his evolving theological education at Crozer Seminary and Boston University. Regarding the former, James Cone has long held that we should not view the years of formal theological training "as the primary resources for understanding King's ideas and actions." He contends, instead, that "the most significant circumstances that shaped King's theology . . . were the oppression of black people and the liberating message of the black church. These two realities—the oppression of blacks and the black church's liberating message of the Gospel— provided King with the intellectual challenge to develop a theology that was Christian and also relevant for the social and political needs of black people."[7] More recently, Keith Miller takes much the same position in arguing that "King's world view and discourse sprang from two major sources: the sermons of Harry Emerson Fosdick and other liberal white preachers; and the African-American folk pulpit of King's father and grandfather, both of whom were folk preachers."[8] There is abundant evidence to support the influence of the black church tradition on King's thought and preaching, although the nature of that influence is more complex than may first appear. For example, during his college years King was undecided about entering the ministry in part because of misgivings about aspects of black religion. According to Garrow, "much black religion, he [King] believed, emphasized emotion rather than ideas and volume rather than elocution. Furthermore, many ministers preached only about the afterlife, rather than about what role the church could play in improving present-day society."[9] This passage suggests that while King was in the black church tradition, he was early on looking for ways to supplement and modify what he saw as problems in that tradition. Thus it would be as equally unreasonable to conclude that the black church tradition served as the sole or the controlling influence on King's theology as it would be to maintain that his theological education was the sole or dominating influence.

The nature of King's theological education at Boston University became a powerful influence that surfaced and resurfaced throughout his public discourse. He completed what we now know to be a substantially flawed doctoral dissertation in 1955, "A Comparison of the Conceptions of God in the Thinking of Paul Tillich and Henry Nelson Wicman."[10] I refer to the instances of plagiarism revealed initially by the *Wall Street Journal* and the *New York Times*.[11] The most complete account to date of the plagiarism and its significance, along with commentary from a variety of King associates and scholars, was published in the June 1991 issue of the *Journal of American History*. This revelation has led to a number of revisionist assessments of King's public writings in particular. Scholars are beginning to draw important distinctions between King's published writings and the body of unpublished sermons and speeches, the latter being considered far more authentic and freer of editing and related problems.[12] The emphasis on speeches and sermons not prepared for publication lends added weight to the "I Have a Dream" speech because of the way it combines a carefully prepared written text in the initial sections of the speech with the spontaneous passages that form the more famous dream sequences in the latter part in the total context of an oral performance. In an especially insightful essay Garrow has posited three aspects of a complex explanation of why King knowingly violated academic rules. The first explanation has to do with a possible lack of expectation by King's professors combined with the fact "that King himself absorbed the lesson that comprehensive regurgitation, rather than individual originality or creativity, was the accepted academic style at Boston University's School of Theology."[13] A second aspect was that King may have been "to a considerable extent going through the motions—preparing and submitting written work that was what he understood his instructors expected but that held little personal meaning or significance for King himself."[14] Last, Garrow suggests "a significant reinterpretation of King before the Montgomery bus boycott," stressing that "King's acquisition of that fundamental sense of mission, calling, and obligation that came to him in Montgomery transformed him into someone whose newly enriched self-understanding gave to his future life an integrity, a dedication, and a sense of purpose reaching well beyond himself that simply had not been present in his life, and in his academic studies, up to that time."[15] The transformative explanation seems especially plausible since King consistently used his life experiences to define and shape his thought. Garrow points to the bus boycott in this formative fashion; we can similarly discern that while nonviolence, for example, is an attractive notion, it becomes fully real for King after he visits India and encounters the method at work in a human context. The March on Washington is in much the same way a crystallizing event, a moment of conflict within and without the movement, a time of special urgency in which the issue of civil rights will need to be defined for specific publics and for the nation at large. The language of the speech draws from King's transformative experiences in Montgomery, Albany, and Birmingham as these allow him to focus on the problem of transforming the cultural understanding of civil rights as a whole.

In spite of the plagiarized passages in his dissertation, it remains clear that the theological sources King encountered at Crozer and

Boston University were strong and significant influences. Indeed, beyond acknowledging the existence of plagiarism itself, we need to explore possible implications about King's rhetorical processes, especially his conception and use of language. David Thelen underscores this point by commenting that "instead of viewing the news as an opportunity to probe how and why a great American used language in this way at this time and place, most commentators worried instead about how much King's plagiarism diminished his greatness and heroism."[16] Building on Bernice Johnson Reagon's idea that King "tried to draw separate worlds together by building borderlands between them where people could mingle instead of collide," Thelen notes that "the challenge for a person who wanted to be heard by people from different cultures was to find a voice for himself that was appropriate to each occasion and that could draw on different languages in ways all groups could recognize and respect."[17] King finds his voice, perhaps his most compelling public voice, in exactly this way in "I Have a Dream."

In view of the plagiarism found in the thematic content of the dissertation, perhaps the most insightful aspect of that work is the method King adopts to critique the positions of both Tillich and Wieman. It is significant that Tillich stands as one of the Western world's most imaginative spokesmen for a view of God as "Being-Itself," immersed in a virtually universal and highly symbolic way in the world. Similarly, Wieman was known as a leading "Personalist" theologian who strongly emphasized a view of God as "creative event." While King was critical of both of these theologians regarding the personality of God, he used many of their insights in formulating the moral foundations for the theme of nonviolent social resistance patterned after the model of God's action in the world. In objecting to what he considered limitations of both theologians, King deliberately seeks a way to reconcile and synthesize the general ideas of both into a larger, more inclusive view. The same tendency to seek a middle way, a synthesis, provides insight into the form and function of sermonic rhetoric. In a detailed study of that aspect of King's formal theological work, James P. Hanigan has observed that "on the question of the personality of God King was equally critical of both men. Essentially both Tillich and Wieman argued that God is above or beyond the human concept of personality."[18] King found it vital to locate divine personality in human events and experiences. Hanigan notes that "what King's criticism of Tillich and Wieman makes evident above all else is a characteristic of his own mind-set, a characteristic which we might call the both-and mind set, as opposed to an either-or mentality."[19]

As a result of this and related theological work King arrived at a definite view of "what the personal God of power and goodness is about in this world."[20]

As King expressed it, God works "to bring goodness to pass . . . and through human beings is striving to achieve a social order that is moral in its nature and capable of expressing love."[21] This idea led to King's view that the kingdom of God was both a present and a future reality. As Hanigan, again, indicates, "as a present reality [for King] it can exist as an inner possession in history. . . . As a future reality it is the idealized social order. . . . Every progress of human life toward that idealized order is an expression of the power of the Kingdom of God in history."[22] Precisely this dynamic tension between the present and future realities of the kingdom are reflected in the "Dream" speech as King focuses on inequities of the past and present and simultaneously creates the vision of a new social order.

King's theology of the kingdom is ideally suited for his role as a proclaimer in the fashion of New Testament kerygma. In this form of discourse the emphasis is placed not on the action of the preacher, but on that which he preaches.[23] It was based on the assumption that God had revealed himself historically in a significant way or event. It was thought to be somewhat distinct from *didache*, or preaching designed mainly to instruct. Indeed, the chief goal of kerygmatic preaching was to announce an encounter between God and man.[24] The textual model for this form of preaching, to which King was thoroughly exposed in his upbringing in the church and in theological education, was Jesus' speaking in the synagogue, cited in Luke 4:16–21. Several important characteristics have been observed: liturgically, that Jesus' sermon was delivered within the established framework of Jewish worship; exegetically, that he spoke from a specific text; prophetically, that he declared the *present* fulfillment of scripture, addressing the present with divine authority; that he created ethical intensification of moral standards; that he emphasized "realized eschatology" in that the promises of God are held to have already been fulfilled and now need to be acted upon; that he used the parabolic method to create symbolic narratives as the structure for shared meanings.[25]

In varying degrees these kerygmatic elements are present in "I Have a Dream" and help explain how the speech operates. The whole oration is set within the framework of an established ceremonial pattern. It came as the climax to a long campaign for civil rights and as an effort to concentrate political and legislative attention on policy issues about civil rights. The details of the March on Washington are especially well documented in recent biographies by Stephen B. Oates and David J. Garrow.[26] Exegetically, King showed considerable skill in employing both a literal and a symbolic text. He grounds the speech literally in the Emancipation Proclamation and in the persona of Abraham Lincoln. In effect, King completes the text by tracing the full implications of emancipation and by presenting his own persona as the symbolic outcome of Lincoln's action. The liturgical and exegetical are artfully combined in that the physical setting for the oration reflected the symbolic power of the verbal message.

At a more overtly symbolic level King draws upon the incipient quality of the concept of the "Dream" as a rhetorical text. This concept was not an entirely new theme in his discourse, although it had never been sharpened and focused in quite so dramatic a fashion. Interestingly, an earlier version of the "Dream" as text appeared in an address given at a public meeting of the Charlotte, North Carolina, branch of the NAACP in 1960. There King announced that his subject was "The Negro and the American Dream" and observed that "in a real sense America is essentially a dream—a dream yet unfulfilled. It is the dream of a land where men of all races, colors, and creeds will live together as brothers. The substance of the dream is expressed in these sublime words: 'We hold these truths to be self-evident, that all men are created equal, that they are endowed by their creator with certain unalienable rights, that among these are life, liberty, and the pursuit of happiness.' This is the dream."[27]

In tracing the development of the speech, Garrow has commented that King had used the dream concept as a peroration on other occasions "at a mass meeting in Birmingham in early April, and in a speech in Detroit's huge civil rights rally in June," but that at the March on Washington, "the words carried an inspirational power greater than many of those present ever had heard before."[28] This power was in part due to King's own sensitivity to his listeners and his ability to translate this occasion to one equivalent to the conditions of orality and audience interaction with which he was so familiar as a kerygmatic preacher. Many of the same participants in the mass meeting in Birmingham, and throughout other parts of the country, had journeyed to Washington for this climactic civil rights march. Thus, while many of them had doubtless heard King refer to the "Dream," the power of the "Dream" as a rhetorical symbol which evoked underlying values and created unifying patterns of identification and inspiration came alive in a new and deeper way on this occasion. In fact, King remembered the speech as involving a clear shift from written text to a more extemporaneous form. In an interview with Garrow, King commented: "I started out reading the speech. . . . just all of a sudden—the audience response was wonderful that day—and all of a sudden this thing came to me that I have used—I'd used it many times before, that thing about 'I have a dream'—and I just felt that I wanted to use it here. I don't know why, I hadn't thought about it before the speech."[29] King's comment may reflect a lack of specific advance strategy, but it is certainly evident that at the deepest level he had processed the fundamental concept of the dream as a powerful symbolic form which became readily available as a motivating idea.

To proclaim that the substance of America is a dream, an essentially unfilled dream at that, is to offer a powerful rhetorical symbol. Like all such symbols its power is partly dependent on the *persona* and character of the speaker, the form in which the symbol is presented, the ideological content it provides for the thoughts and feelings of audiences, and the extent to which it serves as a response to the situational requirements involved. The contours of the dream were defined by King's theology. One author has observed that King's career can be viewed as three stages, each grounded in a clear set of theological positions: The first consists of the development of the mass meeting in black churches in the South as the backbone of the movement; the second is the translation of political actualities into moral, transcendent themes in the 1963 Birmingham campaign and the March on Washington; and the final stage is essentially an enactment of the role of Moses at the edge of the Promised Land in the Memphis campaign and in King's "I've Been to the Mountaintop" speech.[30] Throughout these stages it is the distinctive combination of forceful Old Testament imagery with the adherence to the New Testament version of agape-love that guides and directs King's theology. James McClendon contends that

> it was especially in the Old Testament that he [King] found two elements of his faith, man's own role and the role of God in history, held together in productive tension. Had he emphasized only the humanistic ethic of freedom, King might have been one more Black Militant determined to wring today's revenge from yesterday's injustices. Had he spoken only of God's purpose to redeem, he might have fallen prey to the compensatory religion against which [his mentor] Benjamin Mays had warned. But to this Baptist it was both: man who must act, and God who is acting. Man on his own loses his way, grows weary, discouraged, while passive dependence on God alone is disobedience to God. Either half of the paradox of God-with-man taken alone produces falsehood, but taken together they produce the true vision of the purpose of God and the significance of man's history.[31]

The productive tension between man's role and God's activity in history provides an important clue to the operation of King's rhetoric. Two levels of action are reflected here, one an essentially abstract and cosmic level representing the ongoing action of God and another very concrete specific form of action at the human level, requiring personal choices in particular contexts of opposition to prevailing forms of social injustice. The deliberate decision to break an existing law is a specific form of action; the ultimate justification for doing so grounded in God's continuing role in history is a much more general concept. Nevertheless, the general concept makes the specific action both possible and plausible. For King theology contained both these elements of abstract and particularized action, and he uses this model in shaping the pattern and development of the civil rights movement. It is clearly a form of rhetorical action that mirrors theological action in the sense in which King understood it.

At the level of abstraction King roots the dream in the words of the Bill of Rights. It is thus a constitutional and for that very reason a constitutive idea. For King this idea operated in the sense of a covering law. It is an important element in the "rhetorical depiction" of the dream. As Michael Osborn has noted, rhetoric frequently depicts by the manner in which a concept is presented and the patterns of identification which are held out.[32] By operating at the level of abstraction, King is also able to tap into a larger, ongoing source of public moral consciousness, which is always in a fluid state and becomes sharpened usually in response to a critical challenge or event. King uses the dream concept as a way of providing that challenge and especially to define the nature of the moral crisis involved in the issues of civil rights. Here his references to "the fierce urgency of now" and the repetition of the "now is the time" phrases serve to remind the multiple audiences of the constant moral base of key concepts such as liberty, justice, and equality. Hence the phrase "now is the time to make justice a reality for all of God's children"[33] affirms the underlying value premise that indeed the collection of "God's children" was an inclusive, not exclusive, term, and it clearly covered black as well as white people. At the same time, the phrase is used to attach the predicate "justice" to all people in the general category. By stressing the importance of "now" in this process King also begins to move the symbol of the dream from the abstract level to the level of immediacy and concrete action.

The level of specific action is developed as a form of rhetorical intensification, most dramatically accomplished in the latter sections of the speech where King admonishes listeners, just as biblical prophets were expected to do. The language preceding the famous set of "I have a dream that . . ." statements is actually a summons, a series of specific calls to action: "Go back to Mississippi, go back to Alabama, go back to South Carolina, go back to Louisiana, go back to the slums and ghettos of our northern cities, knowing that somehow this situation can and will be changed."[34] These injunctions are followed by the very specific visionary projections of how the dream with which we are all familiar will be fulfilled: "I have a dream that one day on the red hills of Georgia the sons of former slaves and former slaveowners will be able to sit down together at the table of brotherhood . . . that my four little children will one day live in a nation where they will not be judged by the color of their skin but by the content of their character."[35]

This famous section of the speech where the dream becomes most specific is wrapped at the beginning in a secular abstraction (the reference to living out the true meaning of our national creed "We hold these truths to be self-evident; that all men are created equal") and culminates in a universal theological abstraction ("the glory of the Lord shall be revealed, and all flesh shall see it together").[36] The theological pattern of productive tension permeates this part of the speech. The ease with which King moves from core concepts of justice and equality to specific applications in places such as Alabama and the personae of little children and back again to the larger, guiding themes of justice and unity is a direct reflection of his understanding of the relationship between God and history.

"I Have a Dream" as Oral Form

The power of this speech is contained not only in its theological foundations but also in the particular way in which theology fuses with important dimensions of orality. Clearly, the black church with its long tradition of oral form was a major part of this fusion. King's sensitivity to language, in particular the way language sounds to hearers who are envisioned as active participants in communicative acts, was another major ingredient because it helps us understand both the immediate and lasting powers of the speech. Because the speech takes the pattern of an oral form, it creates several types of meanings: It enables audiences to perform recalling functions at a direct level; it establishes an "agonistic" framework as the psychological and motivational context for civil rights activity; and it carries out an additive function to assist in reinforcement and intensification of beliefs and values. Moreover, through these dimensions of orality the speech both creates and meets expressive and rational expectations on the part of multiple audiences.

We cannot really imagine this speech without remembering how it appears and sounds. The visual presence of King at the backdrop of the nation's capitol and especially the resonance and tone of his voice are inextricably bound up in the power of this speech. As such, it stands as an example of orality delivered in the context of a dominantly literate, that is print-oriented, culture. Orality confronts us with a different kind of literacy, engaging the mind and heart in ways that written speech does not. Perhaps the best account of the similarities and differences in orality and literacy is contained in Walter Ong's book by that title.[37] In it he describes nine characteristics of "primary orality," many aspects of which are displayed in the "I Have a Dream" speech. Such orality is "additive rather than subordinative . . . aggregative rather than analytic . . . redundant . . . close to the human lifeworld . . . agonistically toned . . . empathetic and participatory rather than objectively distanced . . . and is more situational than abstract,"[38] among other things. With these dimensions in mind a close look at King's language is revealing.

The repetition of key phrases obviously recurs throughout the speech. The point is that the repetitions operate in an additive fashion and create aggregate symbols which both penetrate the value frames of hearers and make it easier to recall the basic themes of the speech. Consider the theme of perseverance that King stresses in calling his hearers to continue "walking ahead." He poses the rhetorical question, "When will you be satisfied?" to which he responds with a series of repetitions in the form of "we can never be satisfied as long as . . ." and culminates with a conflation of present and future tenses: "We are not satisfied, and we will not be satisfied until justice rolls down like waters and righteousness like a mighty stream."[39] Each phrase adds a new layer of examples of injustice that serve, in Ong's words, "to keep the mind focused because in the context of orality there is nothing to backloop outside the mind."[40] King's ability to layer language demonstrates a powerful level of intensification, centering the mind of the audience on the single point under discussion.

Beyond the structural aspects of orality, there are psychological dimensions which give orality much of its rhetorical force. In his detailed studies of oral societies, Ong found that oral form frequently was "agonistic" in tone. He meant that oral speech situates knowledge concretely within the human lifeworld and, most importantly, in the context of a struggle, a dynamic polarization of the world of good and evil.[41] We have already seen how King translates abstract moral concepts into images of specific persons and types of actions. In a sense the whole of the speech is an effort to underscore the nature of the moral struggle at stake in the battle for civil rights. Because it is a moral contest, it affects everyone. Acceptance of that argument requires a value choice, and King's language provides the grounding for different persons from diverse perspectives to decide on a common basis. King's reference to enacting the dream in Alabama is especially powerful in this regard. He notes that "I have a dream that one day, down in Alabama, with its vicious racist[s], with its governor having his lips dripping with the words of interposition and nullification, one day right there in Alabama little black boys and black girls will be able to join hands with little white boys and white girls as sisters and brothers."[42] Here the struggle of good versus evil is vividly portrayed at both explicit and implicit levels. At the time of delivery the violence of fire hoses and police dogs in Birmingham was fresh in the collective consciousness of the public. In retrospect, the hostility of Sheriff Jim Clark at Selma as well as the posturing of George Wallace across the state and especially at the University of Alabama were brought to the surface of memory by King's language.

The speech also provides a recurring or enduring context for moral choices quite apart from its immediate impact at the time of delivery. Consider King's selection of "little black boys and black girls" as an operative set of symbols. The possibility for future racial reconciliation pictured in his dream that black and white children would one day exist in brotherhood and sisterhood was quickly placed in the context of a tragic event: the bombing of the Sixteenth Street Baptist Church in Birmingham in September 1963 and the deaths of black children. The depth of the tragedy is reinforced by the articulated symbol of the dream of unity. Yet, it is precisely the idea of the dream that allows the bombing to be seen as part of the ongoing moral struggle. Agony is ontologically tied to innocence. In a very succinct yet constantly powerful way, this part of the speech—and the speech as a whole—holds up the images of innocent suffering as a basic part of the very fabric of the struggle for civil rights. Clearly, there is no distanced objectivity in this language, at least not in the sense of keeping deliberate detachment. King's symbols are the language of involvement, and they create in the minds and hearts of hearers an empathy for sacrifice and involvement, in short, for action. The powerful sense of identification created is a significant dimension of oral form in that audiences hearing and viewing the speech even today are able to relive the moral quality of the struggle and to sense the call to action that the language of the speech brings constantly into focus.

"I Have a Dream" as Moral Argument

The fusion of theology and orality characteristic of this speech creates in the final analysis a form of public moral argument. The nature of that fusion is observed in several specific connections between theology and dimensions of primary orality and merits further comment. In particular, orality and theology are fused through the creation of empathetic identification, the placement of issues within the context of agonistic struggle, and the emerging role of King as traditional mythic voice. As we have previously noted, the theology of the speech is firmly rooted in the New Testament concept of agape-love, the self-sacrificing dedication that formed the basis for King's repeated insistence on maintaining non-violence as the strategy for the movement and for upholding the goal of racial reconciliation. Indeed, while King appears in the form of an Old Testament figure or prophet, hence the frequent allusion to him as Black Moses, he argues in the pattern of New Testament kerygma with its emphasis on the power of agape-love which makes possible the dream of which he speaks.

Significantly, empathetic and participatory identification with the ideas, the moment, and the listener, all of which are major dimensions of primary orality, enlivens the theology of agape-love as King proclaimed it. For example, the very point at which King abandoned his written text and invoked the seemingly spontaneous imagery of the dream was a clear enactment of empathy at all those levels. The context of agonistic struggle also comes into play at this point. Every person who had suffered oppression or been denied a job, a place to eat, an opportunity to vote, a seat on a bus was immediately bonded to each other and to the ideal of the dream as the means of transcending the barriers of oppression. King's language, his vocal tone, his facial expressions, and the sheer totality of his presence in that moment reflected the effects of his message first on himself, then on the listening audience. Even time-distanced viewings of the speech reveal that King is taking the message of nonviolence and the struggle for the dream internally in a serious fashion. This type of internalizing created a high degree of authenticity both for himself and for his message. As King vocalized the internal effects of the message to the larger audience, the sense of communal identification, in Ong's words, was maximized.

The creation of empathy and identification in the context of agonistic struggle was characteristic of much of King's public discourse and reflected a central feature of the tradition of black preaching. In an insightful discussion Hortense Spillers has commented on King's consistent ability in this regard. She cites Mrs. King's reflections about the final moments of the "I Have a Dream" speech, recalling that "when King stopped reading from the text being lifted and carried himself in the overflow of powerful feeling."[43] Spillers further observes that in the style of the black sermon, the preacher would often chide or prompt audiences by repeating key phrases in direct address. Those phrases were energizing and unifying devices as long as the preacher himself was communicating his own experience of the power of the message. In her terms, "The technique was the instrument and generator of the emotional moment, and though the preacher was in charge of the technique, he was not outside or above it. His own word operated upon him as he brought the message to his followers. In that sense, he was one with his followers in a quickened response to the marvel and mystery of God through the Word."[44] This personification is the role of leadership King performs in the final section of the speech where the oral patterns of repetition and agonistic phrasing and expression reach their highest points.

Because of its ceremonial setting it is useful to discern the speech as a climactic ritual act. Indeed, that tendency is sometimes manifest in the yearly remembrances of the speech associated with King's birthday. But if it is ceremonial, it is so in the deeper and more penetrating sense of a cultural landmark, a critical moment in which basic values are defined and sharpened, a moment to which we may return for refinement and redefinition. More than that, the speech remains a recurrent call to action in support of the values undergirding the concepts of justice and equality. It is precisely this sense of argument to which Chaim Perelman called attention in his work on the relationship between epideictic rhetoric and values. He observed, "the orator's aim in the epideictic genre is not just to gain a passive adherence from his audience but to provoke the action wished for or, at least, to awaken a disposition so to act. This is achieved by forming a community of minds which Kenneth Burke, who is well aware of the importance of this genre, calls *identification*."[45] He continues by stressing that the goal of such rhetoric is "to intensify an adherence to values, to create a disposition to act, and finally to bring people to act."[46] This is a useful frame for seeing the argumentative function of King's speech.

Consider the force of this speech in generating political action in support of civil rights legislation. At a pragmatic level this was one of its major purposes and was largely accomplished in a series of indirect effects. The Kennedy administration had been tentative until June 1963 in introducing civil rights legislation. A few months before the speech King sent a telegram to Attorney General Robert Kennedy urgently requesting a meeting with him and President Kennedy: "Dear Mr. Kennedy. I would like very much to have a conference with you and the President to discuss the crisis in race relations formented [*sic*] by the snail like pace of desegregation all across the south. I would like to discuss with you some of the problems we are facing in the south and some of the specific measures that may avert a national calamity. I feel it is urgent that we have such a conference at your earliest convenience. . . ."[47] The paste-up of this telegram contains the handwritten note, "We have to decide what to tell MLK."[48] King viewed as a serious problem the general reluctance to have such a meeting and provide presidential leadership. While the Kennedy administration remained cautious even after the "Dream" speech, there was clearly a different level of awareness about the political importance of civil rights and about King as public leader. The long-awaited civil rights conference was held in the White House shortly after the impact of the "Dream" speech, at which time President Kennedy made a point of explicitly greeting King by repeating, "I have a dream." The legitimacy of civil rights as a major public issue and as an important part of the Kennedy administration's domestic agenda had risen significantly.

Garrow and others confirm that President Kennedy had been concerned about the controversial nature of civil rights as a political issue. Indeed, the administration watched the March on Washington with intense concern. There was much alarm about a speech scheduled to precede King's, an address by John Lewis, leader of the Student Nonviolent Coordinating Committee, which was explicitly critical of the Kennedy administration on civil rights for offering "too little, too late."[49] King was acutely aware of this internal controversy and its potentially destructive effect on the progress of civil rights legislation and the movement as a whole. The rhetorical constraints created by this series of events enables us to realize an important new dimension to the "I Have a Dream" speech, that it was addressed not only to the supporters of civil rights gathered in Washington and to the watching masses in the public at large but also to those factions within the movement representing various degrees of dissent and dissatisfaction.

For example, while there are many powerful passages and memorable phrases in the speech, a set of less-noticed statements in the initial section provides a rhetorical frame for intensification of the moral base of the concept of civil rights and for reassurance and reunification in the face of factional groups presenting alternatives to nonviolent social protest. Dr. King placed the movement in context for both audiences with these words: "But there is something I must say to my people who stand on the warm threshold which leads into the palace of justice. In the process of gaining our rightful place we must not be guilty of wrongful deeds. . . . Again and again we must rise to the majestic heights of meeting physical force with soul force."[50] These sentences reaffirm the moral focus of the movement and underscore the theological foundations of King's view of social justice. They show that moral intensification was directed not only to the broad national audience viewing and hearing the speech but also to the active participants within the movement. In this way King acknowledged and addressed two major rhetorical problems: the need to keep the movement sharply defined in the public mind and the obligation to respond effectively to the mounting pressures to depart from a strict strategy of nonviolent social resistance. This passage, as well as others such as the vivid opening metaphor of the "promissory note" and the visionary projections of the dream itself emphasize the moral concept of "soul force" as the effective alternative both to physical violence and to the forms of discrimination faced in the material world. The language of the speech thus becomes a major means for reaffirming the values central to the civil rights movement and for influencing persons in positions of authority to act positively in support of civil rights.

Doubtless one of those most influenced by the power of King's speech was then vice-president Lyndon B. Johnson. It was left to Johnson during his presidency to translate the moral force of the dream symbol into concrete political legislation. Johnson's willingness and abilities in support of civil rights rank among the high points of his administration, especially his noteworthy address on the Voting Rights Bill of 1965. The Johnson speech on 15 March 1965 came immediately after the protest marches led by King in Selma, Alabama, to gain voting rights for blacks. Those marches were met with some of the most violent opposition in the history of the civil rights movement, and the clubbings and beatings of unarmed marchers were shown dramatically on national television. Here was a visible denial of the dream of which King had spoken. Yet King's words in framing the moral foundation of that dream provided the perspective and tone for Johnson's approach to the issue.

Like King, Johnson employed simple, direct, and very inclusive language: "There is no Negro problem. There is no southern problem. There is no northern problem. There is only an American problem."[51] Like King, Johnson appeals to the Constitution as the basic standard defining the nature and scope of political responsibilities: "our duty must be clear to all of us. The Constitution says that no person shall be kept from voting because of his race or his color. We have all sworn an oath before God to support and defend that Constitution. We must now act in obedience to that oath."[52] Moreover, at the end of the speech Johnson adopts the same imagery of agonistic struggle King had so powerfully dramatized in the "Dream" speech. After noting that the struggle of Negroes is not an isolated experience but part of the common struggle to deal with mutual foes, Johnson reiterated, "and we shall overcome."[53] The language of the civil rights leader, with all its symbolic content, had become the language of the president of the United States. The vocabulary of the oppressed minority had now become a central part of the language of the political majority. These were remarkable transformations, and at least with respect to the specific issue of voting rights, the force of King's vision and the power of the dream were being felt.

The reaffirmation of the values King articulated in "I Have a Dream" carried with it an underlying theme central to the speech and to the civil rights movement as a whole, King's firm belief in the possibility for basic change at both personal and societal levels. The dream is a symbol for the possibility of positive change. For King, it is important to realize that it was no idle symbol that he put forth as a vague abstraction to appease the audiences of the time. The logic of moral concepts is almost always developed, refined, and galvanized within the personal experience of individuals and groups. Such was certainly the case for King, because the dream as a symbol for fundamental change was reflective of his own personal experience in coming to understand and affirm the reality of agape-love. The best evidence for this is dramatically contained in an early document King wrote while a student at Crozer Theological Seminary. In an essay for a class assignment entitled "An Autobiography of Religious Development," King recounts one of the most influential experiences in his late childhood and early adolescence. He writes that at about age six a white playmate with whom he had become friends suddenly disappeared and began attending a different school, breaking their friendship. In King's words, "the climax came when he told me one day that his father had demanded that he would play with me no more. I never will forget what a great shock this was to me. . . . As my parents discussed some of the tragedies that had resulted from this problem [racial relations] and some of the insults they themselves had confronted on account of it, I was greatly shocked and from that moment on I was determined to hate every white person. As I grew older and older this feeling continued to grow. . . . I did not conquer this anti-White feeling until I entered college and came in contact with white students through working in interracial organizations."[54]

Clearly, these are remarkable words for King. This experience had the kind of impact that could have shaped his life in an entirely different direction. His own struggle with racial alienation was extremely difficult. Yet he was able personally to overcome the anti-white hostility that he strongly felt at an early age and open himself to broader and deeper levels of identification with people of all ethnic varieties. This ability marked a fundamental change in his own personal development. It was a deliberate and difficult choice to act in an inclusive and open manner rather than an exclusive and closed fashion. The dream of which he spoke in the speech was a call for exactly the same type of change in society at large, first through its historic institutions of law, commerce, education, and political opportunity, and eventually in its inner attitude and value structures. To understand the "soul force" of the dream was to grasp the knowledge that such fundamental change can and should occur.

Finally, I wish to return to the core idea of oral tradition and the rhetorical significance of the speech as a major event within that tradition. The oral tradition of which this speech is a part is tied to the history of black preaching and even more to the role or orality in slave cultures and, predating that, the prominence of oral forms of communication in West African cultures. In this regard it is useful to view the "Dream" speech as the spoken equivalent of an oral musical form emanating from West Africa, the traditional West Indian calypso. The calypso originated as and still remains one of the primary means of expressing dissent and engaging in social protest. At the heart of calypso is the element of enactment or performance, and at the center of the enactment is the basic structure of what has been labeled the African call-and-response pattern. That pattern manifests itself in different forms, one with special significance being the lyric content and vocal style of traditional calypso music. According to one investigator examining the relationship between musical forms and cultural meanings, "In African call and response, one person will sing a line and the rest will respond by singing a fixed chorus. . . . the call and response pattern shows how music in West Africa involves the whole community— everyone can join in. And calypsoes have the same structure too— each verse ends with a repeated chorus which the crowd soon learns to recognize."[55]

The basic elements of the call-and-response model were developed and refined in the black church in the West from its inception to the present. African slaves retained the dominant aspects of their oral traditions and adapted them to the prevailing institutions to which they had access, most notably the church. As Hebdige observes, "So it was easy for the slaves to insert the old African call and response pattern into the Christian service. Instead of just sitting quietly and listening to the minister, the congregation would add to or cut across his sermon with their own responses. In this way the preacher could 'ride' the developing mood. He could give voice to the feelings, fears and hopes of the people. And together, preacher and congregation formed a bond."[56]

This is an apt description of King's performative role in the "Dream" speech. Viewing it as an oral performance, we are able to understand the speech as an oral text, a performed text which both explains and interprets for immediate and distant audiences the meaning of civil rights as a moral issue. As an oral text the "I Have a Dream" speech carries with it a structure and quality that provide enduring meanings beyond its immediate context, and in many respects the enduring meanings are the most intriguing. The special significance of the speech as an oral text is manifest in several ways: (1) The structure and pattern of language in the speech unite audiences with memorable themes, themes then remembered as part of the conscious reflection and action about civil rights. (2) The oral patterns in the speech, especially the use of heuristic metaphors, create a synthesis of interpretation that writing alone could not do. This is accomplished by directly engaging listeners with value structures that require moral choices. (3) The speech merges the primary realm of sound with the realm of vision to create defining images that energize human memory in a distinctive way. (4) The speech employs a version of what Walter Fisher has termed "narrative rationality"[57] in enacting the stories of injustice, unfulfilled promise, ideal aspiration, sacrifice, and redemption that bond speaker and listener in a lived experience and establish the pattern for future thought and action.

We have already seen a number of distinctive language patterns. Consider the opening story of the "promissory note" of freedom, justice, and equality under the Constitution; the powerful references to a new conception of time contained in "the fierce urgency of now" phrase; and the reiteration of the "I have a Dream that" sequences and the expectations of the future they evoke. These patterns enable audiences to remember, an act that entails conscious reconstruction of past events and associations with a theme that keeps the ideas behind the events alive and functioning. King's language and its oral performance at the central location of American government provide a framework for remembering history. For example, the promises of the Constitution as a defining historical event are recalled to public consciousness in political and moral terms. They allow the struggle for civil rights to be kept alive in memory within the context of similar historical events which are no longer simply events but formative symbols which contain both political and moral dimensions. Underlying all the language patterns of the speech is an implicit image of the timeless battle of good versus evil.

Further, as an oral text the speech brings together sound and sight in a powerful symbolic form. The sound of King's voice, the intonations, the patterns of pause and emphasis all combine to engage memory at a very basic level. Through that engagement patterns of thought and consciousness are shaped. The speech reflects what Ong and others have termed the significance of sound in creating mutuality between speaker and audience. The possibility for such mutuality is centered in the very nature of speech as oral sound. Commenting on this important dimension in an insightful view of Ong's work, Dance has observed that "sound, nested in human orality, is the seat of the intellect. Vision, while extraordinarily important in giving permanence to sound, in allowing distancing and the increase of objectivity, is secondary to sound in the developmental process of human intellection."[58] The primacy of sound is evident in the experiences all persons have when hearing something causing reflection and remembrance. Certainly not all oral forms accomplish this experience. Yet the narration of a story that provides a critical sense of identity or purpose, the depiction of a powerful symbol in public discourse that identifies the values at stake in an otherwise distant problem or issue, operates at this fundamental level. Thus we remember certain things because they have been spoken about in particular ways.

The "I Have a Dream" speech has the added advantage of operating not only at the level of primary sound but also at the level of visual imagery by supplying a corollary texture, a mosaic of sight-sound imagery for those present and for those watching via television. The oral performance of the speech is a combination of hearing King's words and seeing his persona as prophet and spiritual leader, a virtual Black Moses, as he speaks. Together this imagery allows an envisioning of the nature of civil disobedience as a moral action. Through the dimensions of both sound and sight, audiences are invited to experience the actuality of the moral struggle for civil rights for which this speech is a climactic event. Part of the visual force of the speech resulted from its being one of the first nationally televised speeches in the civil rights movement. The influence of television as a visual medium continues even now since many people become exposed to the speech through taped broadcasts and recorded coverage of the original event. In an interesting and somewhat ironic fashion, the emergence of electronic technology for visual forms has created an avenue for the development of what Ong calls secondary orality. In fact, the oral and visual media reinforce each other, making the combination more powerful than either element alone. Ong expresses this development within the context of visuality: "What is distinctive of the visualist development leading to our modern technological culture is that it learns to vocalize visual observation far more accurately and elaborately than primitive man, by vocalizing it manages to intellectualize it, and by intellectualizing it comes to generate further specific visual observation and so on. The visualization we are talking of is thus a visualization strengthened by intimate association with the voice, directly in speech, or indirectly through script."[59] In "I Have a Dream" King provides the kind of direct association with the voice to which Ong refers. Thus the visual images of an unfulfilled constitutional promise, the delaying tactics of the past which require a redefinition of time from chronology to moral urgency, the epic scenes in the battle of good versus evil dramatically displayed in the televised brutality to freedom riders, and the use of fire hoses and police dogs against peaceful demonstrators, especially women and children, in Birmingham are reinforced and driven home as lasting symbols of the struggle. King's voice appropriates these events as central elements of the story of civil rights and gives them perpetual meaning as the story is told and retold.

Viewed in its totality as a rhetorical act, "I Have a Dream" as oral text provides a distinctive example of the power of narration. As Fisher has noted, "The operative principle of narrative rationality is identification rather than deliberation."[60] The story King tells is one of intrinsic values and principles inherent in the democratic tradition. The speech transforms the concepts of justice and equality into encompassing value categories within which the particular episodes in the civil rights struggle are placed. Because the discourse of civil rights is a form of protest, it involves the positing of rival stories to counter the prevailing narratives of separation, inequality and privilege. Fisher notes that frequently in such cases "the rival factions' stories deny each other in respect to self-conceptions and the world. The only way to bridge this gap, if it can be bridged through discourse, is by telling stories that do not negate the self-conceptions people hold of themselves."[61]

By calling attention to the values that underlie civil rights, King's language in the speech affirms rather than negates the self-conceptions of many diverse hearers across ethnic, economic, geographic, religious, and political lines. We remember the speech precisely because it gave us individually and collectively that kind of unifying experience.

Paramount among the terms creating this experience is the idea of the dream itself. Everyone can understand what it is like to dream of a better life, to be treated fairly, to have an equal chance to learn or to succeed. Everyone can identify with the hopes and aspirations of fulfilling an inner potential and becoming a citizen in the fullest sense. The idea of the dream thus brings into play fundamental hopes and values that are critical to self-identity. The negation of the dream is a denial of self-identity. To contemplate the dream King articulates is to apprehend a story for which there is no rival. At the moment of its telling or retelling, the story of the dream holds out a new and larger category of self-conception to hearers, surpassing the boundaries of the rival stories of separate factions. This comprises a significant part of the continuing power of the "I Have a Dream" speech.

Viewed as a whole, then, through its performance as an oral-visual text, the "I Have a Dream" speech carried out an intense pattern of involvement between speaker and audience. This pattern brought about the initial power of identification at the time the speech was first delivered. Each time public audiences hear the words of the speech again or view its powerful unity of sound and visual images, the speech recreates in a remarkably enduring manner the bonding between diverse audiences and the messages of agape-love, non-violence, hope for the future, and the dream of a just society. In this way the fusion of eschatologically grounded theology and orality takes place, a fusion whose energy continues to make the idea of the dream a lasting rhetorical reality.

When "Silence Is Betrayal": An Ethical Criticism of the Revolution of Values in the Speech at Riverside Church

Frederick J. Antczak

> I am convinced that if we are to get on the right side of the world revolution, we as a nation must undergo a radical revolution of values. —Martin Luther King, Jr., at Riverside Church

> To imagine a language means to imagine a form of life. —Ludwig Wittgenstein

One of the most intriguing yet among the most neglected of the addresses of Martin Luther King, Jr., is "A Time to Break Silence," the address he delivered at New York City's Riverside Church 4 April 1967. In this speech Dr. King declared his opposition to American involvement in the war in Vietnam, which alone would have made the speech worthy of attention. It was also here that King began to reenvision and reconstitute the civil rights movement in the larger moral terms that framed his thought and action until his death a year later. But this speech also poses important interpretive difficulties for those who would explore the power of the word in King's career and raises some questions about the limits of our critical repertoire for doing so. The speech and King's whole public career are especially interesting for the way they both call our attention to the tenuous, slippery, sometimes even disturbing relation between rhetorical success and ethical quality.

It is common to see rhetoric as the activity in which we engage when science or logic fails: at best an art based on juggling premises that are not true but merely probable, a second-rate way of handling things that cannot really be known; at worst the ignoble art of persuasion condemned in Plato, a way of using language to deal with people manipulatively, instrumentally, as objects. Under such definitions, apparent rhetorical successes often arise from clear ethical failures: lies or stonewalling or conveniently selective "failures to recall" or distracting or demeaning emotional appeals. But occasionally there appear exceptions that are as puzzling as they are heartening; we are drawn to study them in part to help us make more insightful rhetorical assessments, in part to help us make finer ethical distinctions, in part to advance our understanding of the potentially interanimating and mutually redefining relationship between the two.

What makes Dr. King an especially interesting figure is that across his career, his eloquence seemed to carry an irreducibly ethical component. His public character was essential to his extraordinary ability to call many to endure much—his character as it came to be recognized in the active relation between his words and deeds, a convincing and mutually informative connection between rhetoric and action. It seemed to many that he strained to live his preachings; willingly suffered their consequences, however terrible; and accepted those sufferings publicly. To those he persuaded, he seemed to enact or "incarnate"[1] his message in his interactions with his audience, establishing a public character of a contemporary good man speaking well. But King also had to do his work within the ethical constraints of real circumstances, events, and alternatives, many not of his own making, most beyond his complete control. In the act of composing his discourses, he faced the difficulty of developing a language that made room for both the most idealistic claims of justice and the most specific claims of actual fact and felt need. The speech at Riverside confronts us especially poignantly with the problem of how we are to get at this complex ethical quality of his rhetoric and in what terms we are to describe and evaluate it. In the end, it may also point us to a new ethical dimension of discourse for critics to explore.

King's ethical quality becomes partly accessible biographically; it makes sense to begin by examining the circumstances and events to which the speech might be seen as a response. In these terms, the Riverside speech will indeed prove interesting, for in violating certain ethical expectations—expectations about when and how to break silence—it is one of the most problematic speeches of King's career and perhaps one of the most essential.

King and Vietnam: The Circumstances of Commitment

An examination of concerns extrinsic to the speech surely helps explicate some of its ethical interest. It was still a little surprising in the spring of 1967 to find public figures of any political throw weight willing formally to oppose the American involvement in Vietnam; few civil rights leaders would even consider defying their great patron Lyndon Johnson by taking an explicit stand against his conduct of the war. But even conceding the courage it took to be among the first of his colleagues to venture out so far on this political limb, it may be surprising philosophically that King's stand came so late: one might expect King, as his time's foremost advocate of nonviolence, to oppose all war. Such expectations oversimplify both the scope of his pacificism and the pragmatism of his leadership.

King's stand on Vietnam cannot be understood simply in terms of an undifferentiating opposition to violence per se. Unlike his wife—who joined the antiwar movement early on—and others of his colleagues like Bayard Rustin and James Lawson, King admitted to having been less than a strict pacifist. His reading of Niebuhr allowed him at least to entertain the possibility—in, say, the war against Hitler—that violence might be justifiable in conditions where it was the only means of resisting tyranny.[2] So to understand King's position on the American involvement in Vietnam simply as a pacifist's blanket condemnation of all war would be to understate the specificity and force of his judgment about *this* war by *this* country at *this* time.

It also would underestimate King's pragmatism, for King was never inclined to blanket judgments abstracted from conditions. King was no relativist, but his ideals were—had to be—formulated in a language that was culture specific. Indeed, this quality was the wellspring of its extraordinary power: King thought and spoke in a language that insisted on—and persisted in—congruence with real events, conditions, experiences, feelings, and beliefs. His language drew its capacity for meaning and resonance from the concrete social activities and intellectual influences his audiences shared: the songs they sang, the stories they told, the sufferings they shared. King lived and moved, often quite nimbly, in the "real world" of politics, a world that always includes bargains driven, consequences calculated, and compromises struck. Indeed this attribute was one of the virtues that continued to qualify him for leadership. But one troubling thing circumstances reveal about King's antiwar rhetoric is that such a compromise, a compromise of silence, had been observed for almost two years.

King had questioned the war at least since March of 1965, when during a visit to Howard University he dismissed the growing American involvement as "accomplishing nothing."[3] Around that time FBI bugs overheard King's advisors Bayard Rustin and Stanley Levison urging him to speak his conscience on issues of war and peace.[4] But King knew the FBI had potentially damaging materials concerning his personal life. He was sufficiently worried about the threat of embarrassing revelations that he asked a longtime family friend, Rev. Archibald Carey, Jr., to speak with contacts in the FBI. Carey did so and then advised King to exercise great restraint in public statements about the administration.[5]

Just before the Southern Christian Leadership Conference convention of August 1965, King did make a mild attempt to address the issue, announcing his intention to send letters to LBJ, the leaders of North and South Vietnam, the Vietcong, the U.S.S.R., and China. But these letters were not to argue military or political issues, only to plead in an explicitly personal way for all sides to come to the conference table. At this point King sought no role in any antiwar protests, nor did he see much of a prospect of developing "a peace army right now."[6] As if to confirm this suspicion, the SCLC convention stopped just short of condemning his whole initiative, emphasizing that King spoke only for himself and that the organization did not and would not pursue questions of peace or foreign affairs.[7] In the face of this lack of support, King conceded, "it's physically impossible to go all out on the peace question and all out on the civil rights question."[8] King would maintain this distinction and his silence on Vietnam until the spring of 1967. In the meantime, he had plenty to attend to: There was turmoil within the SCLC, a growing fissure in the movement over the issue of "black power," an enormous new task in Chicago, and a succession of defeats, failures, and bad news for the cause of civil rights.

At this time, the SCLC was unusually beset with both public and personal difficulties. Contributions were falling off precipitously just as several key staffers had to be reprimanded for improvident conduct, most notably Hosea Williams for his handling of the campaign in Birmingham. The behavior of some field staff had become so arrogant and uncompromising as to corrode relations with several local affiliates. Worse, this problem had gone unaddressed by central staff, many of whom were occupied with personality conflicts of their own—between James Bevel and Wyatt Walker, Bevel and Williams, Williams and Randolph Blackwell, and Williams and Andrew Young. These conflicts predictably resulted in internal turmoil, confusion, and side taking. All these problems with his organization demanded more of King's time and contributed to an increasingly serious depression.⁹ Even more disturbing, nonviolence itself seemed threatened as a principle of the movement as the very concepts of power and oratory—not to mention silence—were being reconfigured.

Major riots had occurred in Watts in the summer of 1965 and the next summer in Chicago, Cleveland, Lansing, and other cities. More important, militant leaders and ideas were coming to the fore: Stokely Carmichael had replaced John Lewis as chairman of the Student Nonviolent Coordinating Committee, and Floyd McKissick tightened his hold on the Congress of Racial Equality; in June 1966, when James Meredith was wounded on the March Against Fear, Dr. King went south to continue the march and was joined by Carmichael and McKissick. On the way to a historic rally of some thirty thousand at Mississippi's state capitol, Carmichael first used the slogan "black power" to characterize the evolving goals of the movement. Black power promptly became an issue of division (or perhaps a name for long-fissuring but long-overlooked divisions) in the movement. CORE's national convention immediately promulgated a statement in support of the concept, and the NAACP followed by tartly condemning it. It appeared to an increasingly distraught King that both ends of the spectrum, Roy Wilkins's NAACP as much as the young militants of SNCC and CORE, were welcoming and hastening such cleavage, less for reasons of principle than for institutional and personal motives.¹⁰ King found himself in the precarious position of trying to bridge the sides and hold the movement more or less together—just as he was mounting his first major project in a northern city, the War on Slums in Chicago.

In the past, the success of the civil rights movement had always depended on the political crudity, the symbolic ineptitude of its foils. The unflinching public brutality of a Bull Connor, an Al Lingo, a Jim Clark had always provided a clarifying contrast with the movement's principles of nonviolence. But now for the first time King's organization was moving off its home turf, and it was grappling with a different kind of opponent. If Sheriff Laurie Pritchett could stall the Albany Movement effectively with an only marginally more sophisticated public relations strategy, a big city mayor like Richard J. Daley, adroit in hardball politics and practiced in manipulative public relations, with much of his city's black leadership under his sway and immense tactical advantages in money, manpower, and knowledge of the local political terrain, had the wherewithal to bog things down far more seriously.

While King's work was increasing quantitatively, moreover, it was also confronting him with qualitatively tougher kinds of organizing. The Chicago project was "much larger than anything we've ever touched," with respect both to the sheer size of the place and to the term and tractability of the tasks: "Here, we've got to do more in terms of organizing people into permanent units, rather than on a temporary basis just for demonstrations."[11] Believing that non-violent demonstrations were easily discounted or disregarded in the normal turbulence of urban life, King had to plan a wider variety of initiatives to be sustained over longer periods of time. The project proved every bit as difficult as he foresaw, and even as sympathetic a journal as the *Nation* quickly decided that the movement was nearing its end in Chicago.[12] The *New Republic* faulted King as "pretty much of a failure at organizing" there,[13] and Andrew Kopkind viewed the campaign as King's last stand in the movement, of which "he is not likely to regain command."[14] Bayard Rustin seemed to sum up the Chicago enterprise accurately as "a fiasco."[15]

Then on the heels of all this difficulty came a staggering roll of bad news: Stokely Carmichael had been arrested for inciting a riot in the Summerhill section of Atlanta, as was Hosea Williams several days later; violence had erupted in Grenada, Mississippi, after local officials voided the voter registration accord reached when the Meredith march went through; Johnson's 1966 civil rights bill had died aborning; and the defiantly racist Atlanta restaurateur Lester Maddox had won the Democratic gubernatorial primary of King's home state.

All this took a visible toll on King. As Haynes Johnson remarked, "King seemed to change"; "the tired look and . . . the diffident manner" convinced Johnson "it was not the buoyant, energetic King one had known."[16] Indeed, part of what is worth remarking about the circumstances of King's decision to oppose the war in a new and more serious way is that he brought himself to do so in the most organizationally demanding, politically discouraging, and personally depressing period of his public life.

With all these "internal" problems anguishing him, King could not let go of Vietnam, and he cast about for a language adequate for talking about it. At first, he talked about it as a tactical problem: In the zero-sum game of the federal budget, Lyndon Johnson's domestic promises "top the casualty list of the conflict."[17] But apparently there was another zero-sum game to be played, the trickier one of public opinion. The *New York Times* published a poll claiming that fully 41 percent of respondents admitted that black criticism of the war lessened their support of civil rights.[18] At the same time, Stanley Levison told King that the continuing decline in contributions was attributable in part to the Vietnam War's dislodging civil rights as the foremost concern of American liberals.[19] Indeed, King was already being raked in liberal journals for failing to oppose the war more vocally.[20]

But a fundamentally different consideration began to intrude, one that was to reshape King himself and the way he came to understand and conduct the work of his last year of life. King began to see the two great political issues of his day as connected not only by tactics but also by substantive moral principles and to see each movement as subtly transformed by that connection. He presented his new vision in its fullest form at Riverside, but he had taken several months formulating and rehearsing it.

King's associate Bernard Lee has placed the beginning of this process in January 1967, when King flew to Jamaica for four weeks of solitude to work on another book.[21] There, free for really the first time in his public life from quotidian distractions, King was spurred to meditate at length on the war by a story in the January *Ramparts,* "The Children of Vietnam," in which photographs showed burn wounds suffered by children struck by American napalm. King had always aimed to bring the "beloved community" of his religious convictions into practical being. Now, in the terrible light of these pictures, the war became recognizable as the implacable enemy of that community. It was not merely a competing interest to be calculated, a social vector to be angled. It was the corrosive social solvent of the beloved community's constitutive virtues of steward-ship, solidarity, cooperation, and love, the disastrous answer to its fundamental questions, Who is my neighbor? and What does love require?

To speak to this new enemy and these new conditions required a new language, a reconstitution of the terms of that community. But to speak this language would also require a reconstitution of King's own character and its possibilities, and even of the kind of commu-nity he sought to constitute—to enact, if only for the time of engagement—in his rhetoric.

On a 25 February program in Los Angeles with four anti-war senators (Hatfield, McCarthy, McGovern, and Gruening), King began recharacterizing his opposition to the war by redefining the oppo-nents of the civil rights movement, connecting America's racism to her materialism and militarism. Support for the war now had to be seen as support for the moral abuses of capitalism and white colo-nialism—a reactionary betrayal of all those seeking economic jus-tice anywhere around the world. Then in a 24 March address in Chicago, King extended this new[22] class-oriented language to spe-cific moral inferences; he now argued explicitly that dissent from the war was morally required and that such dissent was now to call upon the same resources of conscience as did civil rights: "We must combine the fervor of the civil rights movement with the peace movement."[23] Then on 31 March, he asked the SCLC's board for a declaration committing the organization to opposing Johnson's policy on the explicit ground that "the evils of capitalism are as real as the evils of militarism and the evils of racism."[24] After vigorous debate, the board voted to table the proposition and let King go his own way. Finally on Tuesday, 4 April, King came to New York's Riverside Church to address a crowd of some three thousand of the Clergy and Laymen Concerned. The speech was assured of being the most extensively covered of his Vietnam statements; hence it was designed to be his most trenchant statement of his position.

As might have been anticipated, it was not a particularly popular position with the administration. At this late stage of his public life, King could depend on the FBI to charge that almost any of his addresses that gained public attention had been ghosted for him by a Communist, sufficient by J. Edgar Hoover's standards of proof and due process to unmask King as "a traitor to his country and his race."[25] He could routinely expect a presidential advisor to report to the increasingly exasperated Johnson that King, "who is inordinately ambitious and quite stupid," had "thrown in with the commies" because he was "in desperate search of a constituency."[26] It was nothing new to hear congressmen with administration connections, most virulently Joe Waggoner, muse in public about how such an address hearkened back to King's alleged Communist training and revealed his leanings toward the International Communist Conspiracy.[27]

King might also have foreseen some bad press, but this address seemed to have struck a special nerve, even with the publications from which he had come to expect the most balanced coverage. *Newsweek* blasted him as "in over his head," improperly and foolishly mixing evangelical passion with simplistic political judgment.[28] *Life* called the speech "a demogogic slander," declaring that King "goes beyond his personal right to dissent when he connects progress in civil rights here with a proposal that amounts to abject surrender in Vietnam"; in this, "King comes close to betraying the cause for which he has worked so long."[29] The *Pittsburgh Courier*, a prominent black newspaper, dismissed the speech as "tragically misleading" American blacks on matters "too complex for simple debate."[30] The *Washington Post* excoriated him for having "diminished his usefulness to his cause, to his country and to his people,"[31] and the *New York Times*, editorializing under the title "Dr. King's Error," accused him of reckless slander that contributed "not to solutions but to deeper confusion."[32] What was more surprising was the virulence with which King's colleagues and friends opened fire on him. Administration insider Carl Rowan raged that King had "delivered a one-sided broadside about a matter on which he obviously has an abundance of indignation and a shortage of information."[33] Ralph Bunche went on record that "I am convinced he is making a very serious tactical error which will do much harm to the civil rights movement"[34]; oddly, in a later private phone call that King found particularly dispiriting, Bunche apologized for his remarks and professed private agreement with King's views on the war, if not his mode of public opposition.[35] Within a week, Whitney Young, Roy Wilkins, Jackie Robinson, and Sen. Edward Brooke had disavowed the position King had taken and the direction in which he was taking the civil rights movement, and the NAACP's sixty-member executive board opposed him unanimously.[36]

Even for so frequent a target of criticism as Martin Luther King, this response was crushing; as used to ill treatment and abuse as he had become, he found this criticism unusually demoralizing. He refrained from public response of any kind for a week, a week during which his advisers found him as hurt and distraught as they could remember seeing him.[37] Yet despite this reaction, the ethically interesting fact remains that King never recanted or defanged the controversial positions he had taken in his Riverside speech; on the contrary, they were to form for the last year of his life fundamental principles by which he tried to reconstitute the movement he had already done so much to advance and the language in which he now meant to advance it.

It would be tempting on these sheerly biographical grounds to celebrate King's choice to break silence, to laud him ethically for publicly taking a hard position in an even harder time and for making a stand on an issue of conscience despite foreseeably excruciating consequences. Such a judgment may be especially enticing for readers who bring certain commitments to the text—those, for example, who already revere King or who accept his condemnation of the war and the American role in it. But this speech reveals particularly starkly the limitations of an extrinsically based ethical criticism; much as we might wish to, it does not seem possible to reach this judgment very decisively on the basis of extrinsic information alone, for a very different ethical reading of this stage of King's rhetorical career remains open and tenable. Given different value commitments on the part of the critic, there appear reasons to consider interpreting the speech as an expedient stab at recovering liberal constituencies that King knew were drifting away or as a desperate attempt to recover his own deteriorating leadership position in the wake of Chicago. One could point out with some persuasiveness that King had taken his time about speaking out, more than two years after he was known to maintain these convictions; and that he finally decided to act only when the movement needed some visible new boost; and that even then, he acted only after having launched what might (at least from someone we know to be so sophisticated in matters of public opinion) be read as carefully calculated trial balloons.

These incommensurable assessments put the critic—at least the critic who seeks to elicit more from the text than refractions of the value commitments he or she brings to it—in a difficult situation. It is this critic's job to seek arguments about the text, and a language for them, that could sustain critical debate and eventually stand as a kind of knowledge, at least pending more compelling arguments to the contrary. But if the critic is to do more than rehearse private prejudices, surveys of the extrinsic determinants surrounding King seem inherently, linguistically insufficient. They cannot from the outside provide an adequate language for describing how those determinants appeared to the agent as he conceived and carried out his action; that is, they cannot reliably say how they seemed to require action at this time and in this situation—rather than in all those similar ones he'd been facing for years, or how he went about formulating the concrete alternatives he chose among, or for what motives it occurred to him to make his choice. Thus they fail to provide an ethical language sufficient for deciding between alternative assessments, or reconciling them, or even reformulating them for a more definitive discussion.

Not only do extrinsic data tell us too little to determine our overall judgments about King, but they especially fail to make specific claims about the quality of this speech, this act itself. Whatever our overall judgment of King may be, it would be less than critical to let it close all questions about the quality of each of his particular actions: after all, even a good person may do better and worse things, a good speaker may give better and worse speeches, and part of what makes one good is caring about the differences.

To assess this speech with respect to such differences, we can tap a critical supplement of a more intrinsic character and orientation. The text itself—like every text—offers us a language of fact, reason, and value, a language of description and evaluation. Even here, we must be careful about what we can really know and steer clear of an intentional fallacy: We will not and cannot know from the text what the existential King actually saw in the world or thought about it. But there is another sort of ethical knowledge we can attain, and there are accessible foci through which to attain it. We might be able to learn a good deal about the moral activities in which this text engages its audience: the ways in which it uses (or misuses) the cultural resources it inherits, the language in which it is composed, and the kind of discussions it begins, sustains, inhibits, and replaces—in short, the rhetorical relation or "discursive community"[38] it constitutes between its implied author "King" and its implied audience.

Since this sort of criticism is descriptive of a text critics hold in common, it will generate knowledge claims that are intersubjectively testable. We may not find much room to wield preconceived values about when and how a rhetor ought to break silence, but we will be able to focus on just how King did—on the qualities, rhetorical and ethical, the text realizes and precludes. From this sort of knowledge of the text, we might even begin to build a more general assessment of King, or at least identify the issues on which a general assessment might turn: From a succession of such judgments across the whole of an orator's work, we could start framing judgments about the "career author King."[39] The implied author King in interaction with his implied audience is still not the same as the existential King but may yet prove to be of ethical interest.

Now the question becomes, What might we learn about the ethical quality of the text if we ask of it, paraphrasing the old civil rights song, not just how it talks the talk, but how it walks the walk?

King's Revolution in Language

The talk King was talking here was nothing less than a call for "a revolution of values" in America; the walk he would walk therefore had to negotiate a powerful moral paradox. For to call for deep change in some American values required of him deep affirmation of others, including the rhetorical values of engagement with the arguments the other way and the essentially democratic effort to make room for both sides—not just the one in command of the platform at a given moment—to say what needs to be said. What's particularly interesting here for ethical criticism is how King's revolution of values required a revolution in language: In order to say what needed to be said, he had to reshape the language of political discourse, conserving its capacities to delineate areas of confluence and compromise while allowing for new kinds of disagreement to be articulated, different interests and different concepts of the right and the prudent to be shared. He had to make new room in it both for claims of justice and virtue of the sort we identify with King and for claims about the kind of communal expedience to which deliberative rhetoric leads. It was a paradox King addressed with characteristic ingenuity if imperfect success.

King as Dynamic Conservator

Martin Luther King, Jr., was his era's—and arguably this century's—most ardent and eloquent articulator of the American dream. He made his most important contributions speaking, again paradoxically, as both its affirmer and its enlarger. When he declared from the steps of the Lincoln Memorial, "I have a dream," it was "a dream deeply rooted in the American dream."[40] This dream drew much of its rhetorically attractive and morally transformative force from its resonance of constitutive American values and their Christian moral heritage; even the famous check metaphor invokes not only the religious virtues of truth telling and promise keeping but also the baseline contractual fidelity of capitalism. Four years later on the issue of Vietnam, King again had to find a rhetoric that both reaffirmed and reinterpreted at least central parts of that dream, in order to articulate what an American community better incorporating those values would be like.

On the face of it, there are places where he fell conspicuously short, at least if we bring into the speech expectations for a conventional calculation of the costs and benefits of changing a particular policy—whether to continue prosecuting the war. But in the relation he enacted with his listeners and readers, the implied author King was engaged in a larger ethical task, with different rhetorical imperatives: to change how Americans deliberate, the very way they recognize benefits and costs, ultimately the way they bring themselves to their constitutive tradition of revolution and bring those traditions into their public talk. The speech not only *urges* a revolution in our values; its moral qualities are evident in the way it attempts to *enact* that revolution in the rhetorical relation King offers his audience, a relation where more troublesome questions must first be addressed and new capacities of discourse are needed to address them. And in examining how King's rhetoric created new possibilities for talk and action—and foreclosed others—we may discover a new dimension of discourse for ethical criticism to explore, indeed a different sense of ethics. The task of ethical criticism here is not to apply any freestanding rules we might import into the text, rules about when and how silence is to be broken; it is instead to describe the relation between the author and audience constituted—if only for the time of engagement—within the text and assess the characters made in that relation for ethical weaknesses and strengths.

If we were to look at the speech for how often it violated rules, easily the most striking thing about what King did at Riverside is how often he seems to reach for the rhetorically expedient—to take the easy way out of relevant questions by assuming an inappropriate rhetorical relation. King often seems to speak to an audience of the already converted and to assume an authority for which he does not appear convincingly qualified: He offers little that could count as proof for his controversial claim that the National Liberation Front is "the only party in real touch with the peasants," for his wonderfully precise knowledge of NLF membership ("less than twenty-five per cent Communist"), for his charge that American officials had long been secretly aware of all this,[41] or for his five-point plan to end the war.[42] Although all his proposals had already been advanced by other prominent diplomatic and military figures, King even neglects to cite them and thereby credential himself or his plan, a move that seems, with reference to the usual rules of discourse, maladroit, even arrogant, and thus startlingly out of character.

He continues this apparent ineptitude by choosing not to describe the costs of the war in the most broadly appealing terms, the billions of dollars spent for no apparent progress, the thousands of body bags filled. Here clearly his strategy is not a reach for the rhetorically easy way. He wants to make room for discourse about a kind of moral stewardship of the living and of the qualities we must husband. Hence he cannot perform a simple cost-benefit analysis but must call attention to more elusive, less quantifiable costs: how American troops are morally disfigured, literally demoralized, by their role in this war, how "we are adding cynicism to the process of death."[43] Indeed he must generate that new, differently value-laden attention to things and teach his audience how to use it.

King here visibly—and, we can only conclude, intentionally—refuses to discuss with us the kind of prudent assessment that in other negotiations he had handled so nimbly. He presents his proposals without anything that might serve as calculation of their prospects for success; indeed he further complicates that very issue. King introduces his proposals on the heels of a long (over 20 percent of the whole text) history of American duplicity toward the North Vietnamese, a history that comprises powerful reasons for them not to credit or cooperate with any American peace plan short of abject surrender. Given the very evidence King adduces so extensively, it seems reasonable to wonder who King is constructing himself to be and what kind of audience would be content without calculation of the plan's realistic prospects.

King also neglects to calculate, or to take what would conventionally be viewed as responsibility for, his plan's potential costs—including military costs, but also the very geopolitical and moral costs he wants us to consider more closely: What would be the immediate risks to our troops of a unilateral cease-fire? What would be the ramifications elsewhere in the world of our being brought, apparently by force, to recognize people whom our diplomats had been branding illegitimate insurgents? What are the likelihoods that the removal of our "foreign" troops would, without a specific agreement, correspond with the removal of the foreign troops of Communist superpowers? What is now to prevent the "dominoes" of Laos and Cambodia and Thailand from falling at the now-to-be-uncountered threat of military domination? Who is King, that he not be bound to consider such issues? Especially in light of the fantastic cruelty that followed our later withdrawal, King concedes conspicuously little about the character of the regime we would in effect be accepting and the moral responsibilities we would thereby take on—little except a disturbing appendix to his plan, "an offer to grant asylum to any Vietnamese who fears for his life under a new regime."[44]

To be fair, the scale and savagery of the disaster, as only partly reflected in those desperate migrations about which we have since come to know, would have astounded almost any predictor of probable consequences; more to the point, we cannot compare what in fact did happen when we left in exhaustion and defeat in 1975 with what might have happened, there and here, had we taken the moral initiative in 1967—or with what might have happened had we tried to stay on longer. To be accurate, moreover, there are textual reasons to suggest that King's fundamental purpose was on a different scale—a purpose that made calculation of such concerns relatively less important for us to do, its terms less appropriate for us to use if we are to bring into the range of our public talk and action the kinds of concerns he is teaching us to recognize. If he were merely attempting to change a particular policy, it would have been appropriate to talk about Vietnam in terms of the conventionally defined expediences of that sort of debate. But this speech attempts a more radical relation between us: King means to reconstitute the mores of our way of life together, beginning as he must with our rhetorical mores. Thinking and talking about policies *as* particular, in moral isolation, is an essential part of our moral problem.

Even reading King's speech this way, we may still find some of his rhetorical decisions to be faults, even moral faults. But we will be disposed to see this and every alleged issue of realpolitik as proper to examine only in the context of a larger moral tradition, our living tradition of revolution, and in light of the universal values that give our tradition its enduring moral significance in the world.

Enacting the Beloved Community: Two Commitments

There are, of course, virtues in the rhetorical community the text offers us. Put in terms of character, we are taught how to follow King's moves and thus how to develop his rhetorical and moral capacities: At least for our time of engagement with the speech, our characters are reshaped, new possibilities for our talk and action explored, old ones demoted. The extensive first part of the speech begins where we are, with our apprehensions about joining King in a protest he freely calls "a vocation of agony"; he recounts his reasons for speaking out, personal and public reasons we might share. But then we are taken through a long history, edging us toward what we are not likely to know or at least to be eager to admit about American involvement in Southeast Asia, with suggestions of what it might tell us about ourselves. His five-point plan only comes appended as an afterthought; it is left undeveloped as if the details of policy should not at this point distract us, as if we must learn to train our attention on not the pragmatics of policy but the character of individual response. King then moves to a discussion of the rightful modes of protest, which in turn opens out onto redefinitions of the moral and political tradition King and his audience share, and of the revolution of values that Americans are called to enact in history as King enacts it in his discourse.

At the outset, King speaks feelingly as one who himself had been torn by fears about this protest of conscience. But he literally takes us through the reasons that compelled him to "move on" and that might teach his listeners how to start moving with him. He starts from an almost conventionally calculative argument about interests: "The war was doing far more than devastating the hopes of the poor at home. It was sending their sons and their brothers and their husbands to fight and to die in extraordinarily high proportions."[45] *Almost* conventionally calculative. The expedient tactic would have been to describe the interests at stake in familiarly racial terms; his audience was disposed to hear him to be referring to blacks when discussing those who had been disproportionately "crippled by our society," sent to "guarantee liberties in Southeast Asia which they had not found in southwest Georgia and East Harlem." Instead he redirects the lines of argument by redefining the fundamental concepts and motives: "I could not be silent in the face of such cruel manipulation of the poor"; "I was increasingly compelled to see the war as an enemy of the poor and attack it as such."[46] Silence about Vietnam is a betrayal not simply of blacks but also of the poor—a betrayal of class and of the revolutionary new value of economic justice.

King next explains how his own roles and the onerous duties they impose—which happen to be some of the attributes his implied audience admires most about him—compel him to protest. If he is to continue, as he expects his intended listeners to wish, to calm ghetto violence by contending that "social change comes most meaningfully through nonviolent action," he must adopt the same stance toward violence by his own government. He takes his charge as civil rights leader from the founding motto of the SCLC, "to save the soul of America";[47] his admirers and followers, even in the civil rights movement, must accept the breadth of that charge if they are to have "any concern for the integrity and life of America today," for America "can never be saved so long as it destroys the deepest hopes of men the world over."[48] King's responsibility goes further: The Nobel Peace Prize he brought home to America "takes me beyond national allegiances" to work for "the brotherhood of man." And ultimately, "I share with all men the calling to be a son of the living God."[49]

Far from making the easier argument and thus treating us expediently, King has taken on a more difficult task: to show us how a seemingly particular question of policy is transformed as a moral concern when placed in ever-widening contexts of duty. To talk coherently about Vietnam in those contexts morally requires us to see and describe things differently, to abandon the conventional terms and objects of calculation. When King considers North Vietnam's intractability at the bargaining table, it makes sense to tell the longer story of America's intractability in its treatment of North Vietnam, chronicling our systematic abandonment of the principle of self-determination in order to side with the exploitative landed classes. If we recognize the poor and the exploited as our neighbors, it makes sense that love requires a willingness to see our actions from those neighbors' point of view and to attend to their implications with respect to the injustices of class. If we recognize as our neighbors those who admire our value of self-determination and self-government, it makes sense—at least this new sort of sense King teaches—that love requires respecting our neighbors' decisions, even if their decision process includes some Communists.

Not that love requires us to abandon entirely our strategic concerns about communism; indeed, "this kind of positive revolution of values is our best defense." We can mount a *more* powerfully anticommunist American revolution if we join King in two commitments he has been enacting with us here. The first is to enlarge our sense of justice to include economic justice: "We must not engage in a negative anticommunism, but rather in a positive thrust for democracy . . . to take offensive action in behalf of justice. We must with positive action seek to remove those conditions of poverty, insecurity and injustice which are the fertile soil in which the seed of communism grows."[50] Valuing people over "machines and computers, profit motives and property rights,"[51] we must develop "person-oriented" solutions to the human problems communism can use to get a foothold and to which materialism, its ineluctable counterparts racism and militarism, and the conventional calculations based on them are perilously insensitive.

The other commitment is King's insistence on nonviolence: "War is not the answer. Communism will never be defeated by the use of atomic bombs or nuclear weapons."[52] In a long paragraph that today's reader might find unnervingly prophetic about the more excruciating entanglements of American foreign policy since 1967, King warns about the consequences of commitments to authoritarian regimes and military solutions in Latin America and with South Africa;[53] in King's revolutionary way of life in language, it becomes possible for him to speak almost prophetically about foreign affairs. But nonviolence applies to each of us as individuals as it does to all of us as a nation. It is important not simply to resist the war but to resist it rightly, "seeking out every creative means of protest."[54] This duty is so binding that King calls students of the ministry to give up their categorical deferments and practice conscientious objection. King does not do the violence of withholding truth from his audience; even this most threatening moral demand is made explicit.

Only in this sort of rhetorical relation can we recognize a way both to "get on the right side of world revolution" and to recover our own revolutionary tradition. This is not a retreat, an act of disengagement or isolation, for it is not a withdrawal from the world or from the material and moral stewardships that distinguish a great nation. It is, rather, a commitment to the same concrete moral capacities King has been demonstrating himself and exercising in us. For the most part, they are as far from expedient as authors and audiences can get. He has not only taken a politically difficult stand in a difficult time; he has also made a moral demand that is so far-reaching that *any* time is a difficult time for it, and every time will demand the qualities of vision and character that the speech rehearses. He has asked of us certain moral commitments while he exercised in us the capacities to make such commitments: to inquire more attentively into the fairness and moral efficacy of our policies, for example; or to address the unjust and destabilizing contrast of poverty and wealth abroad as well as at home and correct the exploitative economic and political arrangements needed to sustain it. He has called us to attend more carefully to what other cultures and peoples can teach us, much as in his own life and thought King had incorporated Gandhi's philosophy of nonviolence and as he led us to do in this speech by having a Buddhist monk call us back to our constitutive traditions of "revolution, freedom and democracy."[55] He has called us to speak more eloquently against the moral devastation that "thing-oriented" profiteering can bring by speaking a language that does not carry its calculative assumptions.

If the speech is described in these terms—its own terms, accessible to us in our participation in the activities in which it engages us—it seems harder to read as a surrender to the morally or rhetorically expedient. More importantly, in its synthesis of moral and political concepts from sources as diverse as the Bible, Gandhi, and the American state papers, it seems a genuine and generously resourceful effort at reconstituting the kind of community contemporary Americans can constitute when they think and talk. So often when we discuss American intellectual history, the conversation reaches Dewey and peters out; but King's resourceful synthesis[56] writes a significant and hopeful new chapter. At the very least, his connection of civil rights to human rights seems our time's most important and beneficial entry into the lexicon of foreign policy and the persuasive vocabulary of international relations.

Yet the speech is not without flaw: What must be judged in King's own terms a serious ethical shortcoming—*must*, lest by critical silence his own values be betrayed—appears in his constitution of audience. King calls the American community to be more inclusive: to make our loyalties "ecumenical rather than sectional," to "develop an overriding loyalty to mankind as a whole," to "call for a world-wide fellowship that lifts neighborly concern beyond one's tribe, race, class and nation."[57] Yet he excludes the so-called enemy from direct participation in the discursive relation he offers: "This speech . . . is not addressed to China or Russia"; "tonight . . . I wish not to speak with Hanoi and the NLF, but rather to my fellow Americans."[58] By conventional calculation of rhetorical tactics, remaining silent toward them makes good sense: Persuading the "enemy" seems too great a task to add to the enormous burden of convincing the American audience. But King has already thrown into question the adequacy of conventional calculation as a way of thinking about the constitution of international relations; why may he now invoke it as a principle of discursive relations? King does pay some lip service to inclusiveness: "Conflicts are never resolved without trustful give and take on both sides."[59] But he accepts for his own rhetoric disturbingly few of the other moral risks of inclusion that he urges upon his audience.

Historians can buttress this criticism at this point, noting that King's exclusiveness of appeal contradicts not only the message of this speech but long-standing themes in his work as well. He always rejected "the presumption of otherness" but here behaves as if he must presume that others of a different place and race would require radically different appeals, would not or could not respond to the appeals we are expected to respond to, and he makes little effort to engage them in doing so. King also consistently rejected ethical relativism and sought a universal ground for ethical judgment. Yet in this speech he articulates no principle of appeal he is willing to apply equally and systematically to both Americans and Vietnamese. In a speech that teaches us to abandon false dichotomies that distinguish "us" against "them," King's consistent rhetorical choices constitute us as a separate, and morally privileged, audience.

In these respects, King has not quite done to others as he would have them do. Here, by his own standards, even a failed attempt would have been less damaging ethically and less implicative practically than the refusal to try. But at least we have been able to note and explicate more of the speech's ethical characteristics and to describe the capacities of such a way of life in language. In such a rhetorical relation, we can worry about preserving our moral traditions and even advancing them in the world, but we can also face the hidden facts of our occasional betrayal of those traditions in the past. We can learn to prophesy, with a disturbing prescience, about the kinds of situations that might entangle and strangle those traditions. We can speak a new language of description and analysis, in this case a language of class, so as to redefine, focus, extend, even recover those traditions. We can learn what it would mean to talk seriously about certain issues of foreign relations and domestic politics without having the range of that discussion delimited and its course determined by a morally inadequate language of calculation. We can learn what it would be like to move and act and speak in terms focused less by materialist, militarist, and racist concerns than on reconstituting and extending the American values of revolution, freedom, and democracy. Ultimately we can catch glimpses—not a definitive picture, but an uplifting and moving vision, with different angles open to our different perspectives—of what is universal in our traditions, what makes them worth sustaining, what is worth sharing with other nations, what can be learned from other peoples, what is the inspiration of God in the affairs of men, and what is the basis of a just and lasting peace among ourselves and with all nations.

King's ethical accomplishment in this text, and in the way of life in language in which it begins to engage us, is to show us what it would be like for us to talk that talk and walk that walk together. To examine that accomplishment might also complicate and enliven even our critical exchange.

Critics disposed to dismiss the speech as essentially an expediential act are confronted in a less escapable way with the ambitious scale of King's moral enterprise; perhaps they will now say more about the ways in which a message so radical that King himself could not bear all the demands of answering it could possibly have been intended by a skillful rhetorician as a way of playing it smart and safe. Critics disposed to venerate King and to find ethical wisdom in his every word are confronted in a less escapable way with his personal and public struggle and partial failure here to strike quite the balance he asked of his audience; perhaps these critics will now say more about the potentially tragic nature of such a struggle, about the moral resources available for it, or about what it is to commit our finite and fallible selves to it, even in perilous situations. Perhaps both kinds of critics will also say more about what it means to deal in rhetorical and ethical fellowship with our mutual failures to do so—convening us, as it were, into a community of critical discourse with the text as its variously approached but commonly held and mutually negotiated res publica.

Would that ethical criticism of this text could give us a glimpse of what a critical beloved community would be, where critical exchange can take place in an undiminished plurality of perspectives, each engaging and extending each other, informed by the way King for the most part has done unto others in his discourse as he would have them do in their actions. For not only did King call for a revolution of values; to a considerable if imperfect extent he enacted that revolution and spoke out of it, showing his audience what the world and our characters could be like in such a language, what could be said and done in such a rhetorical relation.

8

The Last Mountaintop of Martin Luther King, Jr.

Michael Osborn

What I offer here might be called a "critilogue," a critical excursion through a speech, using audiotaped segments both to illustrate and to create a sense of living presence. The procedure goes with what I have called *close criticism*, which "aspires to *appreciation*, an enlightened understanding of *challenges* confronted by rhetors . . . , the *options* available in meeting these challenges . . . , an assessment of the *performance* of rhetoric . . . , a description of the rhetoric as *consummated* (in that evanescent moment when rhetor-audience-message come together) . . . , and the moral, social, political *consequences* of the discourse."[1] If we follow traditional academic directions and attempt to objectify and distance the object of criticism, we run the risk—at least in rhetorical criticism—of losing the subject in the object. This is especially true considering that speeches normally are events that occur within dramatic contexts, are living moments that take their coloration from a symbolic environment that creates their tension and resonance. Such a moment was Martin Luther King, Jr.'s final speech, often called his "Mountaintop" speech.

As I step to the task of "criticizing" this speech, I find myself embarrassed by the role. Clearly, I am well situated to assume the close critical stance. Living in Memphis during that time, I was immersed in the events, the tragic atmosphere, that produced this memorable moment of rhetoric. I experienced the unrelieved tension, the meanness of fearful people and their occasional magnificence, the overall sense of looming explosiveness that often accompany profound social change.

But the speech stands before me like the very mountain from which King symbolically spoke. It was surely an awesome performance. Richard Lentz in his monograph *Sixty-Five Days in Memphis* calls it "one of the finest speeches of his career, matching the eloquence of his 'I have a dream' peroration at the 1963 March on Washington. In it King seemed to foretell his own death."[2] Garry Wills, in a perceptive and sometimes trenchant critique in *Esquire*, argued that it was "one of his great speeches—those speeches that will outlive his labored essays."[3] Adding to my sense of intimidation is the nature of this discourse *as a speech*. If the great poem must seem formidable to the critic, how much more so must be the great oration? For the speech is not a disembodied text. Rather it is a point of complex convergence, in which speaker, auditors, and events can all come together in grand illumination. Time freezes in that moment, and the meaning of its panorama stands revealed: The great speech thus translates into heightened consciousness and even into revelation.

What hubris, then, is required to present oneself as a critic of such a speech? From what hill of vanity must one view Martin Luther King, Jr.'s mountain? My own hill is constructed of small moments, one of which is worth remembering. When I first came to Memphis in 1966, I was asked by a friend to attend a rally announcing the candidacy of the first black candidate for mayor in Memphis. They could get, she said, no other white person to speak in his behalf, and they did not wish him to be seen strictly as a black candidate. So I agreed, but since it was my first such "involvement," I was apprehensive. "What would happen to me?" the kind of concern King shames in his speech as he tells the parable of the Good Samaritan, flashed across my mind. But I went to the rally, and it was huge, and all the audience seemed black. And I stood up finally, among the parade of black speakers, all of whom seemed so powerful and wonderful, an unknown person before an unknown audience, significant, ironically, only because of my race. And I started, "Long ago a man far wiser than any of us said, 'A house divided against itself cannot stand.'" And I paused, and from the collective throat of that great, black, wary audience there came back to me a thunderous "A-MEN!" And I was startled, heckled by my own success. Finally I smiled, and they smiled, recognizing my awkwardness on first entering *their* rhetorical culture, and then I went on. And as I spoke there came to me in a rush what their acceptance meant, how supported I felt as they encouraged me, how large and strong and important I felt, as I talked about white obligation to open the rusted doors of opportunity to those left on the outside.

It was really a small moment, but I learned a great deal from it. Learned what the black church experience meant in forming orators who could speak to listeners who had been systematically degraded and beaten down by each week's experience in racial subjugation. Learned the cultural role of the great bold speaker in representing *what they might be,* relieved of that terrible subjugation. So I take this small experience and a few others like it, magnify them a hundred times, and glimpse for a moment what it might mean to be a Martin Luther King, Jr., beloved and despised, exploited as much by those who loved him as he was hated by those who feared him, as he spoke at the pinnacle and end of his life. And what I see is what follows—my view from the hill.

Much of the greatness of King's final speech on the stormy night of April 3, 1968, lay in what he had to overcome.[4] The strike of the sanitation workers, improbable from the beginning, had become a heavy burden to sustain. Over two months it had endured, involving the lives and destinies of thirteen hundred men and their families. They were poor people, whose salaries qualified them for public welfare. So they had no money, and there had been no preexisting strike fund to support them. They were not a naturally militant group: Most of them had been conditioned both by race and by life to accept a humble role in society. They were hardly the group to start a social revolution. Moreover, they had gone out at just the wrong time: To put the matter bluntly, in the winter uncollected garbage does not stink. It does not create the kind of public pressure that forces a successful conclusion to a strike. Still, from the workers' point of view, it was just the right time: that moment when their accumulation of grievances was simply intolerable and when they must now act or surrender what claim they had on dignity and integrity. When they marched, they often carried signs asserting the simple proposition, "I am a Man." That this was a *metaphor* for many people in Memphis, and that they *had* to assert such a proposition, signified the virulent racism they had to overcome. They were striking both for their jobs and for their identities. But after two months of crisis in Memphis, with no paychecks, the going was very tough indeed.

Then there was King's own embattled situation. He had won the Nobel Prize, but many thought his brand of activism belonged to the past. Hard and brilliant new voices, like that of Malcolm X, questioned and scorned the doctrine of nonviolent protest in America.

King had just experienced a humiliating defeat in Chicago, failing to crack the entrenched institutional racism of housing patterns in that city. Adam Clayton Powell had then rechristened him "Martin Loser King."

As though he needed additional troubles, the first march he had led in Memphis had been a tactical disaster. Poorly organized by local leaders, it had resulted in some petty violence and had disintegrated into a chaos of fleeing demonstrators and pursuing police. King himself had to be transported from the area, leaving the local newspapers to cackle over what they called this latest exhibition of "Chicken-a-la-King." The spectacle seemed to confirm to many critics that King and his movement were dangerous and ineffective anachronisms, raising further doubts about his ability to carry out the grandiose Poor People's Campaign he was planning later that year in Washington.

All these furies were swarming about King's head as he stepped onto the stage at Mason Temple on that final fateful night, and his speech may be savored now as his last triumphant response to them. Mason Temple itself is a cavernous place that can seat a multitude of souls. It is the kind of setting that requires the dramatic, Ciceronian style of oratory to challenge and fill its vastness. On the rainy, stormy night of April 3, only three thousand were in attendance, but these were the faithful, the hard core, the true believers. King had been very tired and reluctant to speak that night. So he had sent Ralph Abernathy in his place, but Abernathy, seeing the audience, called King at the Lorraine Motel and said, "They are your crowd." They needed the message only he could give.

And so he had come, and so he began:

I'm delighted to see each of you here tonight in spite of a storm warning. You reveal that you are determined to go on anyhow. Something is happening in Memphis, something is happening in our world. And you know, if I were standing at the beginning of time with the possibility of taking a kind of general and panoramic view of the whole of human history up to now, and the Almighty said to me, "Martin Luther King, which age would you like to live in? . . ."[5]

Already we see that the "Mountaintop" speech is appropriately named. At the beginning King stands on an implied mountain, outside of time but viewing its panorama up to the present. His only companion is God, with whom he talks and deals directly. He will return to that mountain again as the speech concludes, this time to proclaim his exalted moral vision of the future. He is closely identified with his listeners, but through the metaphor of the mountain he can depart from them and ascend into moral space, there to assume his lonely prophet's stance.

So he tells his audience how he would deal with God's tough question. He would consider especially vital moments in the quest for freedom, beginning in Egypt, going on through Greece and Rome, pausing with Martin Luther in the Renaissance, watching Abraham Lincoln sign the Emancipation Proclamation, and observing Franklin Roosevelt grapple with economic slavery. And he decides:

I would turn to the Almighty and say, "If you allow me to live just a few years in the second half of the twentieth century, I will be happy." [applause]
Now that's a strange statement to make because the world is all messed up, the nation is sick, trouble is in the land, confusion all around. That's a strange statement. But I know somehow that only when it is dark enough can you see the stars. And I see God working in this period of the twentieth century in a way that men in some strange way are responding. Something is happening in our world. The masses of people are rising up, and wherever they are assembled today, whether they are in Johannesburg, South Africa; Nairobi, Kenya; Accra, Ghana; New York City; Atlanta, Georgia; Jackson, Mississippi; or Memphis, Tennessee, the cry is always the same: "We want to be free!" [applause]

Notice here the beautiful diachronic and synchronic effects: King has sketched a rising freedom consciousness through diachronic time, which gradually comes to focus in the present struggle. And then he places this moment at the center of synchronic space, in the freedom quest extending around the world. He lifts the tired heads and hearts of those before him: *They are important!* This is not just some small garbage strike stuck off on the margins of humanity: *This moment is exalted!* (And so are they.)

Lifted with him in this exaltation, they can see the significance of their own crisis as part of the rise of "the colored peoples of the world." They can share King's apocalyptic vision, see that the world's choice is between "nonviolence and nonexistence," see that "if something isn't done and done in a hurry," then "the whole world is doomed." Memphis has become a synecdoche for that dark, vast foreboding, that urgency and trauma. His listeners have become world-historical figures—precisely because they have become figurative, representative. And they can see that in their spiritual journey from Egypt into the now, they have assumed transcendent new identities:

I can remember . . . I can remember when Negroes were just going around, as Ralph has said so often, scratching where they didn't itch and laughing when they were not tickled. [applause] But that day is all over.

[applause] We mean business now, and we are determined to gain our rightful place in God's world. [applause] And that's all this whole thing is about. We aren't engaged in any negative protests and in any negative arguments with anybody. We are saying that "We are determined to be men, we are determined to be people." We are saying, [applause] . . . we are saying that "We are God's children."

In this new religious vision of identity, the origin of the freedom quest in Egypt resonates again. Now they are depicted as on their own exodus out of this new Egypt, escaping from a new Pharaoh. The name "Memphis" itself fortuitously reinforces the prevailing narrative symbolism, which will climax finally with King, their Moses, sharing his last inspired glimpse of the Promised Land.

But first the issues of the present strike, viewed in these dramatic frames:

The issue is injustice. The issue is the refusal of Memphis to be fair and honest in its dealings with its public servants who happen to be sanitation workers. [applause] Now we've got to keep attention on that. That's always the problem with a little violence. You know what happened the other day, and the press dealt only with the window-breaking. I read the articles. They very seldom got around to mentioning the fact that one thousand three hundred sanitation workers are on strike, and that Memphis is not being fair to them, and that Mayor Loeb is in dire need of a doctor. [cheers and applause] They didn't get around to that. Now we're gonna march again and we've gotta march again in order to put the issue where it is supposed to be, and force everybody to see that there are thirteen hundred of God's children here suffering, sometimes goin' hungry, going through dark and dreary nights wondering how this thing is gonna come out. That's the issue. And we've got to say to the nation, "We know how it's coming out." For when people get caught up with that which is right, and they are willing to sacrifice for it, there is no stopping point short of victory! [applause]

One of King's favorite metaphors, that of disease and illness, reechoes in these words. Indeed, Mayor Loeb, already saddled with the Pharaoh figuration, now becomes as well a living synecdoche for the sick society that was contemporary America.[6] This is the same Mayor Loeb who boasted to Garry Wills that there was a "good understanding" between himself and Memphis blacks.

King now puts the heart into listeners by reminding them of glorious successes of the past, and in so doing he defends the power and legitimacy of nonverbal protest as well. Here he remembers, and celebrates, magnificent moments in Birmingham:

I remember in Birmingham, Alabama, when we were in that majestic struggle there, we would move out of the Sixteenth Street Baptist Church day after day. By the hundreds we would move out, and Bull Connor would tell 'em to send the dogs forth, and they did come. But we just went before the dogs singing, "Ain't gonna let nobody turn me around." [cheers] Bull Connor next would say, "Turn the firehoses on." And as I said to you the other night Bull Connor didn't know history. He knew a kind of physics that somehow didn't relate to the transphysics that we knew about, and that was the fact that there was a certain kind of fire that no water could put out. [applause] And we went before the firehoses. We had known water. If we were Baptist or some other denominations we had been immersed, if we were Methodists and some others we had been sprinkled, but we knew water. That couldn't stop us. [applause] And we just went on before the dogs and we would look at them, and we'd go on before the water hoses and we would look at it, and we'd just go on singing "Over my head I see freedom in the air." And then we would be thrown in the paddy wagons, and sometimes we were stacked in there like sardines in a can. And they would throw us in and old Bull would say, "Take 'em off," and they did. And we would just go on in the paddy wagons singin' "We Shall Overcome." And every now and then we'd get in jail and we'd see the jailers looking through the windows being moved by our prayers, and being moved by our words and our songs. And there was a power there which Bull Connor couldn't adjust to. And so we ended up transforming Bull into a steer, and we won our struggle in Birmingham. [applause]

And we've got to go on in Memphis just like that.

This cameo of the past functions as their moral, rhetorical history. It helps to organize and focus time, fusing memory and desire. In rhetoric the past exists in service of the present, so here the story of Birmingham becomes an exemplar for Memphis.

Now King proceeds to tell his listeners exactly what they must do to win this strike, and how they must do it. They must proceed respectfully but with unity and determination. They must find the economic pressure points, and they must build economic strength in the black community as well. And finally, they must invest themselves personally in the desperate plight of the sanitation workers. They must stop by this dangerous road, just as King himself had stopped by Memphis:

. . . We've got to give ourselves to this struggle until the end. Nothing would be more tragic than to stop at this point in Memphis. We've got to see it through. [applause] And when we have our march, you need to be there. If it means leaving work, if it means leaving school, be there. [applause] Be concerned about your brother. You may not be on strike, but either we go up together or we go down together. [applause] Let us develop a kind of dangerous unselfishness.

So he goes on to tell the parable of the Good Samaritan, which functions as a kind of balance for the Children of Israel narrative.

While the latter provides collective identity, the former sets up models of personal conduct to imitate and avoid. Moreover, the Good Samaritan, since he is "of another race," reminds listeners of their own need to maintain tolerance and acceptance:

[Jesus] . . . talked about a certain man who fell among thieves. And you remember that a Levite [Voice says, "Sure."] and a priest passed by on the other side. They didn't stop to help him. And finally a man of another race came by. [Voice says, "Yes sir!"] He got down from his beast, decided not to be compassionate by proxy, but he got down with him, administered first aid, and helped the man in need. Jesus ended up saying, this was the good man, this was the great man, because he had the capacity to project the "I" into the "thou," and to be concerned about his brother.

Now you know we use our imagination a great deal to try to determine why the priest and the Levite didn't stop. At times we say they were busy going to a church meeting, an ecclesiastical gatherin', and they had to get on down to Jerusalem so they wouldn't be late for their meeting. At other times we would speculate that there was a religious law that one who was engaged in religious ceremonials was not to touch a human body twenty-four hours before the ceremony. And every now and then we begin to wonder whether maybe they were not going down to Jerusalem—or down to Jericho rather—to organize a Jericho Road Improvement Association. [laughter] That's a possibility. Maybe they felt that it was better to deal with the problem from the causal root rather than to get bogged down with an individual effect. . . . That's a dangerous road. In the days of Jesus it came to be known as the Bloody Pass. You know it's possible that the priest and the Levite looked over to that man on the ground and wondered if the robbers were still around. [Voices agree, "Yeah."] Or it's possible that they felt that the man on the ground was merely faking, [Voice says, "Uh-huh."] and he was acting like he had been robbed and hurt in order to seize them over there, lull them there for quick and easy seizure. [Voice says, "Oh, yeah."] And so the first question that the priest asked, the first question that the Levite asked, was "If I stop to help this man, what will happen to me?" But then the good Samaritan came by, and he reversed the question: "If I do not stop to help this man, what will happen to him?" That's the question before you tonight: Not, "If I stop to help the sanitation workers, what will happen to my job? Not, "If I stop to help the sanitation workers, what will happen to all of the hours that I usually spend in my office every day and every week as a pastor?" The question is not, "If I stop to help this man in need, what will happen to me?" The question is, "If I do *not* stop to help the sanitation workers, what will happen to them?" That's the question. [long applause]

Let us rise up tonight with a greater readiness. Let us stand with a greater determination. And let us move on, in these powerful days, these days of challenge, to make America what it ought to be. We have an opportunity to make America a better nation . . .

Note here the emergence of the vertical metaphor, signifying both the strength of the rising race and the movement of the speech itself to its own elevated peroration. For now he had come to his conclusion, and who could know—could he?—that it was to be the peroration of his life, that he was actually delivering—as no one else could or would—his own eulogy? He tells first the story of how a "demented black woman" had stabbed him many years ago as he was autographing books in New York. In the hospital they found that the tip of the blade was lodged against his aorta, and the *New York Times* commented that if he had merely sneezed, he would have died. Later, while recovering in the hospital, he had received many kind letters, but one in particular remained in his memory:

But there was another letter [Voices say, "All right."] that came from a little girl, a young girl, who was a student at the White Plains High School, and I looked at that letter and I'll never forget it. It said simply, "Dear Dr. King, I am a ninth grade student at the White Plains High School." She said, "While it should not matter, I would like to mention that I'm a white girl. I read in the paper of your misfortune and of your suffering, and I read that if you had sneezed you would have died. I'm simply writing you to say that I'm so happy that you didn't sneeze." And I want to say tonight . . . [applause] I want to say tonight that I too am happy that I didn't sneeze, because if I had sneezed [Voice says, "All right."] I wouldn't have been around here in 1960 when students all over the South started sitting in at lunch counters. And I knew that as they were sitting in they were really standing up for the best in the American dream and taking the whole nation back to those great wells of democracy which were dug deep by the founding fathers in the Declaration of Independence and the Constitution. If I had sneezed [Crowd replies, "Yeah."] I wouldn't have been around here in 1961 when we decided to take a ride for freedom and ended segregation in interstate travel. If I had sneezed [Crowd says, "Yes."] I wouldn't have been around here in 1962 when Negroes in Albany, Georgia, decided to straighten their backs up. And whenever men and women straighten their backs up they are going somewhere because a man can't ride your back unless it is bent. If I had sneezed [long applause] . . . if I had sneezed I wouldn't have been here in 1963, when the black people of Birmingham, Alabama, aroused the conscience of this nation and brought into being the civil rights bill. If I had sneezed, [applause] I wouldn't have had a chance later in that year in August to try to tell America about a dream that I had had. If I had sneezed, [applause] I wouldn't have been down in Selma, Alabama, to see the great movement there. If I had sneezed, I wouldn't have been in Memphis to see a community rally around those brothers and sisters who are suffering. [Voices say, "Yes sir."] I'm so happy that I didn't sneeze.

And they were telling me . . . [applause] Now it doesn't matter now. [Voice says, "Go ahead."] It really doesn't matter what happens now. I left Atlanta this morning, and as we got started on the plane—there were six of us—the pilot said over the public address system, "We are sorry for the delay, but we have Dr. Martin Luther King on the plane, and to be sure that all of the bags were checked and to be sure that nothing would be wrong on the plane, we had to check out everything carefully, and we've had the plane protected and guarded all night."

And then I got into Memphis, and some began to say the threats, or talk about the threats that were out of what would happen to me from some of our sick white brothers. Well, I don't know what will happen now. We've got some difficult days ahead. But it really doesn't matter with me now because I've been to the mountaintop. [applause] And I don't mind. Like anybody I would like to live a long life. Longevity has its place. But I'm not concerned about that now. I just want to do God's will, and He's allowed me to go up to the mountain, and I've looked over, and I've seen the Promised Land. I may not get there with you, but I want you to know tonight that we as a people will get to the Promised Land. [applause] So I'm happy tonight, I'm not worried about anything, I'm not fearing any man. Mine eyes have seen the glory of the coming of the Lord. [long applause, cheers]

What finally can one say of such a mountain of a speech, viewed from our hill? First, perhaps, that it gives the lie to a view one used to hear quite frequently, that the public oration is a dying art form. King is an orator: On the page his words can seem flat, can lose their iridescence; there the prose patterns sometimes appear overblown and awkward as they strain for inflated effects. It's when you *hear* them that they penetrate to your heart.[7] And it was also in the middle of the action that King was heard best, when the situation stripped his language of all that was unnecessary, leaving such poetry as "Only when it is dark enough can you see the stars."

Such, I would argue, is the language of ritual, as indeed is much of the language of this speech. But the occasion was certainly not epideictic, not at least in any traditional sense of that term. Normally we think of epideictic rhetoric as belonging to an occasion *after* some critical event has already occurred, in which the event is commemorated, celebrated, and interpreted. This occasion, it is clear, was situated *in*, belonged *to*, and constituted a consciousness *of* its moment of crisis. Did King misperceive the rhetorical situation? Clearly not. What defines the ritual of epideictic rhetoric is not so much its place vis-à-vis events, but rather its function, which is to confer or reaffirm social identity. What both races had to confront in Memphis in the spring of 1968 was the changing social identity of black people. In this transition, this exodus out of racism, *Who were they?* and *Who were they to be?* Those questions constituted the crisis of Memphis.

To answer them, King resorted primarily to a biblical story familiar to all in his audience—the flight of the Children of Israel from Egypt. Almost all the circumstances—the extreme poverty of the workers, the setting in Memphis, the especially adamant character of the then-mayor Loeb, the powerful *ethos* of King himself—lent special resonance to this favorite narrative form of the black experience in America. As Malinda Snow has observed, "In the story of the children of Israel in Egypt, . . . [slaves] discovered the central type of their experience, which prefigured their own deliverance from slavery. They merged biblical and contemporary time."[8] Thus as King exercised his inventional option and selected the Children of Israel narrative as the major structural principle of his speech, his choice was far more than an exercise in cleverness. Indeed, ingenuity, a quality we may often associate with inventional excellence, had little to do with the rightness of King's selection. What is more important is that King's listeners had no doubt heard this narrative form explored many times before as figuring and framing their racial experience. While the excellence of this particular version may have seemed unique, its primary virtue was its place within the black rhetorical tradition. For listeners, it transversed time, connecting past with present, confirming their association with generations receding into memory. Central then to the rhetorical experience of this speech was the celebration of rhetorical *ritual*, joining speaker and audience as they acknowledged again what it meant to be black in America and black in Memphis. The narrative tradition made their lives coherent, invested their experience with religious meaning, and gave hope to their cause. As they had prevailed before, in so many dread situations opposed by so many other formidable Pharaohs, they would prevail again. It was the ritual repetition of this narrative then, augmented by the particular eloquence of its statement in this performance, that gave this speech so much of its distinctive power as epideictic utterance.

And yet, appropriate as King's narrative selection was for his audience and for the short-term rhetorical consequences in this situation, we may wonder at its long-term efficacy. No doubt every selection among rhetorical options may have its shadow, its potential negative elements. And we may wonder at the culture-long consequences of continuing to remind people of their slave origins, speaking of them as "children" (even transfigured as "God's children"). The family metaphor had not been kind to black people in America. And King's usage ran the danger of raising the salience again of cultural metaphors that had denigrated adult blacks as "boy," "girl," or at best "uncle." It was the family metaphor that had created the low sense of place for blacks in the racial hierarchy of American society and that confined them to that place. I believe it was these lingering images of debased identity that Malcolm X found most objectionable in King's approach to social reform. Again, I wish not to be misunderstood: I believe that King's narrative selection was correct and astute, his execution superb. But his was a human choice within an imperfect rhetorical world and may well have exacted its price within the spiritual lives of his listeners.

Clearly, the Exodus story did offer hope to King's listeners. The reason for such reassurance, Rosteck has observed, is that the narrative is *predictive:* What it predicts for black people is an American equivalent of the Promised Land.[9] This predictive quality is similar to the deterministic element identified in rhetorical uses of darkness and light metaphors.[10] Both the prediction and the determinism are *conditioned:* The Promised Land will come, and light will follow darkness, *if* (and only if) auditors are true to the speaker's recommendations. Here we must return to the parable of the Good Samaritan and how it functions in this speech vis-à-vis the Exodus narrative. The latter, I observed earlier, offers cultural, collective identity for black people, while the former deals with personal moral obligation. But more than just the counterpart of the Exodus narrative, the Good Samaritan story functions as its enabling condition. The Exodus myth will become reality, will carry listeners to the Promised Land, *if* they are willing to follow with full-hearted commitment the moral example of the Good Samaritan.[11] With King they must "stop by this dangerous road" and embrace the cause of the sanitation workers in the here and now. Through this ingenious combination of biblical narratives, the speech moves from the opening vision of collective identity, these God's children who have inherited the destiny of the Children of Israel, to the close picture of personal moral crisis—of risk and choice—figured in the Good Samaritan story, and back again to the grand concluding image of a people marching toward a land that King alone has been privileged to witness. The movement of the speech is epic as it soars through moral time and space.

Besides its epideictic function as the language of ritual, identity, and moral confrontation, King's speech had the immediate task of reinvigorating a faltering strike action. And so it performed the business of implementing, the work of deciding and sustaining action. It is in such moments that oratory especially comes to the center stage of rhetoric. Nothing can take the place of the actual physical presence of orators in such moments, bringing themselves to bear witness to their own commitment, touching listeners directly with the radiance and fire of their messages, opening the eyes of auditors to the meaning of their lives and to the meaning of the events in which they are engaged. Only the great orator can hold *that* center stage successfully, and King held it with a mastery and grace rarely seen in the long tradition of rhetoric. Clearly, he belongs among the great revolutionary orators. Surely, we have been witness to a phenomenon.

To speak of King's address as exemplifying the rhetoric of implementation is to depart from the close criticism of the speech and our "critilogue" and to step back into what I shall call *perspective criticism.* Here we are concerned with placing King's address within the overall process of rhetoric that was working out its fateful scenario in Memphis during the early months of 1968. To understand this process, I call upon my account of *rhetorical depiction,* which identifies successive phases of *presentation, arousal, group identification, implementation,* and *reaffirmation.*[12] Essentially I argue that the presentation phase of rhetorical process may be most vital, because it affects how we *see* events and thus how we feel, band together, act in response to them, and celebrate them. These phases *enable* each other in successful, coordinated rhetorical campaigns, but when they occur in competing rhetorics, they can *disable* each other. This debilitation explains why all the passionate rhetoric of action generated by black orators during the sanitation strike, including King's several speeches, was finally subverted and limited in effect.

What undercut the reach of such rhetoric was a countervailing rhetoric of presentation that cast events and players according to presuppositions deeply rooted in the culture of racism. Presented in the mass circulation newspapers and on local television "news" programs, this rhetoric developed its power from an irresistible accumulation of stories, human interest features, and editorials, played out day after day during the strike but consistent with plot lines that had already been established, year after year, decade after decade, in the discourse of southern culture. There were, according to Richard Lentz, at least three themes among these powerful cultural plot lines. First, *blame the outsider:* The theme "invoked the belief that outsiders were agitating blacks who otherwise would be content with their lot." Second, *fear of a black uprising:* This theme was "grounded in the concept that during a period of social unrest public order had to be maintained at any cost. . . . The newspaper accounts resurrected in modern dress the fear of servile insurrection that haunted the antebellum South." Third, *racial noblesse oblige:* This theme "was an amalgam of paternalism and another racial stereotype. Blacks were stereotyped as child-like creatures incapable of conducting their own affairs. . . . Whites protected and cared for 'their' blacks, usually by providing some form of largess at the back door." Blacks, in turn, owed them gratitude and rewarded them by being content with a lower station in life. "Thus it was," says Lentz, "that the demands for equality raised by the strikers produced a mixture of puzzlement and shock that blacks would challenge the authority of those who had taken care of them."[13] These plot lines provided molds for depicting the players in the sanitation strike, for describing their motives, and for selecting and connecting their actions in presentation. They helped many Memphians "make sense" of the strike and in effect rigidified the perceptions they predisposed against any counterrhetoric rising from the black community. They limited the reach of King's rhetoric largely to the black community itself, which as this speech shows was developing its own supporting perceptions, plot lines, group togetherness, and agenda for action. What we are describing was clearly a gigantic racial dialectic that reached its point of stasis in Memphis and that would require a cataclysmic event to resolve its almost unbearable tension. The murder of Martin Luther King, Jr., was that event.

While the influence of any oration can be circumscribed in its own time by such countervailing forces as I have described, criticism itself must participate in the final fate of the rhetorical event. Rhetorical artistry is not preserved entire in a monument of words; any surviving text must be fragmentary, dependent for its appreciation on the critical gloss. The critic becomes an archaeologist of the meaning surrounding the rhetorical moment. Therefore, rhetorical criticism is essential to the symbolic afterlife of the artistry it contemplates. Such criticism freezes an evanescent moment for lasting contemplation: On the rhetorical critic's urn, forever shall they speak and listeners be moved. Thus King's speech may address us now, in defiance of the forces that constrained it in its own time. We may learn from his sentiments, apply his precepts to our own exigencies, and witness the tragedy and drama that suffused his life.

I have called King a revolutionary spokesman, and that may lift some eyebrows. What's so revolutionary about wanting to save the American dream and to redeem the national conscience? If we consider just the pure ideology of King's speech, he is as conservative as red, white, and blue. He is not out to overthrow America.

Ah, but that was his secret. He was not a political speaker. He told it to us all along. He was a preacher, a converter of souls. And what he was out to redeem was *cultural sin*, the way people treat each other as human beings, the way they betray their own ideals. As I have put it elsewhere, "His intent therefore was not so much to defeat his opponents as to save them from repudiating their own high principles. As Richard Neuhaus observed, 'A strategy for change that confronts a people with the choice of either accommodating the change or consciously surrendering the values by which they think they live is a most realistic strategy, striking at the heart of society.'"[14]

But we couldn't bear to hear all that, coming from the mouth of a black man. And moreover, a black man who could command a vast black army of humble people who were willing to assume all the risks of their own rising status and all the dangers of our conversion. That is why this really conservative man was so hated, so feared. He threatened to rearrange our social selves and beyond that our very souls. And so we shot him, blew away that great organ voice through an agent, a warped little man who thought, quite reasonably, given the rhetorical circumstances of that time, that he enjoyed moral license to gun down Martin Luther King, Jr. But it was fear and hatred that propelled the bullet—across a darkening street in Memphis on the quiet evening of April 4, 1968.

9

The Call from the Mountaintop: Call-Response and the Oratory of Martin Luther King, Jr.

Robert D. Harrison
Linda K. Harrison

In the spring of 1988, in his quest for the Democratic party's presidential nomination, Jesse Jackson spoke to a crowd of over a thousand people assembled in a hangar at the La Crosse, Wisconsin, airport. We were both in that audience. This was to be Jackson's last campaign stop for the day. He arrived about an hour late, apparently quite tired and hoarse of voice. Shortly after he began to speak, however, his fatigue and raspy tones disappeared. And even though he was under considerable strain, he was not only able to rise to the difficult occasion of addressing an audience late in the day, but he also managed to involve his audience actively in his message. His voice sang out, and we quickly became totally and emotionally involved in the vision he expressed. We felt spiritually uplifted by the words he spoke, and we empathized with his message as well as with his personal situation. In Michael Osborn's terms, we entered a new "rhetorical culture," we literally became one with it, and when we left it we came away with a deeper and fuller appreciation for a different way of being.[1] What we had read about Jackson and his message prior to entering that situation had not prepared us for the vitality of the experience we had encountered. And when that experience had ended, we found it impossible to describe it to those who had not been there.

The problem we have in describing our experience of Jackson's speech is grounded in the difficulty of capturing the experience of *any* speaking event through the written word.[2] That problem is made all the more difficult by virtue of the fact that, among many other factors, Jackson's oratory draws upon an African rhetorical tradition rooted in an oral culture that relies upon its orality as an inherent and essential element in effecting communal interactions and understanding. Until we come to a clearer understanding of the role that such orality plays in the collectivization process, it will be difficult for us to understand the rhetorical presence of such orators as Jesse Jackson. Indeed, in our judgment it is precisely this difficulty that bedevils those who attempt to account for the persuasive power of Rev. Martin Luther King, Jr., as the leader of the civil rights movement in the 1950s and 1960s. King was without a doubt one of the most important American orators of the twentieth century, perhaps in the whole of American history, and yet the analyses of his oratory have been mundane at best, focusing almost exclusively on the intellectual or philosophical content of his words and virtually ignoring the orality of their presentation. The result has been a failure to account fully for the way in which King's presence as an orator animated his listeners to participate in his message as active performers and thus to become one with the message he presented. Our concern in this essay is to address this omission in our historical and critical literature by examining the influences of the African oral tradition known as *nommo* on a selection of King's African-American oratory.

Although it is neither possible nor altogether desirable to deny our own Eurocentric view of the ways in which public discourse functions, we do believe that on occasion it is essential that such a posture be counterbalanced by non-European conceptions of communicative interaction. In order for one to understand African-American oratory as a unique blending of African and Anglo-American communicative practices, we believe that traditional communicative models are essential to account for the Afrocentric perspective. According to Molefi Asante, Afrocentricity is a critical perspective that places "African ideals at the center of any analysis which involves African culture and behavior."[3] The traditional African world view features a unifying interdependence between the spiritual and the material. Balance and harmony in the universe are contingent upon the complementary interplay between these two domains. Put more specifically, African cultural practices rely on the coherence of "persons and things" in all collective activities ranging from music and dance to the nommo.

Nommo represents the special power and presence of the spoken word in Africa's oral culture.[4] According to Asante it refers less to the "object" or idea content of persuasion than to the "generative power of the community." It is in the context of the nommo that the spiritual and material relationships between speaker and audience become one voice, literally performing a collective experience central to the balanced and harmonious maintenance of communal existence. As Asante writes: "In neo-African culture as expressed in North and South America, one gets the feel of this group performance in religious meetings and, indeed, in some secular gatherings. What are conventionally labeled reactions and responses of the audience might be better understood if we spoke of these phenomena as collective actions of participants. *Afro-Americans, viewing a movie, are participating in the events of that movie, not in the oral interpretation sense of 'fulfilling the potential' but in creating the potential. The potential does not exist apart from the participants; thus when an actor or actress is 'being seen' on the movie screen, the 'audience' is being seen.*"[5] From this perspective, public oratory is simultaneously an invitation to unity and creativity. The speaker attains something like power through his or her artistic ability to incite an audience's active, performative affirmation of the expression of community.

Our thesis in this essay is that the speaker-audience interaction that leads to the performance of community in African public discourse is also a significant component in much of Dr. Martin Luther King, Jr.'s oratory. In particular, we maintain that the power of his persuasion was in some measure a function of his ability to induce his audiences to participate in a pattern of performative interaction known as "call-response." In what follows we identify the call-response pattern of interaction as a key element in both African and African-American oral traditions, identify five characteristic oral qualities that invite the audience to participate in a call-response interaction, and then examine several different examples of King's public discourse in light of these qualities as a means of illuminating a significant dimension of his ability to create a sense of community with his followers.

The Cultural Roots of "Call-Response"

Since call-response occurs in varied contexts, we need to provide a broad conceptual framework that will adequately define its cultural and rhetorical dimensions. Jack Daniel and Geneva Smitherman define call-response as an "interacting, spontaneous process" characterized by "verbal and nonverbal interaction between speaker and listener in which" most or all of the "speaker's statements (or 'calls') are punctuated by expressions ('responses') from the listener."[6] It "seeks to synthesize 'speaker' and 'listener' in a unified movement."[7] It is also a creative process that utilizes free and spontaneous expression. While not exclusively African in origins or use, this synthesis clearly reflects the African oratorical experience since it understands the communicative event as a unified whole. The contexts in which this occurs are numerous. We thus find call-response interactions in music, in preaching, and in many ordinary forms of everyday communication in the black community, such as in the practice of "playing the dozens."

Call-response interactions have an undeniably long and rich history that serves to underscore its significance as a communicative phenomenon. Since the 1960s scholars have examined the impact of West African influences on the black American cultural experience.[8] These experiences appear to be linked to the African worldview that embodies concepts such as unity and harmony among all elements of the universe, balance in community experience, rhythm in life and nature, and a movement of the universe in a cyclical rather than a linear fashion. An interactive quality springs from these concepts. For example, all of life's events are characterized by community participation to create an event. Marriages, deaths, storytelling, or even the single transmission of news by drums is accomplished interactively.[9] This early West African influence marks a temporal beginning point to trace the rich antecedents of call-response.

The West African coast contributed the largest number of slaves to the American population. Some of the major African societies known to be influential in this process were the Dahomean, the Ashanti, the Yoruba, and the Mossi. From these groupings scholars have identified cultural characteristics shared in the entire spectrum of African sociopolitical interaction.[10] One of the major shared cultural characteristics is call-response in traditional African music. Even today, it is expressed in contemporary African music by such groups as Toure Kunda or Ladysmith Black Mambazo.[11] Affirming the role of call-response within this cultural context, LeRoi Jones points out that the idea of the solo was not common to the West African music expression.[12] Using the example of these groups we can begin to understand how the power of music is enhanced by interaction between group members and the audience. A lead singer provides the calls, while the group members' responses are repetitive and supportive, often reflecting the tone and intensity of the lead singer. The power or impact of the communication is affected by this interchange.

Conspicuous by its absence, the lack of call-response signals diminished power in traditional African exchanges. Robert Farris Thompson terms call-response "perfected social interaction" and refers to the power potential and the fundamental essence of this interactive system as a "politics of perfection."[13] The hallmark of call-response is the strong sense of community and the group unity and cooperation it engenders. He illustrates these concepts with the following observation: "The poor devil who starts a tale without proper preparation or refinement will find the choral answering to his songs becomes progressively weaker until they ultimately re-form about a man with stronger themes and better aesthetic organization. He is soon singing to himself. The terror of losing one's grip on the chorus is a real one in some African societies, a poignant dimension of social interaction that for some reason is not mentioned in discourse on singing in African music."[14]

Finally, when speaking of oral expressiveness in the traditional African experience, we can refer immediately to the importance of collective activity; achieving accord, balance, and unity; and a lack of distinction between speaker and audience. Asante uses the term nommo from the Dogon tribe to describe the very complex and all-encompassing nature of the African oral tradition. Societal conflict is resolved through discourse that attempts to restore balance; i.e., the speaker continues until "his" audience is "with" him and each other. He coaxes his participants with his creativity, including tone, volume, movement, rate, and rhythm in order to strike a responsive chord within each person and thus achieve a sense of equality and harmony. "The word is productive and imperative, *calling* forth and *commanding*," writes Asante. "Its power derives from the traditional emphasis on the spoken word in African society."[15]

The first blacks to arrive in North America maintained their West African heritage as an important part of their identity. Since the emphasis on oral tradition was so strong, the call-response pattern surfaced in various communication forms. For example, we know that slaves used cries, calls, and field hollers to send messages to one another, to identify themselves, and to maintain communal ties. According to Tilford Brooks, calls played as practical a role in this country as they did in Africa. During the period of American slavery, plantation workers were isolated from one another. The means of maintaining social contact was "by calling back and forth and singing songs together." Frequently a slave would improvise a song and others would help by responding.[16]

Another communication form was the work song. Most West Africans were farmers who had sung work songs to add impetus to the field work. African slaves brought these songs with them to this country and employed them in a similar fashion. Probably purely African at first, the songs changed over time in lyric but not in their call-response form. The Gullah people of the Georgia Sea Islands give us some idea of the sound of the song in its pristine form. The blacks in this setting were largely self-sufficient and thus were best able to preserve their African roots.[17] These roots can be noted by observing the call-response pattern in the work song "Pay Me" as recorded by a group of Gullah singers.[18] Each time the lead singer sings his line, the chorus replies with variations of the same response.

Early spirituals also reflect the use of call-response. One representative example is "Wade in the Water."[19] As the slaves developed their own praise houses and churches, call-response became a prominent feature in gospel songs and in preacher-congregation interactions.[20] Contemporary gospel music still exhibits this basic pattern. Alfred B. Pasteur and Ivory L. Toldson speak to this understanding as they attempt to recreate for the reader an Andre Crouch performance of "Soon and Very Soon (We Are Going to See the King)": "Crouch's vocal leads are answered by a choral mellowness, and are balanced by the powerfully sensuous female lead voice of Danniebelle Hall. Just when you think the tune is finished, it swells with a repetitive choral-chanting of leads and answers (calls and responses). . . . This choral-chant is accompanied only by mouth basses, toe taps, and hand claps, leaping suddenly back through time to authentic African influences, 'jazzing' the music."[21]

In the black church, the call-response of the singing leads to the call-response between preacher and congregation. The singing conditions the audience for the interactive process that follows. Asante writes that congregants are prepared on an emotional and physical level through song and are thus more receptive to the preacher. Song then serves to make the congregation more cohesive: "In mounting the platform to speak to a religious audience, the black preacher does not challenge *Nommo* but uses it, becomes a part of it, and is consumed in the fire of speech and music."[22] The power of the spoken word reaches its pinnacle with the introduction of the preacher.

During slavery the preacher's role as lead singer took on importance because secular outlets for emotional expression so vital in an oral culture had been repressed. Ben Sidran writes that "the group actionality was generated by the vocal and rhythmic response of the congregation (they were all lead singers, group singers, and rhythm singers) and the musical-religious ritual became the most important single experience in the daily life of the slave, much as it had been in preslavery Africa."[23]

As the church evolved, call-response continued to enhance the cohesion of the congregational community. The interactive, spontaneous quality of preacher and congregation cannot easily be communicated on paper, but Daniel and Smitherman provide in the following a good slice of the dynamics involved in the traditional service:

Following this "warming up" period of invoking the spirit, and other intermediate parts of the service, the preacher gets into his service by issuing his initial call: "My theme for today is waiting on the Lord." The congregation responds with "Take your time," "Fix it up, Reb.," "Come on up, now," or simply "Preach, Reb." When the preacher's calls get stronger and more emotional, you can see the spirit moving over there in the Amen Corner, and hear the congregation urging him on with "Go, 'head, now!" "Yessuh!" "Watch yo-self, now!" and such nonverbal responses as nodding of heads, clapping of hands, stomping of feet, jumping up and down, jerking the body, holy dancing, "shouting." While the preacher is moving his congregation through the Power of the Word, the congregation's verbal and body responses are also moving him to a higher level of emotional feeling and understanding of the Magic of the Word. Many's the time the Black preacher has been heard to say, "I sho was gon take it easy today, but the folks made me preach."[24]

From this excerpt we can identify the strength of the call-response dynamics upon the participants. The preacher and congregation work together to intensify the experience for all who participate. Audience members and speaker are caught up in the developing emotional fervor. The preacher sets the process in motion and directs its progress, while the congregation provides the energy to sustain the process. We can also see why the pulpit would become the most logical place for the development of leadership in the black community.

It is clear that the black church furnished strong leaders for the community. It is interesting to recognize that preachers assumed leadership roles in political, social, and intellectual as well as spiritual arenas.[25] This combined role is instructive because it is consistent with the Afrocentric notion of the unity of all aspects of life. Moreover, it reflects the Afrocentric idea that the spiritual realm achieves prominence over the material domain and that those educated within the spiritual realm become the leaders. This tradition had a strong impact on Dr. Martin Luther King, Jr.'s style of oratory, a point underscored by Coretta Scott King when she wrote, "His (Martin Luther King, Jr.'s) style of preaching grew out of the tradition of the Southern Baptist ministers, with cadences and timing which he had learned from his father and other ministers as long as he could remember."[26]

The Function of Call-Response in King's Oratory

Recalling our initial definition of call-response, we can now consider King's oratory in light of its interactive, spontaneous qualities characterized by the verbal and nonverbal interaction between him and the audience. King's audiences frequently punctuated his "calls" with various expressions.[27] Furthermore, call-response helped to create a sense of community by synthesizing King and his audience into a unified movement for civil rights.[28]

Informed by a rich heritage that had been passed down from previous generations, King expressed both self and culture in his oratory. It was an oratory given life by call-response. Responses naturally varied according to the setting (secular versus religious) and audience composition. Even though "that's right" may have replaced "amen," the fundamental call-reponse pattern in King's oratory remained intact.[29]

How did King and his audience work together to build the desired result? To help us to arrive at an understanding, we listened to and watched samples of King's speeches, including audio recordings of "We Shall Overcome" and "On Police Brutality" and video recordings of "How Long? Not Long" and "I Have a Dream."[30] It is necessary to note that some of the extant primary materials feature either eliminated or reduced aural or visual responses to King's oratory. An important rhetorical element of King's oratory is missing because of this deletion.

Anaphora

Anaphora, or the repetition of words and phrases within successive sentences, heightens the emotional climate. With its characteristic redundancy as a reflection of the oral culture from which it springs, it is a mutual cue for audience and speaker. Support and encouragement evolve from the "calling forth."

There are numerous examples of anaphora in King's speeches. For example, in "On Police Brutality," the phrase "If you can accept it . . ." emerges at the beginning of several sentences.[31] In his "We Shall Overcome" speech, "We shall overcome because . . ." is repeated.[32] In the "How Long? Not Long?" speech, King returns to "How long? Not long."[33] Along with the repeated lines of "I have a dream . . . ," "We can never be satisfied . . . ," "Go back to . . . ," and "With this faith . . . ," King says "Let freedom ring . . ." at least eleven times in his "I Have a Dream" speech:

. . . let freedom ring from the prodigious hilltops of New Hampshire. Let freedom ring from the mighty mountains of New York. Let freedom ring from the heightening Alleghenies of Pennsylvania. Let freedom ring from the snow-capped Rockies of Colorado. Let freedom ring from the curvaceous slopes of California. But not only that. Let freedom ring from Stone Mountain of Georgia. Let freedom ring from Lookout Mountain of Tennessee. Let freedom ring from every hill and molehill of Mississippi; from every mountainside, Let freedom ring; and when this happens, and when we allow freedom [to] ring, when we let it ring from every village and every hamlet, from every state and every city, we will be able to speed up that day when all of God's children—Black men and White men, Jews and Gentiles, Protestants and Catholics—will be able to join hands and sing in the words of the old Negro spiritual, "Free at last, free at last; thank God Almighty, we are free at last."[34]

It is interesting to note that many of his speeches became known by specific anaphora. Indeed, the titles of the speeches reflect the most powerful repeated phrases. The phrases become metonymic representations for the very experience of the speech. The number of times that anaphora appears seems to be directly proportionate to the intensity of audience response or to the circumstances. Each successive phrase is marked by changes in pitch, in volume, and in rhythm. Each change helps to move the audience to a higher emotional state. For example, King's audience participated in the anaphora by mirroring his frequent calls of "How long? Not long. . . ."[35] In "On Police Brutality," on the other hand, his anaphora was limited to fewer repetitions.[36] He was attempting to cool tempers. In even more of a contrast, his address to the American Jewish Committee shows how the absence of anaphora changed the listener's involvement with the speech. In this instance, there were no audible responses.[37] The lack of anaphora in his speech before the committee is very revealing. Even with anaphora, the call-response characteristic of "How Long? Not Long" would not be duplicated under these circumstances. The audience in the American Jewish Committee address was generally more reserved and more conservative. Indeed, anaphora does not necessarily and magically evoke a particular response. Any type of response is conventional, learned, and cultural. King probably saw the inclusion of anaphora as altogether inappropriate in this case. He was a rhetor who was sensitive to the presence of audience. Thus the specific cultural context altered what he did. When he saw and heard and felt the responses of certain audiences, nommo was there, and what occurred was a "calling forth *with*" those present rather than a "speaking *to*" an audience. King's anaphora reinforced particular ideas in the speech, motivated the audience to participate in the event, and enhanced the prospect of acceptance of the message. Also, in the American Jewish Committee address, another closely linked feature of call-response was less prominent. This is called vocal creativity.

Vocal Creativity

King's vocal creativity reacted with the responses of his audience. King's vocal creativity was spontaneous, not planned. This characteristic reflected his feeling for what he was saying and how the audience was responding to him. With vocal creativity there are changes in tone, rate, loudness, emphasis, intonation, and duration of words and phrases.[38] This characteristic is closely intertwined with anaphora, since the repeated words and phrases are the only things that remain constant, while the way in which these words and phrases are presented changes. Smitherman calls vocal creativity a component of "tonal semantics." She points to the importance of this phenomenon in black English since it affects deep levels of understanding. With tonal semantics, according to Smitherman, "the effect achieved is the conveyance of a psycho-cognitive message."[39] Thus this feature of style is not simply a cognitive element, but it also has an affective component. The vocal creativity found in King's oral discourse is yet another manifestation of its cultural roots. African languages, unlike English, "have a very complex, highly sophisticated system of tone," writes Smitherman. Speakers of African languages depend "on the tone with which they pronounce syllables, sounds and words to convey their meaning."[40]

If we listen to King's repeated phrases, we hear obvious changes in emphasis on certain words, the rate at which words are spoken, the elongation or duration of words and phrases, and the intensity at which the words and phrases are produced. In "I Have a Dream," when he says "down in Alabama," each word is drawn out very slowly so that the phrase becomes "d-oow-n in Al-a-bama." Then he quickens the pace, ending with "I have a *dream* today." This last part is introduced with more emphasis. The crowd responds with shouting, applause, and whistling. In the same speech, his first utterance of "let freedom ring" appears at the end of a sequence of thought. It is nearly lost among the other words because of lack of tonal emphasis and intensity. Soon thereafter, however, the repetitions of the phrase take on a new identity as King gives different expression to them each time.[41]

It is important to note that we have isolated anaphora as a means to examine King's vocal creativity. Yet this creativity appears throughout his speeches. By definition, it is virtually impossible to convey this characteristic on paper. We can only hint at what it "looks like." What we hope to convey, though, is that vocal creativity brought together the participants in the speaking event. The step, the next characteristic, should help to define the emotional commitment shared by the interactants in that relationship.

The Step

Lyle Mayer defines a step as a variation in pitch between words or syllables. "The voice skips, jumps, or leaps from one pitch to another, either up or down." The step carries greater emphasis than the inflection. It permits the speaker "to give greater prominence to important words or phrases or, conversely, to give lesser prominence to unimportant words and phrases."[42]

To illustrate what the step looks like in King's discourse, here are two examples from "How Long? Not Long": At the end of the speech King repeats the phrase "Glory Hallelujah" four consecutive times. He says:

Glory Hallelujah!"

Glory Hallelujah!

Glory Hallelujah!

"Glory Hallelujah!

This reflects a step-up pattern. Each successive phrase is given greater emphasis through the movement upward in pitch.

In the same speech, King's repetition of "How long? Not long" shows a different pattern: He says,

"How long? Not long   How long? Not long

. . .   . . ."[43]

This reflects a step-down, step-up pattern. The repeated phrase is given greater prominence than the words separated by those phrases.

The step was evident in both speaker and audience and seemed to reflect emotional involvement. King's higher pitch and ever-increasing vocal intensity were matched by audience responses that included, among other things, more robust shouting, whistling, and clapping.

The intensity of the interactions seemed to vary according to the particular circumstances of the speech event. For example, one can easily contrast the "On Police Brutality" speech with the speaking event that occurred in Montgomery after the third Selma march. The first instance reveals little evidence of the step. When it does occur, there is little difference between the step up and the step down.[44] There is a softening of emotional impact. In the second case, the step pattern is less subtle. As Dr. King shouts "How long?

Not long . . . ," his audience joins in more frequently and with matching enthusiasm.[45]

The step seems linked to the frequency of anaphora. The more repetitions, the greater the change in pitch and intensity. Notably the "I Have a Dream" speech contains the most anaphora from among the speeches we sampled. This speaking event also provides us with the best examples of the step.

King begins in a calm, even, low key. It is soon replaced by frequent changes in pitch and loudness. By the time he begins to utter the repetitive phrase "We can never be satisfied"—about half way through the event—he is already beginning to heighten the emotional climate and seems to be accepting the audience's response as part of the process. He pauses for audience clapping and whistling. Then he either picks up the intensity or softens it depending upon the emphasis he seeks to give to the words.[46]

The step reflects the intensity of the interaction. It is not, of course, strictly limited to this. Cadence, on the other hand, among other things, seems to set up the pattern that determines when the audience will respond. Cadence is a fourth characteristic quality of the call-response pattern.

Cadence

Cadence, much like the pounding of the human heart or the measure marked on an African drum, meted out King's words. Realizing that an oral tradition informed the communication process between King and his audience, we can best define cadence (or rhythm) by examining its purpose rhetorically in an oral culture. Walter Ong observes, "In a primary oral culture, to solve effectively the problem of retaining and retrieving carefully articulated thought, you have to do your thinking in mnemonic patterns, shaped for ready oral recurrence. Your thought must come into being in heavily rhythmic, balanced patterns, in repetitions or antitheses, in alliterations and assonances."[47] These mnemonic patterns are the essence of cadence.

Cadence is present throughout King's speeches. One of the clearest examples, however, is from his "How Long? Not Long" speech at Montgomery in 1965. Heavy with formal verse, anaphora, balanced phrasing, and alliteration, the rhythm is easily discernible. The anaphora of "How long? Not long because . . ." sets up a distinct pattern, as does the verse from William Cullen Bryant: "Truth forever on the scaffold." King also voices familiar Biblical phrases. They are easily remembered and easily repeated. He concludes with a pattern of strong, even quality as he shouts the refrain of "Glory Hallelujah!"[48] The rhythm was such that there was little opportunity for lack of audience response. The cadence of repeated words and phrases, the pattern of familiar verse and texts drew people into the event.

As with the other characteristics within call-response, cadence can be linked with anaphora. The repeated phrase sets up a pattern that invites response. One might even compare the emphasized phrase to listening to a marching band when the big bass drum takes over and commands our attention. Not only does the drum catch our attention, but also it gets us excited and involved in the parade.[49] In effect, the anaphora establishes a rhythmic pattern so that the audience knows what to expect and how to respond. This response in the black community came from a long tradition of orality, not from a predetermined plan. In fact, spontaneity is one of the hallmarks of call-response.

Spontaneous response can also be seen and heard in King's audiences by observing their synchronous kinesic and paralinguistic behaviors. This is the final characteristic quality of the call-response pattern that we advance.

Synchronous Kinesic and Paralinguistic Behaviors

Synchronous kinesic and paralinguistic behaviors feed one another. Marianne LaFrance and Clara Mayo write of the different ways in which synchrony appears in interaction. There is "movement synchrony" where people move in unison and reflect each other's movements. "Posture synchrony" is where people sit or stand in similar positions as they interact. "Vocal synchrony" is when one's vocal behavior takes on the oral characteristics (e.g., rate, loudness) of the other interactant. LaFrance and Mayo suggest that all these forms of synchrony reveal a desire to get involved.[50]

In a segment from King's "I Have a Dream" speech, we see a microcosm of the audience by virtue of the camera's picking up the interaction between King and a man who seems to be clergy. This occurs during the "let freedom ring" anaphora sequence. This man appears in the lower right-hand corner of the screen. In most of the sequence the man faces King, while at other times he faces the audience. We see the man as the speech moves toward a climax. He punctuates King's statements not only with verbal responses but also with body gestures; e.g., he uses forceful arm gesticulation and forward body lean. King, in turn, responds to his audience's increasing intensity with more head movement, e.g., shaking the head and thrusting the head back, and arm movement, e.g., extending and waving his arms, while vocally building to a crescendo.[51]

Still another example reflecting how synchronous kinesic and paralinguistic behaviors feed one another occurs in King's speech on the steps of the Montgomery capitol at the conclusion of the third Selma march in 1965. Again, we see a microcosm of the audience by scrutinizing a man standing adjacent to King. The man is on the stage facing the audience. Not only is he mirroring King's movements (i.e., he is looking down and swaying and thrusting his arms) and his words (i.e., with equally intense utterances of "How long" and "Not long"), but he also reflects the larger audience's behavior. We see him turning toward others for affirmation and hear him say "Yes, sir," with the crowd.[52]

The Interactive Qualities of Call-Response and the Power of King's Oratory

The five characteristic qualities of call-response that we have chosen to address are not found in isolation within King's speeches. Much as call-response is a dynamic process wherein speaker and audience become a unified whole, so too its characteristic components coalesce. It is therefore a somewhat artificial move to isolate not only the elements that define it but also the means by which it is activated. Put simply, call-response is the sum total of all the means that activate it, including the persons involved. If we choose to examine anaphora in King's speeches, we are also likely to find, for example, vocal creativity, the step, cadence, and synchronous kinesic and paralinguistic behaviors all working in an interactive fashion with the audience.

The five characteristic qualities together create mutually rising intensity that echoes back to the concept of nommo in African oral cultures and becomes a vital part of interactions within a variety of communication contexts. For example, Pasteur and Toldson comment on this interaction when they write, "Black audience participation in the forms of verbal approval, verbal commands, hand-clapping, foot-stomping, finger-popping, and other forms, is not only tolerated but also encouraged by the performer and considered a conduit for the flow of the audience's emotional, aesthetic impulses, which in their collective totality form an emotional power that spurs the artist to perform at high achievement levels."[53] The accord achieved can be directly linked to every aspect of call-response.

Perhaps the best tribute to the power of call-response as an interactive process exemplified by King and his audience lies in the tell-

telling way in which it could shape a speaking event. The emotional involvement engendered through call-response was sometimes so stirring that it compelled King to modify his discourse.[54] Coretta Scott King recalls that King often changed his prepared text because of the intense interaction of the moment.[55] In his Memphis address of 3 April 1968, the emotional response, the exaltation, and the action and reaction between King and his audience were so intense that he had to break off his speech.[56]

The intensity of the audience's reaction also caused him to depart from his text during his "I Have a Dream" speech.[57] While many writers focused on what King said, by so doing they have missed the most creative aspect of the event—the mounting give-and-take between the speaker and the huge audience.[58] King exemplified a speaker fully aware of nommo and the power with which it was imbued. Call-response was not an isolated part of this experience. It was an essential dynamic that brought together diverse peoples to a sense of unity. The implications regarding the significance of nommo, and thus call-response, can be seen here because this was not a church-related event, nor was it one that involved only the black community. Yet by visually and aurally examining the video-tapes of King's discourse, we can witness the effect of the interaction to unify and uplift all the participants.

King begins his speech with a quiet, even delivery. He eloquently and briefly speaks of the history of American blacks since the Emancipation Proclamation, and then he leads into the metaphor of a "promissory note" that has gone bad for "citizens of color." The sense of urgency and the need for response really commence when King speaks with increased intensity about the "urgency of *now.*" He begins to say the phrase "now is the time" with forceful emphasis. The audience responds with greater affirmations, such as verbal encouragement and applause. King alternates fervor with quieter tones throughout the middle portion of the speech. This pattern seems to heighten audience awareness. When he speaks of injustices toward blacks, he repeats the phrase "we cannot be satisfied. . . ." Here the crowd again replies with cheers, applause, and affirmations. When he begins the "I have a dream" sequence, the audience and King are as one. Although the individual responses are difficult to decipher on tapes, shouts like "Keep on dreaming!" do escape from the multitude of sounds. King's speech is capped when he says "let freedom ring" again and again throughout the final portions. He has built his intensity to a shout, and the crowd is equally thunderous in its response. The fervor is so intense that it seems as though by some unknown mutual consent between the participants, it *must* end here, at a point where all seem to be as one. Coretta

Scott King affirms this, writing that "the feeling that they had of oneness and unity was *complete*."[59] How was it that this communal sense was created? Those who had African roots were already familiar with the uplifting and unifying effects of call-response. They had experienced it in their churches. They had sung it in the streets while marching for civil rights. They had used it in everyday communication throughout their lives. So when King mounted the podium and began to speak, the people were creating *with him* an event that will long be remembered as a landmark in the communication experience. The occasion marked a kind of cultural sharing with people from other cultures participating in the experience.

Conclusion

We have offered a view of the significant role that call-response plays in the oratory of Martin Luther King, Jr. As a primary element in nommo, the all encompassing power of the African oral culture, call-response and its characteristic qualities of anaphora, vocal creativity, the step, cadence, and synchronous kinesic and linguistic behaviors work to bring audience and speaker together to shape the message and its impact.[60] Call-response and the broader concept of nommo reflect the Afrocentric ideals of balance and harmony among opposites—whether they be elements of the spiritual and material realms or speaker and audience. King's oratorical power was influenced by those Afrocentric ideals as tempered by the black experience in America. Although the elements that we find here may resemble those characteristics of other oral cultures, we must remember that those characteristics are deeply rooted in a world view that helps to account for the special significance of what transpires.

As Melbourne Cummings and Jack Daniel suggest, there is a need to develop an archives in which culturally coded communication events can be preserved and by which significant black orators may be recognized.[61] After our frustration with the incompleteness and the poor condition of some of the materials that we found, we agree that there is a need for a systematic collection and storage of audio and video tapes. The rationale is to protect authentic and detailed reproduction of the events, since these materials enhance our appreciation for and study of the speaker, audience, and culture. As Michael Osborn noted when he wrote about reading the prose patterns of King's discourse, it is necessary to hear them in order to be caught up with them.[62] Being caught up in them provides a better understanding of the dynamics involved.

But why preserve these materials at all? Why are they important? One reason we propose is that the study of these materials can lead to a stronger bridge to interethnic communication. As Michael Hecht, Sidney Ribeau, and J. K. Alberts write, "An understanding of cultural differences and attendant communication differences can lead to the development of strategies for managing interethnic interaction. Certainly these strategies will not eliminate interethnic communication barriers, but they can provide skills for managing these differences more effectively."[63]

Specifically, with the study of call-response we can enhance understanding of creative ways to stimulate audience involvement, thus creating more meaningful speaking events. Also, the preservation of materials will insure that call-response with all its African underpinnings can be recognized as a vibrant historical and viable communication component of the societal fabric. We have seen that it can affect people of diverse cultural backgrounds in a positive way.

Specific to African Americans, the study of call-response and King's oratory can provide a greater appreciation for the cultural heritage of their oral tradition. Call-response and the Afrocentric philosophy of communication reflect a rich legacy that must be nurtured and expressed within our educational systems.[64] We agree with Smitherman's assertion that call-response can be effectively employed within the classroom setting. She states that black children may learn more easily if call-response is applied in teaching them because it is an integral part of their communication experience even before they start school.[65]

Finally, since King's oratory reflects so many characteristics and qualities that are African in origin, it needs to be studied further from the Afrocentric perspective. The hope is that this new corpus of research will help to bring about fresh insight into the nature of his ability to unite diverse people and to influence the behavior of an entire community.

Notes

Introduction

1. Robert Jewett and John Shelton Lawrence, *The American Monomyth*, 2d ed. (Lanham, Md.: University Press of America, 1988), 169–97.

2. See Clayborne Carson, "Martin Luther King, Jr.: Charismatic Leadership in a Mass Struggle," *Journal of American History* 74 (1987): 436–81; and Nathan Irvin Huggins, "Martin Luther King, Jr.: Charisma and Leadership," *Journal of American History* 74 (1987): 477–81.

3. See Kenneth Smith and Ira Zepp, Jr., *Search for the Beloved Community* (Valley Forge, Pa.: Judson, 1974).

4. The first volume of the King papers, being prepared under the senior editorship of Clayborne Carson and the sponsorship of the Martin Luther King, Jr., Center for Nonviolent Social Change, Inc., appeared in print just as the essays in this volume were going to press. *Called to Serve, January 1929–June 1951*, vol. 1 of *The Papers of Martin Luther King, Jr.*, ed. Ralph E. Luker and Penny A. Russell (Berkeley: University of California Press, 1992).

5. The art and practice of preaching predate Christianity, but it is the Judeo-Christian sermon developed primarily during the Middle Ages that serves as the basis for our contemporary understanding and practice of the sermonic form. See George A. Kennedy, *Greek Rhetoric Under Christian Emperors* (Princeton: Princeton University Press, 1983), 182–83, 282–86; and James J. Murphy, *Rhetoric in the Middle Ages: A History of Rhetorical Theory from St. Augustine to the Renaissance* (Berkeley: University of California Press, 1974), 269–356.

6. The general role of sermonic discourse in American political society is characterized implicitly in a number of places. See Sacvan Bercovitch,

The American Jeremiad (Madison: University of Wisconsin Press, 1978); Robert N. Bellah, *The Broken Covenant: American Civil Religion in Time of Trial* (New York: Seabury Press, 1975); Roderick P. Hart, *The Political Pulpit* (West Lafayette, Ind.: Purdue University Press, 1977); and Garry Wills, *Under God: Religion and American Politics* (New York: Simon and Schuster, 1990). On the political role of sermonic discourse in African-American society, see Henry Mitchell, *Black Preaching* (New York: J. B. Lippincott, 1970), 65–71; Mary Frances Berry and John W. Blassingame, *Long Memory: The Black Experience in America* (New York: Oxford University Press, 1982), 98–101; and David Howard-Pitney, *The Afro-American Jeremiad: Appeals for Justice in America* (Philadelphia: Temple University Press, 1990).

7. Richard M. Weaver, *Language Is Sermonic: Richard M. Weaver on the Nature of Rhetoric*, ed. Richard L. Johannnesen et al. (Baton Rouge: Louisiana State University Press, 1970), 211.

8. Michael Osborn, "Rhetorical Depiction," in *Form, Genre, and the Study of Political Discourse*, ed. Herbert W. Simons and Aram A. Aghazarian (Columbia: University of South Carolina Press, 1986), 79–107.

9. See Michael Calvin McGee, "A Materialist's Conception of Rhetoric," in *Explorations in Rhetoric: Studies in Honor of Douglas Ehninger*, ed. Ray E. McKerrow (Glenview, Ill.: Scott, Foresman, 1982): 23–48; and Celeste Michelle Condit and John Louis Lucaites, "The Rhetoric of 'Equality' and the Expatriation of African-Americans, 1776–1826," *Communication Studies* 42 (1981): 1–2.

10. Donald C. Bryant, "Rhetoric: Its Function and Scope," *Quarterly Journal of Speech* 39 (1953): 401–24. See also Michael C. McGee, "In Search of 'The People': A Rhetorical Alternative," *Quarterly Journal of Speech* 61 (1975): 235–49; John S. Nelson, "Political Foundations for Rhetoric of Inquiry," in *The Rhetorical Turn*, ed. Herbert W. Simons (Chicago: University of Chicago Press, 1990), 258–89; and John Louis Lucaites and Celeste Michelle Condit, "The Rhetorical 'Foundation' of Equality in American Political Discourse," in *Taking Political Talk Seriously*, ed. John S. Nelson, forthcoming.

11. Cf. Celeste Michelle Condit's three functions of epideictic experience in "The Functions of Epideictic: The Boston Massacre Orations as Exemplar," *Communication Quarterly* 33 (1985): 284–99; and Michael Osborn's five functions of rhetorical style in *Orientations to Rhetorical Style* (Chicago: Science Research Associates, 1976), 1–8.

12. Kenneth Burke, *A Rhetoric of Motives* (1950; reprint, Berkeley: University of California Press, 1962), 55. Cf. Jose Ortega y Gassett's notion of "usage" in *Men and People*, trans. Willard R. Trask (New York: W. W. Norton, 1957), 192–272.

13. Chaim Perelman and L. Olbrechts-Tyteca, *The New Rhetoric: A Treatise on Argumentation*, trans. John Wilkinson and Purcell Weaver (Notre Dame, Ind.: University of Notre Dame Press, 1969), 77–82.

14. See Celeste Michelle Condit, "Crafting Virtue: The Rhetorical Construction of Public Morality," *Quarterly Journal of Speech* 73 (1987): 79–97.

15. See Richard Bauman, *Verbal Art as Performance* (Prospect Heights, Ill.: Waverly Press, 1977), 28–35.

16. Cf. Lawrence W. Rosenfield's notion of the "radiance of being" in "The Practical Celebration of Epideictic," *Rhetoric in Transition: Studies in the Nature and Uses of Rhetoric,* ed. Eugene White (University Park: Pennsylvania State University Press, 1980), 131–56. Note, however, two important differences. First, while Rosenfield locates the phenomenological presence of "being" in the speaker's invitation to an audience to heed the meaning of their shared existence, we treat it as the *joined* public display of community by the combination of speaker and audience. Community thus becomes a feeling in the presence of the rhetorical interaction itself. Second, Rosenfield characterizes the "radiance of being" as a more or less extraordinary rhetorical phenomenon; we treat the enactment of community as a more common rhetorical experience, though by no means do we see it as inherent to every rhetorical interaction.

17. Taylor Branch, *Parting the Waters: America in the King Years, 1954–63* (New York: Simon and Schuster, 1988), 123–24.

18. Virtually all of King's biographers go into great detail characterizing the various sources of his social activism. See, for example, Branch, *Parting the Waters,* 39–142; Stephen B. Oates, *Let the Triumph Sound: The Life of Martin Luther King, Jr.* (New York: Harper and Row, 1982), 3–51; David Lewis, *King: A Biography* (Urbana: University of Illinois Press, 1978), 3–45; and James H. Cone, *Martin & Malcolm & America: A Dream or a Nightmare* (Maryknoll, N.Y.: Orbis Books, 1991), 19–37.

19. See E. Franklin Frazier, *The Negro Church in America* (1964; reprint, New York: Schocken Books, 1974), 26–34; and George P. Rawick, *From Sundown to Sunup: The Making of the Black Community* (Westport, Conn.: Greenwood Press, 1972), 30–52.

20. Frazier, *The Negro Church in America,* 47–49.

21. The influence of the black church experience in King's political discourse in this simple sense is noted in several places. See Lewis V. Baldwin, "Martin Luther King, Jr., the Black Church, the Black Messianic Vision," *Journal of the Interdenominational Theological Center* 12 (Fall 1984/Spring 1985): 93–108; Lewis V. Baldwin, "The Minister as Preacher, Pastor, and Prophet: The Thinking of Martin Luther King, Jr.," *American Baptist Quarterly* 7 (1988): 79–97; James H. Cone, "Martin Luther King, Jr., Black Theology—Black Church," *Theology Today* 41 (1984): 409–20; and Hortense J. Spillers, "Martin Luther King and the Style of the Black Sermon," *Black Scholar* 3 (1971): 14–27.

22. Frazier, *The Negro Church in America,* 35–51.

23. C. Eric Lincoln makes a similar point in *The Black Church Since Frazier* (New York: Schocken Books, 1974), 108–9. See also Anthony E. Cook, "Beyond Critical Legal Studies: The Reconstructive Theology of Dr. Martin Luther King, Jr.," *Harvard Law Review* 103 (1990): 1022.

24. The claim that King was a communist sympathizer generally derived from his association with Stanley Levison, a one-time ally of the leaders of the American Communist party, and is chronicled in most of King's biogra-

phies. The most complete sources are Branch, *Parting the Waters*, 468–69, 565–66, 853–919 passim, and David J. Garrow, *Bearing the Cross: Martin Luther King, Jr., and the Southern Christian Leadership Conference* (New York: William Morrow, 1986), 195, 200, 222, 235, 361. See also Adam Fairclough, "Was Martin Luther King a Marxist?" *History Workshop Journal* 15 (1983): 117–25. The virulence of the charges increased once King announced his opposition to the war in Vietnam.

25. The point is well documented. See, for example, Garrow, *Bearing The Cross*, 91–98, 134–38, 166, 269–70; and Adam Fairclough, *To Redeem the Soul of America: The Southern Christian Leadership Conference and Martin Luther King, Jr.* (Athens: University of Georgia Press, 1987).

26. The best source on the liberal pressures imposed on King is Branch, *Parting the Waters*, esp. 524–887 passim; on the tensions between King and SNCC see Garrow, *Bearing the Cross*, 404–41; and Manning Marable, *Race, Reform, and Rebellion: The Second Reconstruction in Black America, 1945–1982* (Jackson: University Press of Mississippi, 1985), 71–75, 104–6. For an insider's view on the relationship between King and SNCC see Mary King, *Freedom Song: A Personal Story of the 1960s Civil Rights Movement* (New York: William Morrow, 1987).

27. Ira G. Zepp, Jr., *The Social Vision of Martin Luther King, Jr.* (Brooklyn, N.Y.: Carlson, 1989), 207–11. Zepp provides a detailed description of the historical and theological roots of King's beloved community on pp. 207–34. See also Cook, "Beyond Critical Legal Studies," 1023–40.

28. In this context it is notable that the primary attacks made against King from the liberal white community focused on "means" rather than "ends," typically indicting his commitment to nonviolent massive resistance as designed to promote violence. See James A. Colaiaco, "Martin Luther King, Jr., and the Paradox of Nonviolent Direct Action," *Phylon* 47 (1986): 16–28.

29. For black Americans this paralleled the conversion experience of slavery. See Cook, "Beyond Critical Legal Studies," 1022.

30. The role of the mass media in the civil rights movement has yet to be adequately investigated. An important first step occurs in Richard Lentz, *Symbols, the News Magazines, and Martin Luther King* (Baton Rouge: Louisiana State University Press, 1990).

31. See Garrow, *Bearing the Cross*, 431–525.

32. Martin Luther King, Jr., "Where Do We Go from Here," in *A Testament of Hope: The Essential Writings of Martin Luther King, Jr.*, ed. James Melvin Washington (San Francisco: Harper and Row, 1986), 250–51. Cf. "Transcript of 'Face to Face' Television News Interview (1967)" *A Testament of Hope*, 409.

33. Howard-Pitney, *The Afro-American Jeremiad*, 165. King's treatment of the issue of gradualism and its effect on the civil rights movement is dealt with provocatively in J. Robert Cox, "The Fulfillment of Time: King's 'I Have a Dream' Speech," and Robert Hariman, "Time and the Reconstitution of Gradualism in King's Address: A Response to Cox," in *Texts in Context: Critical Dialogues on Significant Episodes in American Political*

Rhetoric, ed. Michael C. Leff and Fred J. Kauffeld (Davis, Calif.: Hermagoras Press, 1989), 181–204, 205–17.

34. See Richard Lischer, "The Word That Moves: The Preaching of Martin Luther King, Jr.," *Theology Today* 46 (1989): 180; and Cone, *Martin & Malcolm & America,* 283–314.

35. The theoretical foundations of Afrocentricity are outlined in Molefi Kete Asante, *Afrocentricity: The Theory of Social Change* (Buffalo, N.Y.: Amulefi Press, 1980); and idem, *The Afrocentric Idea* (Philadelphia: Temple University Press, 1987). See also the essays in Bruce Williams and Orlando L. Taylor, eds., *International Conference on Black Communication* (Bellagio, Italy: Rockefeller Foundation, 1980). For earlier, case-based studies that emphasize the rhetorical dimensions of the Afrocentric experience, see Jack L. Daniel and Geneva Smitherman, "How I Got Over: Communication Dynamics in the Black Community," *Quarterly Journal of Speech* 62 (1976): 26–39; and Geneva Smitherman, *Talkin and Testifyin: The Language of Black America* (Detroit: Wayne State University Press, 1977).

36. The issue of King's plagiarism is taken up in some detail in a special forum in the *Journal of American History* 78 (1991): 11–123, edited by David Thelen and titled "Becoming Martin Luther King, Jr.—Plagiarism and Originality: A Round Table." See in particular Martin Luther King, Jr., Papers Project: "The Student Papers of Martin Luther King, Jr.: A Summary Statement on Research," 23–40; David J. Garrow, "King's Plagiarism: Imitation, Insecurity, and Transformation," 86–92; John Higham, "Habits of the Cloth and Standards of the Academy," 106–11; Bernice Johnson Reagon, "'Nobody Knows the Trouble I See'; or 'By and By I'm Gonna Lay Down My Heavy Load,'" 111–19; and Keith D. Miller, "Martin Luther King, Jr., and the Black Folk Pulpit," 120–23.

37. Henry Louis Gates, Jr., *The Signifying Monkey: A Theory of Afro-American Literary Criticism* (New York: Oxford University Press, 1988).

Chapter 1

A College of Liberal Arts and Sciences Award from Arizona State University provided financial assistance for this research project. I also thank my research assistants Mary Anne Elia and Linda Van der Wal.

1. Stephen B. Oates, *Let the Trumpet Sound: The Life of Martin Luther King, Jr.* (New York: Harper and Row, 1982), 289.

2. Harvard Sitkoff, *The Struggle for Black Equality* (New York: Hill and Wang, 1981), 60.

3. See Keith D. Miller, "Composing Martin Luther King, Jr.," *PMLA* 105 (1990): 70–82.

4. Eugene Genovese, *Roll, Jordan, Roll: The World the Slaves Made* (New York: Vintage, 1976), 252.

5. Frederick Douglass, *The Life and Times of Frederick Douglass* (1892; reprint, London: Collier-Macmillan, 1962), 159–60. See also Albert Rabo-

teau, *Slave Religion* (New York: Oxford University Press, 1978), 246–51; and Genovese, *Roll, Jordan, Roll,* 248–51. In *Negro Slave Songs in the United States* (New York: Citadel, 1969), Miles Mark Fisher emphasizes the spirituals' theme of earthly liberation.

6. See Genovese, *Roll, Jordan, Roll,* 252–54.

7. John Lovell, *Black Song* (New York: Macmillan, 1972), 228.

8. For "My Army Cross Over" and "O the Dying Lamb," see Thomas Higginson, "Negro Spirituals," in *The Negro and His Folklore in Nineteenth-Century Periodicals,* ed. Bruce Franklin (Austin: University of Texas Press, 1987), 85–86, 88. For other spirituals, see Lovell, *Black Song,* 229–55.

9. Lawrence Levine, *Black Culture and Black Consciousness* (New York: Oxford University Press, 1977), 30–55.

10. Ibid., 31.

11. For detailed discussions of typology, see George Landau, *Victorian Types, Victorian Shadows* (Boston: Routledge, 1980); and Earl Miner, *Literary Uses of Typology: From the Late Middle Ages to the Present* (Princeton, N.J.: Princeton University Press, 1977).

12. Desmond Tutu, *Hope and Suffering* (Grand Rapids, Mich.: Eerdman's, 1985), 56–57.

13. Genovese, *Roll, Jordan, Roll,* 252.

14. Lovell, *Black Song,* 234.

15. Levine, *Black Culture,* 38.

16. Molefi Kete Asante, *The Afrocentric Idea* (Philadelphia: Temple University Press, 1987), 89.

17. Among other influences, this sermonizing reflects African culture. See Asante, *Afrocentric Idea,* 65.

18. William Pipes, *Say Amen, Brother!: Old-Time Negro Preaching* (Westport: Conn.: Negro Universities Press, 1951), 111.

19. L. J. Coppin, *Fifty Years of Religious Progress: An Emancipation Sermon* (Philadelphia: African Methodist Episcopal Book Co., 1913), 39.

20. Tony Heilbut, *Gospel Sound* (New York: Simon and Schuster, 1971), 301; J. M. Gates, *Moses in the Wilderness,* Matrix, 3649-1, Victor 20421, 1926; C. L. Franklin, *Moses at the Red Sea,* Chess 19, ca. mid-1950s.

21. See James English, *The Prophet of Wheat Street: The Story of William Holmes Borders, a Man Who Refused to Fail* (Elgin, Ill.: Cook, 1973), 74.

22. Bruce Rosenberg explains in *Art of the American Folk Preacher* (New York: Oxford University Press, 1970) that the practice of circulating sermons emerged largely as the result of the demands of an oral tradition for formulaic language. According to Rosenberg, oral traditions of many cultures insist upon formulaic language because of the innate demands of orality. Rosenberg also attributes the practice of circulating sermons to the need to facilitate congregational participation in worship services. While folk preachers do facilitate such participation, Rosenberg ignores the all-important rhetorical, theological, and epistemological functions of sacred time, typology, and self-making in the folk pulpit. Moreover, he overlooks the social and political positions of blacks. Such sermons as "Moses at the Red Sea," "Eagle Stirs Her Nest," and "Dry Bones in the Valley" excited African-American congregations because the topic of the revival/

deliverance of the Israelites from captivity in Egypt, the wilderness, or Babylon related directly to their own captivity in the semislavery of segregation. Folk homilists did not deliver these *specific* sermons because oral culture in general creates formulaic language or because preachers wanted to facilitate congregational participation. Instead, *masters of the folk pulpit preached "Moses at the Red Sea," "Eagle Stirs Her Nest," and "Dry Bones" because their people were still enslaved.* Rosenberg works hard to apply to the black folk pulpit a general theory of formulaic language in oral culture. But he fails to appreciate the distinctive features of black folk preaching.

23. Franklin, "Dry Bones in the Valley," in *Give Me This Mountain*, ed. Jeff Todd Titon (Urbana: University of Illinois Press, 1989), 80–88; Gates, *Dry Bones in the Valley*, Victor 1, 35810-A, DLC 0242/1594, n.d.; E. O. S. Cleveland, "Dry Bones in the Valley," in *The Eagle Stirring Her Nest* (N.p.: n.p., 1946), 31–37; Rosenberg, *Art*, 28.

24. See Charles Lyell, "A Negro Church in Savannah," in *The Negro American: A Documentary History*, ed. Leslie Fishel and Benjamin Quarles (Glenview, Ill.: Scott, Foresman, 1967), 135–36; Rosenberg, *Art*, 28; Gates, *The Eagle Stirs Her Nest*, Matrix 400302-B, Okeh 8582, 1928; Franklin, *Eagle Stirring Her Nest*, Chess 61, 62, 63, n.d.

25. Cleveland, "The Eagle Stirring in Her Nest," in *The Eagle Stirring Her Nest*, 71.

26. Martin Luther King, Sr. (with Clayton Riley), *Daddy King: An Autobiography* (New York: William Morrow, 1980), 85–86; Lerone Bennett, *Confrontation: Black and White* (Chicago: Johnson, 1965), 229–30; and Donald Smith, "Martin Luther King, Jr.: Rhetorician of Revolt" (Ph.D. diss., University of Wisconsin, 1964), 21.

27. Martin Luther King, Jr., *Martin Luther King Treasury* (Yonkers, N.Y.: Educational Heritage, 1964), 265.

28. See interviews conducted by the author in 1987 and 1988 with Gardner Taylor, William Holmes Borders, Sarah Reed, James Kemp, J. H. Edwards, Arthur and Laura Henderson, and Jethro English. With the exceptions of Taylor and Borders, all these people are long-time members of the Ebenezer Baptist Church who knew King throughout most or all of his life. The best source on Borders's life is English, *The Prophet of Wheat Street*.

29. For King scholars who attribute King's social theology primarily to his exposure to Rauschenbusch, see in particular Oates, *Let the Trumpet Sound*, 25–26; Kenneth Smith and Ira Zepp, Jr., *Search for the Beloved Community* (Valley Forge, Pa.: Judson, 1974), 33–45; John Ansbro, *Martin Luther King, Jr.: The Making of a Mind* (Maryknoll, N.Y.: Orbis, 1982), 151–60; and William R. Miller, *Martin Luther King, Jr.* (New York: Avon, 1969), 27–28.

30. See Keith D. Miller, *Voice of Deliverance: The Language of Martin Luther King, Jr., and Its Sources* (New York: Free Press, 1992).

31. Although King's collection of sermons, *Strength of Love*, (1963; reprint, Philadelphia: Fortress, 1981), does not include these lyrics, they appear in the transcripts of the vast majority of his oral sermons, transcripts found in the archives of the King Center in Atlanta. See, for example, Martin Luther King, Jr., "How Long?" reprinted as "Our God Is Marching

On," in *A Testament of Hope: The Essential Writings of Martin Luther King, Jr.*, ed. James Melvin Washington (San Francisco: Harper and Row, 1986), 227–30.

32. See Keith D. Miller, *Voice of Deliverance*, 142–58.

33. During King's childhood Borders protested segregation and raised money to bury victims of lynching. Later he organized racial protests in Atlanta and constructed a multi-million-dollar low-income housing project across the street from his church. See English, *The Prophet of Wheat Street*. Unlike other King scholars, Taylor Branch pays some attention to Borders. See his *Parting the Waters: America in the King Years, 1954–63* (New York: Simon and Schuster, 1988).

34. Lovell, *Black Song*, 535–36.

35. Wyatt Walker, *Somebody's Calling My Name: Black Sacred Music and Social Change* (Valley Forge, Pa.: Judson, 1979), 57, 180.

36. Mahalia Jackson (with Evan Wylie), *Movin' On Up* (New York: Hawthorne, 1966), 196.

37. Robert Norrell, *Reaping the Whirlwind: The Civil Rights Movement in Tuskegee* (New York: Random House, 1986), 93–94; and Ralph Abernathy, *And the Walls Came Tumbling Down* (New York: Harper, 1989), 195–96.

38. Quoted in Aldon Morris, *The Origins of the Civil Rights Movement* (New York: Free Press, 1984), 98.

39. Quoted in Charles Hamilton, *Black Preacher in America* (New York: Morrow, 1972), 132–33.

40. Martin Luther King, Jr., *Where Do We Go from Here: Chaos or Community?* (New York: Harper, 1967), 170.

41. Martin Luther King, Jr., "Death of Evil on the Seashore," in *Strength of Love*, 78.

42. Ibid., 79.

43. Ibid.

44. Ibid., 80.

45. Ibid., 81.

46. Ibid.

47. Ibid.

48. Ibid., 82.

49. Ibid.

50. Ibid., 84.

51. Keith D. Miller, "Martin Luther King, Jr., Borrows a Revolution," *College English* 48 (1986): 249–65.

52. King, "Death of Evil on the Seashore," 82.

53. Martin Luther King, Jr., "I've Been to the Mountaintop," reprinted as "I See the Promised Land," in *A Testament of Hope*, 279–88. In *At the River I Stand: Memphis, the 1968 Strike, and Martin Luther King* (Memphis, B & W Books, 1985), Joan Turner Beifuss provides an excellent account of the Memphis strike beginning before King's decision to enter the controversy and continuing until its settlement.

54. King, "I've Been to the Mountaintop," 279.

55. Ibid., 279–80.

56. Ibid., 280.
57. Ibid., 280–81.
58. Ibid., 281.
59. Ibid., 282.
60. Ibid.
61. Ibid.
62. Ibid., 280.
63. Ibid., 286.
64. Levine, *Black Culture*, 51.

Chapter 2

1. Among scholarly treatments are Haig Bosmajian, "Rhetoric of Martin Luther King's Letter from Birmingham Jail," *Midwestern Quarterly* 8(1967): 127–43; James A. Colaiaco, "The American Dream Unfulfilled: Martin Luther King, Jr., and the 'Letter from Birmingham Jail,'" *Phylon* 45 (1984): 1–18; Richard P. Fulkerson, "The Public Letter as a Rhetorical Form: Structure, Logic, and Style in King's 'Letter from Birmingham Jail,'" *Quarterly Journal of Speech* 65 (1979): 121–36; Mia Klein, "The Other Beauty of Martin Luther King, Jr.'s 'Letter from Birmingham Jail,'" *College Composition and Communication* 32 (1981): 30–37; Wesley T. Mott, "The Rhetoric of Martin Luther King, Jr.: Letter from Birmingham Jail," *Phylon* 36 (1975): 411–21; and Malinda Snow, "Martin Luther King's 'Letter from Birmingham Jail' as Pauline Epistle," *Quarterly Journal of Speech* 71 (1985): 318–34. The most exhaustive study of King is David J. Garrow, *Bearing the Cross: Martin Luther King, Jr., and the Southern Christian Leadership Conference* (New York: William Morrow, 1986). The most readable and, I think, most striking interpretation of King is Taylor Branch, *Parting the Waters: America in the King Years, 1954–63* (New York: Simon and Schuster, 1988).

2. Garrow discusses extensively the role of ghostwriting in King's speeches and essays. See *Bearing the Cross*, 73, 111–12, 280, 299, 312, 649 n. 21, 650 n. 28, and 679 n. 9.

3. In a phone conversation with the author (2 June 1988), Garrow expressed some reservations about whether King wrote the letter, and if so, how much of the letter was written by King. Garrow believes the FBI-tapped conversation between King and Levison (*Bearing the Cross*, 670–71 n. 18) is good evidence that he did write some or all of the letter, and absent explicit evidence to the contrary, Garrow treats the letter as if it were written by King. Subsequent phone conversations by the author with Arthur Shores and Clarence Jones (20 June 1988) and Addine Drew (27 June 1988), each of whom was involved at some stage in the production of the letter, raised no questions about authenticity, and in fact each asserted categorically that the letter was King's work exclusively. Jones said that had King needed a ghostwriter he would have asked Jones to talk it over with Levison and make suggestions. Jones, who was in Birmingham at the time of the letter's

writing, said no such request was made of him. Wyatt T. Walker (by phone, 12 July 1988) says that the letter was "99.44 percent" King's and that he served only as translator of King's "chicken scratch handwriting." A duplicated copy of King's original letter is in the Albert Boutwell Papers, Birmingham Public Library Archives. With few exceptions (typographical) it parallels the first full text publication in the *Christian Century*, 12 June 1963. The copy of the letter that appears in Martin Luther King, Jr., *Why We Can't Wait* (New York: Harper and Row, 1963), 77–100, is edited substantially for syntax but maintains the argumentative integrity of each sentence in the original letter.

4. King would not have received the *Birmingham News* until some time in the afternoon of 13 April at the earliest. All published copies of the letter bear the date of 16 April. However, it is likely that King kept writing after turning over the initial body of the letter on the sixteenth to Clarence Jones. See Branch, *Parting the Waters*, 738. King remained in jail until Saturday, the twenty-second. Moreover, since the letter received no notice for at least a month, it is possible that revisions continued to be made in the text.

5. Branch, *Parting the Waters*, 602.

6. Garrow, *Bearing the Cross*, 201–19; and King, *Why We Can't Wait*, 34–35.

7. *Time*, 27 September 1963.

8. *Birmingham News*, 3 April 1963.

9. W. C. Patton to Roy Wilkins, 22 December 1965, NAACP Papers, Library of Congress.

10. Paul Rilling interoffice memo, 28 February 1962, Southern Regional Council Papers, Birmingham Public Library Archives.

11. Quoted in Arthur M. Schlesinger, Jr., *Robert Kennedy and His Times* (Boston: Houghton Mifflin, 1978), 328.

12. *Birmingham News*, 17 January 1963. Interview with Rabbi Milton Grafman, 22 June 1988.

13. Drew's story conflicts with Walker's. Neither remembers the other having anything to do with the actual production of the letter. In a phone interview with the author (27 June 1988) and in a conversation with Marvin Y. Whiting, archivist and curator of manuscripts in the Birmingham Public Library (reported in a letter from Whiting to Michelle Vachon, 15 February 1988), Drew recounts her version of the letter's production. She remembers having received portions of the manuscript from King on two occasions, once in the jail and once during a court appearance, and, with the permission of Dr. Lucius Pitts of Miles College, having the letter typed at the college. Of course, both accounts may be true; that is, both Walker with his secretary working in an office furnished by A. G. Gaston on the east side of Kelly Ingram Park and Drew with White working at Miles College could have produced a copy of the letter. However, it is odd that neither knew of the other's work, especially since Walker was in overall command of operations. Moreover, both parties could not have been transcribing at the same time from King's original notes. It is also strange that only one copy of the original transcribed text survives. Had two copies been made simultaneously, or nearly so, there would likely have been discrepancies between

the two texts. The text that does survive appears to be the one produced by Walker because it is Multilithed, the process used in Gaston's office. Finally, it is possible, even likely, that Drew was involved with having some later version of the letter typed, perhaps between King's court appearance on Saturday, 22 April, and the letter's first excerpted appearance in the *New York Post Magazine* on 19 May, or its publication by the American Friends Service Committee. This scenario would account for her having something to do with the letter's production but not with the original effort.

14. Grafman interview, 22 June 1988.

15. In Mathew H. Ahmann, ed., *Race: Challenge to Religion* (Chicago: Henry Regnery Co., 1963), 155–69.

16. David Vann to Robert F. Kennedy, 19 January 1963, Burke Marshall Papers, John Fitzgerald Kennedy Presidential Library.

17. King, *Why We Can't Wait*, 64–65.

18. Garrow, *Bearing the Cross*, 236.

19. George Brown Tindall, "The Central Theme Revisited," in *The Southerner as American*, ed. Charles Grier Sellers, Jr. (Chapel Hill: University of North Carolina Press, 1960), 104–29. Tindall's thesis was in turn influenced by Gunnar Myrdal, *An American Dilemma: The Negro Problem and Modern Democracy*, 2 vols. (1944; reprint, New York: Pantheon Books, 1972), esp. ch. 1, sec. 13; ch. 21; and app. 2, sec. 3 and 4.

20. David W. Southern, *Gunnar Myrdal and Black-White Relations: The Use and Abuse of an American Dilemma, 1944–1969* (Baton Rouge: Louisiana State University Press, 1987), 231–32.

21. Alan Knight Chalmers Papers, Mugar Library, Boston University, passim.

22. Southern, *Gunnar Myrdal and Black-White Relations*, 187–224.

23. Garrow, *Bearing the Cross*, 670–71 n. 18.

24. Emphasis added. Part of King's frustration with moderates stemmed from a theological view that social problems were far more tractable than personal sins. In fact, as Branch sees it, King believed that a commitment to doing social good helped "the public man to redeem the private man." *Parting the Waters*, 702.

25. King, *Why We Can't Wait*, 107.

26. *New York Times*, 16 November 1978, 20, and *Atlanta Journal and Constitution*, 19 November 1978.

27. Howell Raines, *My Soul Is Rested: Movement Days in the Deep South Remembered* (New York: G. P. Putnam's Sons, 1977), 161. This quotation is additional evidence that King may not have written all of the letter. Shuttlesworth's ego notwithstanding, it seems forward, even for him, to have thought that the document should be signed "by all of us" unless he thought the letter to have been written by a group of those present in Birmingham.

28. Daniel C. Thompson, *The Negro Leadership Class* (Englewood Cliffs, N.J.: Prentice-Hall, 1963), x.

29. Norman C. Jimerson to Southern Regional Council, quarterly report, Alabama Council on Human Relations, 16 July 1963, Southern Regional Council Papers, Birmingham Public Library Archives. As early as the Al-

bany, Georgia, campaign, King talked about the neutrality of time "to the history of moral causes." Branch, *Parting the Waters*, 545.

30. Ahmann, *Race*, 164.

31. *Birmingham News*, 3 April 1988.

32. King, *Why We Can't Wait*, 117.

33. Raines, *My Soul Is Rested*, 161.

Chapter 3

1. Malinda Snow, "Martin Luther King's 'Letter from Birmingham Jail' as Pauline Epistle," *Quarterly Journal of Speech* 71 (1985): 327–29.

2. Ibid., 318.

3. Martin Luther King, Jr., *Why We Can't Wait* (New York: Harper and Row, 1963, 1964), 69–70.

4. David J. Garrow, *Bearing the Cross: Martin Luther King, Jr., and the Southern Christian Leadership Conference* (New York: William Morrow, 1986), 246.

5. *Birmingham Post Herald*, 13 April 1963, 10, as cited in Snow, "Martin Luther King's Letter," 321; and *Birmingham News*, 13 April 1963.

6. John Walton Cotman, *Birmingham, JFK, and the Civil Rights Act of 1963* (New York: Peter Lang, 1989), 34–36.

7. Theodore C. Sorensen, *Kennedy* (New York: Harper and Row, 1965), 490.

8. Lloyd F. Bitzer, "The Rhetorical Situation," *Philosophy and Rhetoric* 1 (1968): 1–14.

9. Richard E. Vatz, "The Myth of the Rhetorical Situation," *Philosophy and Rhetoric* 6 (1973): 154–61. For an analysis of the relationship between "situation" and "argument," see Michael C. McGee, "The Fall of Wellington: A Case Study of the Relationship Between Theory, Practice, and Rhetoric," *Quarterly Journal of Speech* 63 (1977): 28–42.

10. B. L. Ware and Wil A. Linkugel, "They Spoke in Defense of Themselves: On Generic Criticism of Apologia," *Quarterly Journal of Speech* 59 (1973): 273–83.

11. Martin Luther King, Jr., "Letter from Birmingham Jail," in *Why We Can't Wait*, 78.

12. Ibid., 77–78.

13. Ibid., 77–100.

14. Ibid., 88–89.

15. Ibid., 92.

16. Ibid., 82–83. For an analysis of King's use of recent, historical, and spiritual dimensions of time to explain his and others' actions, to express a variety of liberal ideologies, and to appeal to the readers' consciences, see Ronald E. Lee, "The Rhetorical Construction of Time in Martin Luther King, Jr.'s 'Letter from Birmingham Jail,'" *Southern Communication Journal* 56 (1991): 279–88. For contrasting views of King's references to time in "I Have a Dream" as an argument against white voices of gradualism or as

an argument in favor of black voices of moderation, see J. Robert Cox, "The Fulfillment of Time: King's 'I Have a Dream' Speech (August 28, 1963)," 181–204; and Robert Hariman, "Time and the Reconstruction of Gradualism in King's Address: A Response to Cox," 205–17, in *Texts in Context: Critical Dialogues on Significant Episodes in American Political Rhetoric,* ed. Michael C. Leff and Fred J. Kauffeld (Davis, Calif.: Hermagoras Press, 1989).

17. King, "Letter from Birmingham Jail," 79.

18. Ibid., 96.

19. Ibid., 84–86.

20. Ibid., 85.

21. Ibid., 85–86.

22. Ibid., 86–88.

23. Ibid., 94.

24. Taylor Branch, *Parting the Waters: America in the King Years, 1954–63* (New York: Simon and Schuster, 1988).

25. Kenneth O'Reilly, *"Racial Matters": The FBI's Secret File on Black America, 1960–1972* (New York: Free Press, 1989).

26. Police Department Reports to Chief Jamie Moore, box 13, 1963, Eugene T. "Bull" Connor Papers, Birmingham Public Library Archives.

27. R. S. Whitehouse to Jamie Moore, 7 May 1963, 10 May 1963, Connor Papers, box 13; and O'Reilly, *Racial Matters,* 87.

28. B. A. Allison to Jamie Moore, 14 May 1963, Connor Papers, box 13.

29. B. R. Goforth and J. C. Wilson to Jamie Moore, 6 March 1963, Connor Papers, box 13.

30. R. S. Whitehouse and R. A. Watkins to Jamie Moore, 5 April 1963, Connor Papers, box 13.

31. Ibid.

32. Ibid.

33. Ibid.

34. R. S. Whitehouse and R. A. Watkins to Jamie Moore, 10 April 1963, Connor Papers, box 13.

35. B. A. Allison and R. A. Watkins to Jamie Moore, 10 April 1963, Connor Papers, box 13.

36. R. S. Whitehouse and R. A. Watkins to Jamie Moore, 12 April 1963, Connor Papers, box 13.

37. Ibid.

38. Branch, *Parting the Waters,* 371.

39. Martin Luther King, Jr., "Speech to the Alabama Christian Movement for Human Rights," 3 May 1963. Audio tape recording, Birmingham Public Library Archives.

40. Chaim Perelman and L. Olbrechts-Tyteca, *The New Rhetoric: A Treatise on Argumentation,* trans. John Wilkinson and Purcell Weaver (Notre Dame, Ind.: University of Notre Dame Press, 1969), 54–55.

41. King, "Letter from Birmingham Jail," 78–99.

42. Ibid., 91.

43. David L. Lewis, *King: A Critical Biography* (Urbana: University of Illinois Press, 1970), 188.

44. Snow, "Martin Luther King's Letter," 329.

45. King, "Letter from Birmingham Jail," 94.

46. See, for example, Kennedy's "Annual Message to the Congress on the State of the Union," 11 January 1962, and "Remarks Recorded for the Ceremony at the Lincoln Memorial Commemorating the Centennial of the Emancipation Proclamation," 22 September 1962, both in volume 2 of *Public Papers of the Presidents of the United States, John Fitzgerald Kennedy,* 3 vols. (Washington, D.C.: Government Printing Office, 1963). See also Kennedy's responses to the specific questions of reporters. A comparison of these three annual volumes reveals a clear shift in interest in speaking about civil rights on the part of the president. In 1961 he spoke on the issue only twice; in 1962, seven times; and in 1963, on thirty-two separate occasions.

47. Sorenson, *Kennedy,* 476–90.

48. O'Reilly, *Racial Matters,* 20.

49. Ibid., 39–40.

50. Ibid., 116.

51. Ibid., 66.

52. Branch, *Parting the Waters,* 711.

53. O'Reilly, *Racial Matters,* 121.

54. Ibid., 64.

55. Branch, *Parting the Waters,* 693.

56. Richard L. Johannesen, *Ethics in Human Communication,* 2d ed. (Prospect Heights, Ill.: Waveland Press, 1983), 1.

57. Perelman and Olbrechts-Tyteca, *The New Rhetoric,* 75.

58. *Birmingham Post Herald,* 10.

59. King, "Letter from Birmingham Jail," 77–100.

60. Ibid., 78–81.

61. Ibid., 83–84.

62. Ibid., 85–86.

63. Ibid., 87–90.

64. Martin Luther King, Jr., "Letter from Birmingham City Jail," in *A Testament of Hope: The Essential Writings of Martin Luther King, Jr.,* ed. James Melvin Washington (San Francisco: Harper and Row, 1986), 299. King removed the sentence containing the headlight/taillight metaphor in his "polished" version of the letter reprinted in *Why We Can't Wait.* Washington reprints the original text.

65. Ibid., 96.

66. Edward D. Steele, "Social Values in Public Address," *Western Journal of Speech Communication* 22 (1958): 38–42; "Symposium: Value Theory and Rhetoric," *Western Journal of Speech Communication* 26 (1962): 70–91, 133–45; Ralph T. Eubanks and Virgil L. Baker, "Toward an Axiology of Rhetoric," *Quarterly Journal of Speech* 48 (1962): 161; Richard M. Weaver, *The Ethics of Rhetoric* (Chicago: Henry Regnery, 1953), 23; Karl R. Wallace, "The Substance of Rhetoric: Good Reasons," *Quarterly Journal of Speech* 49 (1963): 239–49. See also Milton M. Rokeach, *Beliefs, Attitudes, and Values* (San Francisco: Jossey-Bass, 1968), 157; Kenneth Burke, *Permanence and Change* (1935; reprint, Indianapolis: Bobbs-Merrill, 1965), 1–7; Clyde

Kluckhohn, "Values and Value-Orientation in the Theory of Action: An Exploration in Definition and Classification," in *Toward a General Theory of Action*, ed. Talcott Parsons and Edward A. Shils (Cambridge: Harvard University Press, 1951), 388–433; Henry Margenau, "The Scientific Basis of Value," in *New Knowledge in Human Values*, ed. Abraham H. Maslow (New York: Harper and Row, 1959), 38–51; and Paul Tillich, "Is a Science of Human Values Possible?" in *New Knowledge in Human Values*, 189–96. For recent syntheses see both Douglas Ehninger and Gerard A. Hauser, "Communication of Values," 720–48, and Roderick P. Hart, "The Functions of Human Communication in the Maintenance of Public Values," 749–91, in *Handbook of Rhetorical and Communication Theory*, ed. Carroll C. Arnold and John Waite Bowers (Boston: Allyn and Bacon, 1984).

67. Weaver, *Ethics of Rhetoric*, 23.

68. Kenneth Burke, *A Rhetoric of Motives* (1945; reprint, Berkeley: University of California Press, 1969), 187–88.

69. Perelman and Olbrechts-Tyteca, *The New Rhetoric*, 80–83.

70. Branch, *Parting the Waters*, 744.

71. Ibid., 755.

72. The letter was reprinted by the American Friends Services Committee and in numerous publications, such as *Christian Century* 80, 12 June 1963; *Ebony*, 18 August 1963; *Time* 83, 3 January 1963; and *Negro History Bulletin* 27 (March 1964).

Chapter 4

1. The only full-length, published, rhetorical studies of this speech, to my knowledge, are J. Robert Cox, "The Fulfillment of Time: King's 'I Have a Dream' Speech (August 28, 1963)," 181–204, and Robert Hariman, "Time and the Reconstitution of Gradualism in King's Address: A Response to Cox," 205–18, in *Texts in Context: Critical Dialogues on Significant Episodes in American Political Rhetoric*, ed. Michael C. Leff and Fred J. Kauffeld (Davis, Calif.: Hermagoras Press, 1989). See also Lloyd E. Rohler, "Martin Luther King's 'I Have a Dream,'" in *Great Speeches for Criticism and Analysis*, ed. Lloyd E. Rohler and Roger Cook (Greenwood, Ind.: Alistair Press, 1988), 329–36.

2. Michael Osborn, "Archetypal Metaphor in Rhetoric: The Light-Dark Family," *Quarterly Journal of Speech* 53 (1967): 115–26.

3. Arthur Hastings, "Metaphor in Rhetoric," *Western Speech* 34 (1970): 181–94; N. Lamar Reinsch, Jr., "An Investigation of the Effects of the Metaphor and Simile in Persuasive Discourse," *Speech Monographs* 38 (1971): 142–45; John Waite Bowers and Michael Osborn, "Attitudinal Effects of Selected Types of Concluding Metaphors in Persuasive Speeches," *Speech Monographs* 33 (1966): 147–55.

4. William J. Jordan, "A Reinforcement Model of Metaphor," *Speech Monographs* 39 (1972): 223–26; William J. Jordan and Margaret L. McLaughlin, "The Metaphorical Dimension in Descriptive Language," *Human Communication Research* 2 (1976): 182–91.

5. William E. Rickert, "Winston Churchill's Archetypal Metaphors: A Mythopoetic Translation of World War II," *Central States Speech Journal* 28 (1977): 106–12.

6. Jane Blankenship, "The Search for the 1972 Democratic Nomination: A Metaphorical Perspective," in *Methods of Rhetorical Criticism: A Twentieth-Century Perspective*, 2d ed., ed. Bernard L. Brock and Robert L. Scott (Detroit: Wayne State University Press, 1980), 321–45.

7. See Kathleen Hall Jamieson, "The Metaphoric Cluster in the Rhetoric of Pope Paul VI and Edmund G. Brown, Jr.," *Quarterly Journal of Speech* 66 (1980): 51–72; and Michael P. Graves, "Functions of Key Metaphors in Early Quaker Sermons, 1671–1700," *Quarterly Journal of Speech* 69 (1983): 364–78. Both Jamieson and Graves have examined clusters of metaphors in texts, but they have not explored the relationship which may have united those clusters. As a direction for future research, Jamieson suggests exploring the possibility that "one cluster or element may exercise esemplastic power over the others" (p. 72).

8. Osborn suggested this perspective when he urged examination of the role of metaphors in rhetorical invention to determine if a rhetor's recurrent metaphors reflected "an underlying unit of imaginative outlook on public questions." See "Archetypal Metaphor in Rhetoric," 397.

9. Jonathon Culler, *The Pursuit of Signs: Semiotics, Literature, Deconstruction* (Ithaca, N.Y.: Cornell University Press, 1981); Michael Riffaterre, *The Semiotics of Poetry* (Bloomington: Indiana University Press, 1978).

10. Riffaterre, *Semiotics of Poetry*, 19.

11. Ibid., 164.

12. Culler, *Pursuit of Signs*, 83

13. Sherry B. Ortner, "On Key Symbols," *American Anthropologist* 75 (1973): 1138–46.

14. Michael Calvin McGee, "The 'Ideograph': A Link Between Rhetoric and Ideology," *Quarterly Journal of Speech* 66 (1980): 1–16.

15. Doris Graber, *Politics and Verbal Behavior* (Urbana: University of Illinois Press, 1976).

16. I would not, of course, contend that any text has a single "correct" or simple meaning. Rather I would assume that each audience member tends to perceive a unity of meaning in a text.

17. Kenneth Burke, *The Philosophy of Literary Form: Studies in Symbolic Action*, 3d ed. (1941; reprint, Berkeley: University of California Press, 1973): 138–68.

18. Kenneth Burke, "Scope and Reduction: The Representative Anecdote," in *A Grammar of Motives* (1945; reprint, Berkeley: University of California Press, 1969), 59–62. For critical applications of this concept, see Barry Brummett, "The Representative Anecdote as a Burkean Method Applied to Evangelical Rhetoric," *Southern Speech Communication Journal* 50 (1984): 1–23; and Charles Conrad, "Agon and Rhetorical Form: The Essense of 'Old Feminist' Rhetoric," *Central States Speech Journal* 32 (1981): 45–53.

19. George Lakoff and Mark Johnson, *Metaphors We Live By* (Chicago: University of Chicago Press, 1980).

20. Here I am aware one could argue that the matrix of the speech is a simple declarative statement, not a metaphor. But since King expressed his philosophy metaphorically within the speech, I feel justified in conceptualizing the matrix as a metaphor. Moreover, I have chosen the word "covenant" deliberately, in preference to other words used to refer to the establishment of governments, e.g., compact, contract. I believe, as I shall argue, that "covenant" suggests a bond between individual citizens and the state, which the other terms do not, and which, I think, is central to King's political philosophy.

21. Anna Howard Shaw, "The Fundamental Principle of a Republic," in *Anna Howard Shaw: Suffrage Orator and Social Reformer*, ed. Wil A. Linkugel and Martha Solomon (New York: Greenwood Press, 1991), 147–64.

22. Mario Cuomo's and Jesse Jackson's speeches to the 1984 Democratic National Convention are reprinted in Rohler and Cook, *Great Speeches for Criticism and Analysis*, 80–87, 101–10.

23. Cox reaches a similar conclusion in his analysis of the use of time in the speech. See "The Fulfillment of Time."

24. Richard P. Fulkerson, "The Public Letter as a Rhetorical Form: Structure, Logic, and Style in King's 'Letter from Birmingham Jail,'" *Quarterly Journal of Speech* 65 (1979): 121–36.

25. For a fuller explanation of the journey motif, see Northrop Frye, *Anatomy of Criticism: Four Essays* (Princeton: Princeton University Press, 1973). For a critical application of this view, see Martha Solomon, "The 'Positive Woman's' Journey: A Mythic Analysis of the Rhetoric of STOP ERA," *Quarterly Journal of Speech* 65 (1979): 262–74.

26. Stephen B. Oates, *Let the Trumpet Sound: The Life of Martin Luther King, Jr.* (New York: New American Library, 1982), 256.

27. Ibid., 244–46.

28. Ibid., 251–53.

29. Ibid., 258.

30. Ibid., 256–57; Coretta Scott King, *My Life with Martin Luther King, Jr.* (New York: Holt, Rinehart, and Winston, 1969), 236.

31. Oates, *Let the Trumpet Sound*, 255–62. In a taped interview with Donald Hugh Smith in the King archives in Atlanta, King notes that he was inspired by the crowd response and added the dream sequence extemporaneously. Other elements in this lengthy passage had appeared in his various speeches, books, and essays.

32. Ortner, "On Key Symbols," 1344.

33. Hugh Dalziel Duncan, *Symbols in Society* (Oxford: Oxford University Press, 1968), 98.

34. Ortner, "On Key Symbols," 1341.

35. David Henry, "The Rhetorical Dynamics of Mario Cuomo's 1984 Keynote Address: Situation, Speaker, Metaphor," *Southern Speech Communication Journal* 53 (1988): 105–20.

36. Oates, *Let the Trumpet Sound*, 70.

37. Kenneth Burke, *Language as Symbolic Action: Essays on Life, Literature, and Method* (Berkeley: University of California Press, 1966), 44–61.

38. Oates, *Let the Trumpet Sound,* 70, 71, 132, 167–68.

Chapter 5

Portions of this essay are reprinted from John Louis Lucaites and Celeste Michelle Condit, "Reconstructing <Equality>: Culturetypal and Countercultural Rhetorics in the Martyred Black Vision," *Communication Monographs* 57 (1990): 5–24.

1. "*Playboy* Interview: Martin Luther King, Jr. (1965)," in *A Testament of Hope: The Essential Writings of Martin Luther King, Jr.,* ed. James M. Washington (San Francisco: Harper and Row, 1986), 377.

2. This is a fairly common, popular assessment of King's legacy. See, for example, William Robert Miller, "Gandhi and King: Trail Blazers in Nonviolence," *Fellowship* 35 (1969): 5–7; James Sellers, "Love, Justice and the Non-Violent Movement," *Theology Today* 18 (1962): 65–69; Loudan Wainwright, "Martyr of the Sit-Ins," *The Negro History Bulletin* 24 (1961): 147–51; and James A. Colaiaco, *Martin Luther King, Jr.: Apostle of Militant Nonviolence* (New York: St. Martin's Press, 1988). The point has also been emphasized by rhetorical and communication scholars who frequently treat King's promotion of a rhetoric of "conscience" and "creative protest" as truly revolutionary. See Edwin Black, "The 'Vision' of Martin Luther King," in *Literature as Revolt and Revolt as Literature: Three Studies in the Rhetoric of Non-Oratorical Forms: Proceedings of the Fourth Annual University of Minnesota Spring Symposium in Speech Communication, May 3, 1969* (Minneapolis: University of Minnesota Press, 1970), 7–16; and Michael Osborn, "'I've Been to the Mountaintop': The Critic as Participant," in *Texts in Context: Critical Dialogues on Significant Episodes in American Political Rhetoric,* ed. Michael C. Leff and Fred J. Kauffeld (Davis, Calif.: Hermagoras Press, 1989), 165–66, reprinted as chapter 8 of this volume.

3. See, for example, Martin Luther King, Jr., "Pilgrimage to Nonviolence (1960)," 35–40; "Love, Law, and Civil Disobedience (1961)," 43–53; and "Nonviolence: The Only Road to Freedom (1966)," 54–62, all in *A Testament of Hope.*

4. In our vocabulary the word "equality" functions in American political discourse as an "ideograph." Ideographs are abstract words or short phrases that signify the normative, collective commitments of community. As abstractions their meanings are of course open to debate and discussion, but to be a member of a particular community is to commit oneself to a belief in its ideographs at least at the level of the signifier. Thus, for example, in American political discourse hawks and doves might argue over the meaning of "national security" as a motivation for action in a particular situation, but there will be no debate over the importance of national security as a commitment of community. Taken in their entirety, the ideographs for a particular community constitute its political ideology. Ideo-

graphs are only one of a number of elements in the public vocabulary, but they are especially significant because they typically serve in discourse as the primary purpose or motivating terms for public action and behavior. Because ideographs are frequently drawn from ordinary discourse, they are terms that can have both ideographic and nonideographic meanings. Hence the word "liberty" can refer in its ideographic sense to one of the primary political commitments of community for the members of liberal-democratic societies, in which case it must be understood in the historical context of its usage in public discourse as such, or it can refer in its nonideographic sense to a general philosophical concept or the general feeling of being free. In order to avoid confusion, we identify specifically ideographic representations of "equality" by placing it inside quotation marks. See Michael Calvin McGee, "The 'Ideograph': A Link Between Rhetoric and Ideology," *Quarterly Journal of Speech* 66 (1980): 1–16; Michael Calvin McGee, " 'Not Men, But Measures': The Origins and Import of an Ideological Principle," *Quarterly Journal of Speech* 64 (1978): 141–55; Celeste Michelle Condit, "Democracy and Civil Rights: The Universalizing Influence of Public Argumentation," *Communication Monographs* 54 (1985): 1–18; and John Louis Lucaites, "Constitutional Argument in a National Theater: The Impeachment Trial of Dr. Henry Sacheverell," in *Popular Trials: Rhetoric, Mass Media, and the Law,* ed. Robert Hariman (Tuscaloosa, Ala.: University of Alabama Press, 1990), 31–54.

5. We use the "foundation" metaphor in the context of recognizing that all social and political "foundations" are inherently metaphorical and rhetorical. In their way, the rhetorical foundations of society are more like the genetic foundations of families which change and adapt from one generation to the next than they are like the foundations of a building intended to remain unchanged against the ravages of time. See John Louis Lucaites and Celeste Michelle Condit, "The Rhetorical 'Foundations' of Equality in American Political Discourse," in *Taking Political Talk Seriously,* ed. John S. Nelson, forthcoming; and John S. Nelson, "Political Foundations for Rhetoric of Inquiry," in *The Rhetorical Turn,* ed. Herbert W. Simons (Chicago: University of Chicago Press, 1990), 258–89.

6. The debate over what Jefferson "really" meant by this phrase is loud and contentious. We draw our conclusion from our general sense of Jefferson's rhetorical and political sensitivities and his private letters where he makes the point quite explicitly. On the various debates see Stephen E. Lucas, "Justifying America," in *American Rhetoric: Context and Criticism,* ed. Thomas W. Benson (Carbondale: Southern Illinois University Press, 1989), 85–86. See also "Thomas Jefferson to John Randolph, 25 August 1977," and "Thomas Jefferson to John Randolph, 29 November 1775," in *The Papers of Thomas Jefferson: Volume 1: 1760–1776,* ed. Julian P. Boyd (Princeton: Princeton University Press, 1950), 240–43, 268–67; and "Thomas Jefferson to Henry Lee, 8 May 1825," in *The Writings of Thomas Jefferson: Memorial Edition,* vol. 16, ed. Albert Ellery Bergh (Washington, D.C.: Thomas Jefferson Memorial Association of the United States, 1904), 117–19. See also Dumas Malone, *Jefferson: The Virginian,* vol. 2 (Boston: Little, Brown, 1948), 220–24.

7. Gunnar Myrdal, *An American Dilemma: The Negro Problem and Modern Democracy*, 2 vols. (1944; reprint, New York: Pantheon Books, 1972), 2:3–25, 670–72.

8. The actual terms of the *Brown* decision were that "separate educational facilities are inherently unequal." See *Brown* v. *Board of Education of Topeka, Kansas*, 347 U.S. 463 (1954).

9. This of course is not to deny that the public meaning of the word is often hotly contested, as the contemporary debate over affirmative action policies seems to indicate. Rather, we simply mean to point to its ideographic status as a defining commitment of community at the level of the signifier. See J. R. Pole, *The Pursuit of Equality in American History* (Berkeley: University of California Press, 1978); Andrew Flew, *The Politics of Procrustes: Contradictions of Enforced Equality* (Buffalo, N.Y.: Procrustes Books, 1981), 21–28; Kenneth Karst, "Why Equality Matters," *Georgia Law Review* 17 (1983): 245–89; Bryan Turner, *Equality* (London: Tavistock, 1986), 18–29; Herman Belz, *Equality Transformed: A Quarter-Century of Affirmative Action* (New Brunswick, N.J.: Transaction Press, 1991); and Aaron Wildavsky, *The Rise of Radical Egalitarianism* (Washington, D.C.: American University Press, 1991).

10. The literature here is extensive. See, for example, the treatment of equality in John Rawls, *A Theory of Justice* (Cambridge, Mass.: Belknap Press, 1971); R. H. Tawney, *Equality* (1931; reprint, London: George Allen and Unwin, 1964); Richard Sennett and Jonathon Cobb, *The Hidden Injuries of Class* (New York: Vintage Books, 1972); Sidney Verba and Gary G. Orren, *Equality in America: The View from the Top Down* (Cambridge: Harvard University Press, 1985), 5–6; Erik Olin Wright, "Race, Class, and Income Inequality," *American Journal of Sociology* 83 (1978): 1368–97; and Peter Westen, *Speaking of Equality: An Analysis of the Rhetorical Force of 'Equality' in Moral and Legal Discourse* (Princeton: Princeton University Press, 1990).

11. We are influenced here by Donald C. Bryant's notion that the function of rhetoric is to "adjust ideas to people and people to ideas" and Michael Calvin McGee's notion that rhetoric represents an experiential negotiation of the tension between symbolic and material environments. See Donald C. Bryant, "Rhetoric: Its Functions and Scope," *Quarterly Journal of Speech* 39 (1953): 401–24; and Michael C. McGee, "In Search of 'the People': A Rhetorical Alternative," *Quarterly Journal of Speech* 61 (1975): 235–49.

12. We inscribe the word "(re)vision" with parentheses around the prefix in order to call attention to the fact that King's portrait of American "equality" was less an attempt to revise the meaning of that term in the sense of changing it to accommodate new and different conditions than it was an attempt to persuade his listeners "once again" to envision what American equality means. This is not to concede that there was an absolute, foundational "equality" to be envisioned, but only to indicate (a) that King's argument presumed the existence of such a foundation in the rhetorical culture he was addressing and (b) that he sought to employ his audience's acceptance of that presumption as a means of authorizing his own agenda.

13. For a detailed analysis of this rhetorical engagement and the paradox of

"equality," see Celeste Michelle Condit and John Louis Lucaites, *Crafting Equality: America's Anglo/African Word* (Chicago: University of Chicago Press, 1993).

14. See, for example, W. E. B. Du Bois's discussion of the "double consciousness" of African Americans in *The Souls of Black Folks* (1903; reprint, New York: Fawcett, 1961), 43–53. The topic is taken up in a slightly different vein by Henry Louis Gates, Jr., *The Signifying Monkey: A Theory of Afro-American Literary Criticism* (New York: Oxford University Press, 1988), 207–9, 239–40.

15. See John Phillip Reid, *The Concept of Liberty in the Age of the American Revolution* (Chicago: University of Chicago Press, 1988); and Condit and Lucaites, *Crafting Equality.*

16. See Pole, *The Pursuit of Equality in American History,* esp. 112–47.

17. See Molefi Kete Asante, *The Afrocentric Idea* (Philadelphia: Temple University Press, 1987), 3–18 and 164–67; and James D. Anderson, "Black Cultural Equality in American Education," in *Equality and Social Policy,* ed. Walter Feinberg (Urbana: University of Illinois Press, 1978), 42–65.

18. Du Bois, *The Souls of Black Folks,* 45.

19. See James H. Cone, *Martin & Malcolm & America: A Dream or a Nightmare* (Maryknoll, N.Y.: Orbis Books, 1991).

20. Although the rhetorics of Malcolm X and Martin Luther King, Jr., have been studied by a number of rhetorical analysts from a variety of critical and theoretical perspectives, we find it curious that no one addresses the material presence or rhetorical significance of the commitment to "equality"—either formally or functionally—in their public discourse. On Malcolm X, see John Illo, "The Rhetoric of Malcolm X," *Columbia University Forum* (1964): 5–12; *Malcolm X and the American Negro Revolution: The Speeches of Malcolm X,* ed. Archie Epps (London: Peter Owen, 1968), 47–99; Robert L. Scott, "Justifying Violence: The Rhetoric of Militant Black Power," *Central States Speech Journal* 19 (1968): 96–104; Finley C. Campbell, "Voices of Thunder, Voices of Rage: A Symbolic Analysis of Malcolm X's Speech 'Message to the Grass Roots,'" *Communication Education* 19 (1970): 101–10; Arthur L. Smith and Stephen Robb, eds., *The Voice of Black Rhetoric* (Boston: Allyn and Bacon, 1971), 3; Thomas W. Benson, "Rhetoric and Autobiography: The Case of Malcolm X," *Quarterly Journal of Speech* 60 (1974): 1–13; and Hank Flick and Larry Powell, "Animal Imagery in the Rhetoric of Malcolm X," *Journal of Black Studies* 18 (1988): 435–51. On Martin Luther King, Jr., see Donald H. Smith, "Martin Luther King, Jr., Rhetorician of Revolt" (Ph.D. diss., University of Wisconsin, 1964); Donald H. Smith, "Martin Luther King, Jr.: In the Beginning from Montgomery," *Southern Speech Communication Journal* 34 (1968): 8–17; Black, "The 'Vision' of Martin Luther King"; Haig Bosmajian, "Rhetoric of Martin Luther King's Letter from Birmingham Jail," *Midwest Quarterly* 8 (1967): 127–43; Richard P. Fulkerson, "The Public Letter as a Rhetorical Form: Structure, Logic, and Style in King's 'Letter from Birmingham Jail,'" *Quarterly Journal of Speech* 65 (1979): 121–36; and Malinda Snow, "Martin Luther King's 'Letter from Birmingham Jail' as Pauline Epistle," *Quarterly Journal of Speech* 71 (1985): 318–24; J. Robert Cox, "The Fulfillment of

Time: King's 'I Have a Dream' Speech (August 28, 1963)," in *Texts in Context: Critical Dialogues on Significant Episodes in American Political Rhetoric*, ed. Michael C. Leff and Fred J. Kauffeld (Davis, Calif.: Hermagoras Press, 1989), 181–204; Ronald E. Lee, "The Rhetorical Construction of Time in Martin Luther King, Jr.'s 'Letter from Birmingham Jail,'" *Southern Communication Journal* 56 (1991): 279–88; Osborn, "'I've Been to the Mountaintop': The Critic as Participant"; Kurt W. Ritter and James R. Andrews, *The American Ideology: Reflections of the Revolution in American Rhetoric* (n.p.: Speech Communication Association, 1978), 106–14; and Keith D. Miller, *Voice of Deliverance: The Language of Martin Luther King, Jr., and Its Sources* (New York: Free Press, 1992).

21. Malcolm X, "The Black Revolution" (8 April 1964), in *Malcolm X Speaks*, ed. George Breitman (New York: Grove Press, 1966), 51.

22. Ideographs frequently operate enthymematicly, either evoking or being evoked by the particular narratives and/or clusters of culturally acknowledged characterizations with which, over time, they have become associated. Hence, just as the smell of rain on a spring day can elicit the presence of "life-as-a-child" or a particular youthful romantic interlude in the consciousness of a fifty-year-old person, so can the story of Nathan Hale recall the commitment to "liberty" for one reared in the United States. See John Louis Lucaites, "Flexibility and Consistency in Eighteenth-Century Anglo-Whiggism: A Case Study of the Rhetorical Dimensions of Legitimacy" (Ph.D. diss., University of Iowa, 1984), 227–28; Kenneth Burke, *The Philosophy of Literary Form* (1941; reprint, Berkeley: University of California Press, 1973), 1–137; Michael Osborn, *Orientations to Rhetorical Style* (Chicago: Science Research Associates, 1976), 16; and Michael Osborn, "Rhetorical Depiction," in *Form, Genre and the Study of Political Discourse*, ed. Herbert W. Simons and Aram A. Aghazarian (Columbia: University of South Carolina Press, 1986), 79–107.

23. All quotes from "I Have A Dream" are taken from an audio recording of the speech in the authors' possession and have been verified against the transcription contained in *A Testament of Hope*, 217–20.

24. See Condit and Lucaites, *Crafting Equality*, esp. part 2, "Rhetorical Integrations."

25. Malcolm X and Alex Haley, *The Autobiography of Malcolm X* (New York: Grove Press, 1966), 272.

26. Ibid., 275. Emphasis added.

27. Malcolm X, "To Mississippi Youth" (31 December 1964), in *Malcolm X Speaks*, 139.

28. Malcolm X, "The Ballot or the Bullet," in *Malcolm X Speaks*, 23–44.

29. Anthony E. Cook, "Beyond Critical Legal Studies: The Reconstructive Theology of Dr. Martin Luther King, Jr.," *Harvard Law Review* 103 (1990): 985–1040 contains a compelling analysis of the rhetorical dimensions of King's beloved community.

30. Martin Luther King, Jr., "Letter from Birmingham Jail," in *Why We Can't Wait* (New York: Harper and Row, 1964), 82–83.

31. See John Louis Lucaites and Celeste Michelle Condit, "Recon-

structing <Equality>," 5–25; and "Malcolm X: The Limits of the Rhetoric of Revolutionary Dissent," *Journal of Black Studies*, 23 (1993): 291–313.

32. *New York Times*, 29 August 1963, 1.

33. The significance of the "universalizing" function of public argument is elaborated in Chaim Perelman and L. Olbrechts-Tyteca, *The New Rhetoric: A Treatise on Argumentation*, trans. John Wilkinson and Purcell Weaver (Notre Dame: University of Notre Dame Press, 1969), 17–62. See also James Crosswhite, "Universality in Rhetoric: Perelman's Universal Audience," *Philosophy and Rhetoric* 22 (1989): 157–73; and Condit, "Democracy and Civil Rights."

34. See Michael C. McGee, "In Search of 'The People.'"

35. On the mythic and rhetorical dimensions of the American dream, see James Oliver Robertson, *American Myth, American Reality* (New York: Hill and Wang, 1980), 127–208, 258–70; and Walter R. Fisher, "Reaffirmation and Subversion of the American Dream," *Quarterly Journal of Speech* 59 (1973): 160–67. On the rhetorical dimensions of the Christian cycle of guilt, purification, and redemption, see Kenneth Burke, *Permanence and Change* (1935; reprint, Berkeley: University of California Press, 1984), passim; and idem, *The Rhetoric of Religion: Studies in Logology* (Berkeley: University of California Press, 1970), passim.

36. Archetypal metaphors seem to have a special rhetorical potency, particularly when seeking to establish the stability and legitimacy of group identity, because they frame and constitute present conditions in terms of "experiences and motives that repeat themselves at fundamental levels of awareness in the lives of all people." According to Osborn, the primary sources of archetypal metaphors are derived from the fundamental human experience of water and the sea, light and darkness, the human body, war and peace, animals, the family, mountains, sexuality, and the relationships between above and below and forward and backward. See Osborn, *Orientations to Rhetorical Style*, 16–19, 28. See also idem, "Archetypal Metaphor in Rhetoric: The Light-Dark Family," *Quarterly Journal of Speech* 53 (1967): 115–26; and idem, "The Evolution of the Archetypal Sea in Rhetoric and Poetic," *Quarterly Journal of Speech* 63 (1977): 347–63.

37. Rhetorical characterizations are the normalized labels attached to concrete acts, scenes, agents, and agencies in the public vocabulary of a particular rhetorical culture. They integrate the denotations and cultural connotations affiliated in the public discourse of a community with a particular act, scene, agent, and so on, so as to embody and evoke a "taken for granted" stereotype. So, for example, the phrase "welfare mother" essentializes the image of an unemployed, pregnant, black, single woman with several children, living in an urban ghetto and using her welfare checks to buy cigarettes and alcohol. The phrase "urban ghetto" essentializes the image of a neighborhood populated almost exclusively by non-Anglo ethnic minorities, controlled by street gangs and drug dealers, and consisting of run-down apartment dwellings and burned-out buildings. Both of these examples represent fairly negative rhetorical characterizations, but that need not be the case. Rhetorical characterizations can be positive as well,

as in the stereotypical images that we affiliate with terms like "supermom" or "residential neighborhood." See Lucaites and Condit, "Reconstructing <Equality>," 7–8; and Kenneth Burke, *A Grammar of Motives* (1945; reprint, Berkeley: University of California Press, 1969), esp. 127–322.

38. Martin Luther King, Jr., "Love, Law, and Civil Disobedience (1961)," in *A Testament of Hope*, 45.

39. King arrives at this characterization in his public renunciation of America's involvement in the war in Vietnam on 4 April 1967. It represents an important stage in his attempt to universalize the commitment to "equality" beyond the particular demands of the civil rights movement and deserves far more attention than we can give it here. See "A Time to Break Silence (1967)," in *A Testament of Hope*, 238.

Chapter 6

Portions of the research for this essay were made possible by a Travel to Collections Grant from the National Endowment for the Humanities. The author extends special thanks to the archival staffs at the Library and Archives, Martin Luther King, Jr., Center for Nonviolent Social Change, Atlanta, Georgia, and the Department of Special Collections of Mugar Memorial Library, Boston University, Boston, Massachusetts, for their assistance and cooperation in gaining access to major documents.

1. Martin Luther King, Jr., "I Have a Dream," advance text, as delivered at the March on Washington, 28 August 1963. The complete text is usefully reprinted in Richard L. Johannesen, Ronald Allen, and Wil A. Linkugel, eds., *Contemporary American Speeches*, 6th ed. (Dubuque, Iowa: Kendall/Hunt, 1988), 301–33. References to the text of "I Have a Dream" will be cited from this source.

2. Gerhard Kittel, *Theological Dictionary of the New Testament*, vol. 2, trans. Geoffrey W. Bromiley (Grand Rapids, Mich.: Wm. B. Eerdmans, 1964), 697.

3. Rudolf Bultmann, *Theology of the New Testament*, vol. 2, trans. Kendrick Grobel (New York: Charles Scribner's Sons, 1955), 112.

4. Jürgen Moltmann, *The Theology of Hope* (New York: Harper and Row, 1967), 21.

5. David J. Garrow, *Bearing the Cross: Martin Luther King, Jr., and the Southern Christian Leadership Conference* (New York: William Morrow, 1986), 50.

6. W. J. Weatherby, *James Baldwin: Artist on Fire* (New York: Donald L. Fine, 1989), 138.

7. James H. Cone, "Martin Luther King, Jr., Black Theology–Black Church," *Theology Today* 41 (1984): 409–20, reprinted in *Martin Luther King, Jr.: Civil Rights Leader, Theologian, Orator*, 3 vols., ed. David J. Garrow (Brooklyn, N.Y.: Carlson Pub., 1989), 3:206. See also in the same volume, idem, "The Theology of Martin Luther King, Jr.," *Seminary Quarterly Review* 40 (1986): 21–39 at 215–33.

8. Keith D. Miller, "Martin Luther King, Jr., and the Black Folk Pulpit," *Journal of American History* 78 (1991): 120–21.

9. Garrow, *Bearing the Cross*, 37.

10. Martin Luther King, Jr., "A Comparison of the Conceptions of God in the Thinking of Paul Tillich and Henry Nelson Wieman" (Ph.D. diss., Boston University, 1955). This is scheduled for publication in volume 2 of the *Papers of Martin Luther King, Jr.*, forthcoming from the University of California Press. For a detailed account of the nature and extent of King's plagiarism, see Martin Luther King, Jr., Papers Project, "The Student Papers of Martin Luther King, Jr.: A Summary Statement on Research," and "Appendix," which includes major segments from the dissertation along with the written reports of the first and second readers on King's dissertation committee, in *Journal of American History* 78 (1991): 23–40.

11. Peter Waldman, "To Their Dismay, King Scholars Find a Troubling Pattern," *Wall Street Journal*, 9 November 1990, 1ff. This disclosure was followed by a burst of stories including Anthony DePalma, "Plagiarism Seen by Scholars in King's Ph.D. Dissertation," *New York Times*, 10 November 1990, 1ff. Clayborne Carson, the director of the Martin Luther King, Jr., Papers Project, responded in "Documenting Martin Luther King's Importance—and His Flaws," *Chronicle of Higher Education*, 16 January 1991, A52.

12. For interesting correspondence on this matter, see Lewis V. Baldwin, *There Is a Balm in Gilead: The Cultural Roots of Martin Luther King, Jr.* (Minneapolis: Fortress Press, 1991), 12, 13.

13. David J. Garrow, "King's Plagiarism: Imitation, Insecurity, and Transformation," *Journal of American History* 78 (1991): 89.

14. Ibid., 89, 90.

15. Ibid., 90, 91.

16. David Thelen, "Becoming Martin Luther King, Jr.: An Introduction," *Journal of American History* 78 (1991): 14.

17. Ibid., 15, 16.

18. James P. Hanigan, *Martin Luther King, Jr., and the Foundations of Nonviolence* (Lanham, Md.: University Press of America, 1984), 79.

19. Ibid., 80.

20. Ibid., 89.

21. Ibid.

22. Ibid.

23. This view and the essential features of New Testament kerygma are developed by C. H. Dodd, *The Apostolic Preaching and Its Developments* (New York: Harper and Row, 1964).

24. Ibid.

25. Ibid.

26. See especially Stephen B. Oates, *Let the Trumpet Sound: The Life of Martin Luther King, Jr.* (New York: Harper and Row, 1982), 256–76; and Garrow, *Bearing the Cross*, 231–86.

27. Martin Luther King, Jr., "Address at Charlotte, N.C., Branch Chapter of NAACP," 25 September 1960, Library and Archives, Martin Luther King, Jr., Center for Nonviolent Social Change, Atlanta, Georgia, 1.

28. Garrow, *Bearing the Cross*, 283.

29. Ibid.

30. James McClendon, *Biography as Theology* (New York: Abingdon Press, 1974), 85.

31. Ibid., 80–86. This is an especially insightful view of King's theology and its implications for his social-political role.

32. Michael Osborn, "Rhetorical Depiction," in *Form, Genre, and the Study of Political Discourse*, ed. Herbert W. Simons and Aram A. Aghazarian (Columbia: University of South Carolina Press, 1986), 79–107.

33. King, "I Have a Dream," 301.

34. Ibid., 302.

35. Ibid.

36. Ibid.

37. Walter J. Ong, *Orality and Literacy: The Technologizing of the Word* (London: Metheun, 1982).

38. Ibid., 36–57.

39. King, "I Have a Dream," 302.

40. Ong, *Orality and Literacy*, 39.

41. Ibid., 43–44.

42. King, "I Have a Dream," 302.

43. Hortense Spillers, "Martin Luther King and the Style of the Black Sermon," *Black Scholar* 3 (1971): 26.

44. Ibid., 26.

45. Chaim Perelman, *The New Rhetoric and the Humanities* (Dordrecht, Holland: D. Reidel, 1979), 7.

46. Ibid.

47. Text of telegram 30 May 1963, Papers of Burke Marshall, box 8, Special Correspondence—Martin Luther King, Jr., John Fitzgerald Kennedy Presidential Library, Waltham, Massachusetts.

48. Ibid.

49. Garrow, *Bearing the Cross*, 281–82.

50. King, "I Have a Dream," 301.

51. Lyndon B. Johnson, "Voting Rights Address of March 15, 1965," in *Great Issues in American History*, vol. 3, ed. Richard and Beatrice Hofstadter (New York: Random House, 1982), 460.

52. Ibid.

53. Ibid., 461.

54. Martin Luther King, Jr., "An Autobiography of Religious Development," in *The Papers of Martin Luther King, Jr.*, Vol. 1, ed. Clayborne Carson (Berkeley: University of California Press, 1992), 362–63.

55. Dick Hebdige, *Cut 'N' Mix: Culture, Identity, and Caribbean Music* (New York: Metheun, 1987), 39.

56. Ibid., 47.

57. Walter R. Fisher, "Narration as a Human Communication Paradigm," *Communication Monographs* 51 (1984): 9.

58. Frank E. X. Dance, "Ong's Voice: 'I,' the Oral Intellect, You, and We," *Text and Performance Quarterly* 9 (1989): 185–98.

59. Walter J. Ong, *Interfaces of the Word: Studies in the Evolution of Consciousness and Culture* (Ithaca, N.Y.: Cornell University Press, 1977), 129.

60. Fisher, "Narration," 9.

61. Ibid., 14.

Chapter 7

1. I am indebted to Rev. Dr. Joseph L. Roberts, Jr., associate of Martin Luther King, Jr., and present pastor of the Ebenezer Baptist Church, for the notion that King "incarnated" his message. The conversation took place at the scholarly conference "The Power of the Spoken Word: The Oratory of Dr. Martin Luther King, Jr.," 9 January 1988. As will become clear, I mean "incarnation" less in the sense in which it currently is used in hermeneutics than in the sense in which Kenneth Burke and James Boyd White have introduced and refined it for rhetorical studies.

2. Martin Luther King, Jr., *Stride Toward Freedom* (New York: Harper, 1958), 91–93.

3. *Baltimore Sun*, 3 March 1965, 2.

4. FBI file 100-106670-1373, 13 May 1965.

5. David J. Garrow, *Bearing the Cross: Martin Luther King, Jr., and the Southern Christian Leadership Conference* (New York: William Morrow, 1986), 425.

6. *Southern Courier*, 20 August 1965, 1.

7. "SCLC Summary," in the King Papers, Martin Luther King, Jr., Center for Nonviolent Social Change, Atlanta, Georgia.

8. *New York Times*, 15 August 1965, 73.

9. Garrow, *Bearing the Cross*, 460–63.

10. Ibid., 463.

11. Stephen B. Oates, *Let the Trumpet Sound: The Life of Martin Luther King, Jr.* (New York: Harper and Row, 1982), 432.

12. *The Nation*, 25 July 1966, 68.

13. *The New Republic*, 17 September 1966, 9.

14. *New York Review of Books*, 24 August 1967, 3–6.

15. *The New Republic*, 17 September 1966, 9.

16. *Washington Post*, 2 April 1978, 38.

17. Garrow, *Bearing the Cross*, 470.

18. *New York Times*, 14 April 1966, 1.

19. Stanley Levison to King, 20 May 1966, King Papers, MLK Center.

20. *Christian Century*, 16 March 1966, 331–32.

21. Garrow, *Bearing the Cross*, 543.

22. This class orientation seems to have been new only to King's public character. At the King Conference and elsewhere, Mrs. King has attested that he had voiced such concerns in private as long before as their courtship but that his leadership was always so pragmatic as not to get intolerably far ahead of what public opinion would sustain. But critics of King's public

discourse must obviously be primarily concerned with what he said *in public.*

23. *Washington Post,* 26 March 1967, 1.

24. Garrow, *Bearing the Cross,* 552.

25. U.S. House of Representatives, *Investigation of the Assassination of Dr. Martin Luther King, Jr.,* Hearings, VI, 296.

26. John Roche, Memo to the President, 5 April 1967, White House Central Files, Lyndon B. Johnson Presidential Papers, Johnson Library, Austin, Texas.

27. *Congressional Record,* 3 May 1967, 2.

28. *Newsweek,* 17 April 1967, 46.

29. *Life,* 21 April 1967, 4.

30. *Pittsburgh Courier,* 15 April 1967, 10.

31. *Washington Post,* 15 April 1967, 12.

32. *New York Times,* 7 April 1967, 20.

33. *Cleveland Plain Dealer,* 14 April 1967.

34. *New York Times,* 13 April 1967, 1.

35. Garrow, *Bearing the Cross,* 554.

36. Oates, *Let the Trumpet Sound,* 422.

37. Ibid.

38. For a study of relations with texts as a neglected critical metaphor, see Wayne C. Booth, "'The Way I Loved George Eliot': Friendship with Books as a Neglected Critical Metaphor," *Kenyon Review* 2 (1980): 1–27. See also idem, *The Company We Keep: An Ethics of Fiction* (Berkeley: University of California Press, 1988), 169–98. For an articulation of the critical concept of "textual community," see James Boyd White, *When Words Lose Their Meaning: Constitutions and Reconstitutions of Language, Character and Community* (Chicago: University of Chicago Press, 1984), 14–20. I extend Booth's and White's concepts to apply to multiple texts in ongoing discourse over time, so as to illuminate and explicate individual authors' rhetorical character, their distinctive habits and mores of discourse, and the ethical possibilities available in interaction with them. It is a methodological ambition of this chapter to make more explicit what may still be implicit in the ethical criticism of these critics and to make those contributions more directly relevant to the study of public address in the traditional sense. For a more extended treatment of the basic concepts behind ethical criticism of public address, see Frederick J. Antczak, "Discursive Community and the Problem of Perspective in Ethical Criticism," in *Conversations on Communication Ethics,* ed. Karen Joy Greenberg (Norwood, N.J.: Ablex Press, 1991), 75–85.

39. Wayne C. Booth, *Critical Understanding: The Powers and Limits of Pluralism* (Chicago: University of Chicago Press, 1979), 270. Of course even dealing with the implied author of texts across a whole career, we still do not have knowledge of the existential King. But I would claim that the career author is a more enduring critical interest than the existential author. Consider an analogy to the familiar debates in literary studies about the "real" authorship of Shakespeare's plays. No matter whether the historical author was actually Sir Francis Bacon or the Earl of Oxford, I suggest that

the much more interesting and productive questions remain, surrounding the implied Shakespeare we infer by reading his plays and wondering at his continuing, amplifying, and interanimating insights into the human condition. In the same way, it may be interesting to pursue the existential King, for historical purposes. But it is the purpose of this essay to suggest how rhetorical purposes can be richly rewarded by pursuing the King constructed in texts and the rhetorical community he offered (and continues to offer) his audiences.

40. Martin Luther King, Jr., "I Have a Dream (1963)," in *A Testament of Hope: The Essential Writings of Martin Luther King, Jr.*, ed. James Melvin Washington (San Francisco: Harper and Row, 1986), 219.

41. Martin Luther King, Jr., "A Time to Break Silence (1967)," in *A Testament of Hope*, 237.

42. Ibid., 239.

43. Ibid., 238.

44. Ibid., 239.

45. Ibid., 233.

46. Ibid.

47. Ibid.

48. Ibid., 234.

49. Ibid.

50. Ibid., 241.

51. Ibid., 240.

52. Ibid., 241.

53. Ibid., 240.

54. Ibid., 239.

55. Ibid., 238.

56. Of course, King currently stands accused of being too resourceful in his syntheses, with recent disclosures of unattributed appropriations in his doctoral dissertation. An imporant response to these charges of plagiarism is Keith D. Miller, *Voice of Deliverance: The Language of Martin Luther King, Jr., and Its Sources* (New York: Free Press, 1992). Miller puts King's use of language—as well as his theology and politics—in the context of the African-American folk church and characterizes King's work as a blending of the black oral and white written traditions.

57. King, "A Time to Break Silence," 242.

58. Ibid., 232.

59. Ibid.

Chapter 8

1. Michael Osborn, "A Philosophy of Criticism" (Paper presented at the annual meeting of the Eastern Communication Association, April 1988).

2. Richard Lentz, *Sixty-Five Days in Memphis: A Study of Culture, Symbols, and the Press*, Journalism Monographs, no. 98 (August 1986), 29.

3. Garry Wills, "Martin Luther King: Blessed Be the Name of De Lawd," *Esquire*, August 1968, 128.

4. The facts in the description that follows of the rhetorical situation of King's speech are drawn from Lentz, *Sixty-Five Days in Memphis*; Joan Turner Beifuss, *At the River I Stand: Memphis, the 1968 Strike, and Martin Luther King* (Memphis: B & W Books, 1985); John Bakke, "A Study of Establishment Rhetoric During the Sanitation Strike in Memphis, 1968" (Missouri Valley Collection, Brister Library, Memphis State University, Memphis, Tennessee) and from the personal experience of the author.

5. All quotations from "I've Been to the Mountaintop" are taken from an audiotape of the speech in the author's possession. An accurate transcription of that speech is contained in Michael C. Leff and Fred J. Kauffeld, eds., *Texts in Context: Critical Dialogues on Significant Episodes in American Political Rhetoric* (Davis, Calif.: Hermagoras Press, 1989), 311–22.

6. Richard P. Fulkerson has remarked on King's attraction to archetypal metaphors, including images of disease and health, and technological imagery in his "The Public Letter as a Rhetorical Form: Structure, Logic, and Style in King's 'Letter from Birmingham Jail,'" *Quarterly Journal of Speech* 65 (1979): 131. Such archetypal and culturetypal images, as I would identify them, connect King's vision to the timeless and the timely, to the eternal as well as to the now. The technological (culturetypal) images lend their subjects relevance and are what Fulkerson would call "adaptive." The archetypal images invest their subjects with feeling and authenticity, functioning in Fulkerson's account as "affective" and "ethical."

7. In these judgments I concur with Edwin Black, who observes that King "was often a clumsy and overblown stylist" but concludes concerning "I Have a Dream": "Show me a man who can *hear* that speech and not be stirred to his depths, and I'll show you a man who has no depths to stir." "The 'Vision' of Martin Luther King," in *Literature as Revolt and Revolt as Literature: Three Studies in the Rhetoric of Non-Oratorical Forms* (Minneapolis: University of Minnesota Press, 1970), 9.

8. Malinda Snow, "Martin Luther King's 'Letter from Birmingham Jail' as Pauline Epistle," *Quarterly Journal of Speech* 71 (1985): 319.

9. Thomas Rosteck, "I've Been to the Mountaintop: The Linkage of Narrative, Metaphor and Argument in Martin Luther King's Final Speech" (Paper presented at the annual convention of the Speech Communication Association, Denver, Colorado, November 1985).

10. Michael Osborn, "Archetypal Metaphor in Rhetoric: The Light-Dark Family," *Quarterly Journal of Speech* 53 (1967): 115–26.

11. See the discussion of parable in general, and the Good Samaritan parable in particular, in William G. Kirkwood, "Storytelling and Self-Confrontation: Parables as Communication Strategies," *Quarterly Journal of Speech* 69 (1983): 58–74; and idem, "Parables as Metaphors and Examples," *Quarterly Journal of Speech* 71 (1985): 422–40.

12. Michael Osborn, "Rhetorical Depiction," in *Form, Genre, and the Study of Political Discourse*, ed. Herbert W. Simons and Aram A. Aghazarian (Columbia: University of South Carolina Press, 1986), 79–107.

13. Lentz, *Sixty-Five Days in Memphis*, 8.

14. Richard John Neuhaus, letter to the editor, *Commonweal* 88, 31 May 1968, 342, as cited in Osborn, "Rhetorical Depiction," 94.

Chapter 9

We thank the following people for their contributions to this study: J. Jay Scott, residence hall director, University of Wisconsin–La Crosse; John Shaw, Vincent Voice Library, Michigan State University; and Dave Wolf, Audio-Visual Services, University of Wisconsin–La Crosse.

1. Michael Osborn, "'I've Been to the Mountaintop': The Critic as Participant," in *Texts in Context: Critical Dialogues on Significant Episodes in American Political Rhetoric*, ed. Michael C. Leff and Fred J. Kauffeld (Davis, Calif.: Hermagoras Press, 1989), esp. 150–51, reprinted in this volume as chapter 8.

2. See Roderick P. Hart, "Contemporary Scholarship in Public Address: A Research Editorial," *Western Journal of Speech Communication* 50 (1986): 286.

3. Molefi Kete Asante, *The Afrocentric Idea* (Philadelphia: Temple University Press, 1987), 6.

4. Africa does not represent the only oral culture, and thus it is important to note that many of the characteristics of African oral culture, such as the use of mnemonic patterns to assist cultural memory or of vocal redundancy, audience participation, and empathy to achieve community, will appear elsewhere. Our point is that these qualities need to be understood as part of a larger Afrocentric system defined by the performative moment of the nommo as a philosophical system. See Walter J. Ong, *Orality and Literacy: The Technologizing of the Word* (London: Methuen, 1982), 31–77; and Asante, *Afrocentric Idea*, 59–80.

5. Asante, *Afrocentric Idea*, 66–67. Emphasis added.

6. Jack L. Daniel and Geneva Smitherman, "How I Got Over: Communication Dynamics in the Black Community," *Quarterly Journal of Speech* 62 (1976): 27. See also Geneva Smitherman, *Talkin and Testifyin: The Language of Black America* (Detroit: Wayne State University Press, 1977).

7. Daniel and Smitherman, "How I Got Over," 33.

8. Melville J. Herskovits, among others, spoke of this relationship as early as the 1940s, but a plethora of studies appeared during the 1960s. See, for example, Arthur L. Smith, "Markings of an African Concept of Rhetoric," *Today's Speech* 19 (1971): 13–17.

9. See Daniel and Smitherman, "How I Got Over," 26–34.

10. See Arthur L. Smith, ed., *Language, Communication and Rhetoric in Black America* (New York: Harper and Row, 1972).

11. While Ladysmith Black Mambazo is from South Africa, the group reflects the even broader concept of pan-African cultural similarities. For an example, listen to Ladysmith Black Mambazo, *Inala*, Shanachie Records Corp., 1986.

12. LeRoi Jones, *Blues People* (New York: William Morrow, 1969), 69.

13. Quoted in Daniel and Smitherman, "How I Got Over," 34.

14. Ibid.

15. Smith, "Markings of an African Concept of Rhetoric," 16. Emphasis added.

16. Tilford Brooks, *America's Black Musical Heritage* (Englewood Cliffs, N.J.: Prentice-Hall, 1984), 49.

17. See Robert McCrum, William Cran, and Robert MacNeil, *The Story of English* (New York: Elizabeth Sifton Books–Viking, 1986), 208–10.

18. For the lyrics, see Alan Lomax, *The Folk Songs of North America* (Garden City, N.Y.: Doubleday, 1960), 530. For a Gullah recording, hear *Georgia Sea Islands Songs*, New World Records, 1977.

19. Lomax, *The Folk Songs of North America*, 470–71.

20. For a view of the repressive effects that slavery brought about in this setting, see Cal M. Logue, "Transcending Coercion: The Communicative Strategies of Black Slaves on Antebellum Plantations," *Quarterly Journal of Speech* 67 (1981): 34–35; and Grace Sims Holt, "Stylin' Outta the Black Pulpit," in *Rappin' and Stylin' Out*, ed. Thomas B. Kochman (Urbana: University of Illinois Press, 1972), 190.

21. Alfred B. Pasteur and Ivory L. Toldson, *Roots of Soul* (Garden City, N.Y.: Anchor Press/Doubleday, 1982), 201–202.

22. Arthur L. Smith, "Socio-Historical Perspectives of Black Oratory," *Quarterly Journal of Speech* 56 (1970): 269.

23. Ben Sidran, *Black Talk* (New York: Holt, Rinehart, and Winston, 1971), 19.

24. Daniel and Smitherman, "How I Got Over," 36.

25. Lomax, *Folk Songs of North America*, 468. See also Holt, "Stylin' Outta the Black Pulpit," 195.

26. Coretta Scott King, *My Life with Martin Luther King, Jr.* (New York: Holt, Rinehart, and Winston, 1969), 6.

27. See ibid.; Flip Schulke and Penelope O. McPhee, *King Remembered* (New York: W. W. Norton, 1986); and *Montgomery to Memphis*, videotape from the Martin Luther King, Jr., Center for Nonviolent Social Change, Atlanta, Georgia, n.d.

28. It would be misleading to conclude that King's oratory was the only example of call-response during these times. Call-response was a central component of the freedom and protest songs employed at marches, sit-ins, and other demonstrations throughout the civil rights movement as a means of making collective unity and spiritual uplift immediately "present." For some examples of this communicative form, hear *Freedom Songs: Selma, Alabama*, Folkway Records, FH5594, and see *Montgomery to Memphis*.

29. See Arthur L. Smith, *Rhetoric of Black Revolution* (Boston: Allyn and Bacon, 1969): 65–66; Daniel and Smitherman, "How I Got Over," 37; and the discussion of the varied purposes of response in Smitherman, *Talkin and Testifyin*, 107.

30. For example, Martin Luther King, Jr., "We Shall Overcome" and "On Police Brutality," on *We Shall Overcome! Martin Luther King, Jr.*, Phoenix 10 Records, 1984. See also "How Long? Not Long" and "I Have a Dream" in *Montgomery to Memphis*.

31. King, "On Police Brutality."

32. King, "We Shall Overcome."

33. King, "How Long? Not Long."

34. King, "I Have a Dream."

35. King, "How Long? Not Long."

36. King, "On Police Brutality."

37. Hear Martin Luther King, Jr., "Address to the American Jewish Committee," on *We Shall Overcome! Martin Luther King, Jr.*

38. See for example, Lyle V. Mayer, *Fundamentals of Voice and Diction,* 7th ed. (Dubuque, Iowa: William C. Brown, 1985), esp. 186–212.

39. Smitherman, *Talkin and Testifyin,* 135.

40. Ibid.

41. King, "I Have a Dream."

42. Mayer, *Fundamentals of Voice and Diction,* 195.

43. King, "How Long? Not Long."

44. King, "On Police Brutality."

45. King, "How Long? Not Long."

46. King, "I Have a Dream."

47. Ong, *Orality and Literacy,* 34.

48. King, "How Long? Not Long."

49. Cf. Smitherman's discussion of "talk singing" in *Talkin and Testifyin,* 137–42.

50. Marianne LaFrance and Clara Mayo, *Moving Bodies: Nonverbal Communication in Social Relationships* (Monterey, Calif.: Brooks/Cole-Wadsworth, 1978), 74–76.

51. King, "I Have a Dream."

52. King, "How Long? Not Long." We should note that repeated phrases may vary with each speech. Sometimes they mime the speaker's words. At other times they become chorus-like with more than one participant employing identical wording. At still other times wording may be highly individual. In any case, the effect is the same, i.e., to synthesize the speaker and the listener in a unified movement.

53. Pasteur and Toldson, *Roots of Soul,* 113.

54. King showed remarkable sensitivity to those around him. Note, for example, his speeches following the 30 January 1956 bombing of his own home and the speech that followed the beating of Rev. James Reeb on 7 March 1965. See *Montgomery to Memphis* for insight on these and other examples related to this concern.

55. Interview with Coretta Scott King, 10 January 1988, King Center, Atlanta, Georgia.

56. See *Montgomery to Memphis;* and King, *My Life with Martin Luther King,* 316. We should also note that King did not always work from a prepared text.

57. See, for example, Schulke and McPhee, *King Remembered,* 154–55; and King, *My Life with Martin Luther King,* 239.

58. Osborn, "I've Been to the Mountaintop."

59. King, *My Life with Martin Luther King,* 240. See also William R. Miller, *Martin Luther King, Jr.: His Life, Martyrdom and Meaning for the World* (New York: Weybright and Talley, 1968), 166.

60. Asante, *Afrocentric Idea,* 66.

61. Melbourne S. Cummings and Jack L. Daniel, "Scholarly Literature on the Black Idiom," in *International Conference on Black Communication,*

ed. Bruce E. Williams and Orlando L. Taylor (Bellagio, Italy: Rockfeller Foundation, 1980), 123.

62. Osborn, "I've Been to the Mountaintop," esp. 160.

63. Michael L. Hecht, Sidney Ribeau, and J. K. Alberts, "An Afro-American Perspective on Interethnic Communication," *Communication Monographs* 56 (1989): 386.

64. See Elkin Sithole, "Black Folk Music," in *Rappin' and Stylin' Out*, ed. Thomas B. Kochman (Urbana: University of Illinois Press, 1972), 82.

65. See Smitherman, *Talkin and Testifyin*, esp. 219–22.

References

Primary Documents

Speeches, Pamphlets, and Other Writings of Martin Luther King, Jr.

"Address at Charlotte, N.C., Branch Chapter of NAACP, 25 September 1960." Martin Luther King, Jr., Papers, 1950–1968. Library and Archives, Martin Luther King, Jr., Center for Nonviolent Social Change, Atlanta, Georgia.

"An Autobiography of Religious Development." King Papers Collection, box 106, 11–13, Mugar Memorial Library, Boston University.

Called To Serve, January 1929–June 1951. Vol. 1 of *Papers of Martin Luther King, Jr.* Edited by Ralph E. Luker and Penny A. Russell. Berkeley: University of California Press, 1992.

"A Comparison of the Conceptions of God in the Thinking of Paul Tillich and Henry Nelson Wieman." Ph.D. diss., Boston University, 1955.

"Death of Evil on the Seashore." In *Strength to Love*, 58–65.

"How Long? Not Long." In *Montgomery to Memphis*, videotape, King Center Archives. For a written text of the speech, see "Our God is Marching On! [Selma, Alabama, Speech] (1963)." In *A Testament of Hope*, 227–31.

"I Have a Dream (1963)." In *A Testament of Hope*, 217–20; *Contemporary American Speeches*, 6th ed., edited by Richard L. Johannesen, et al., 301–03. Dubuque, Iowa: Kendall/Hunt, 1988. For a videotape version of the speech, see *From Montgomery to Memphis*, Library and Archives, Martin Luther King, Jr., Center for Nonviolent Social Change, Atlanta, Georgia.

"I've Been to the Mountaintop." In *Critical Dialogues on Significant Epi-*

sodes in American Political Rhetoric, edited by Michael C. Leff and Fred J. Kauffeld, 311–21. Davis, Calif.: Hermagoras Press, 1989. Reprinted as "I See The Promised Land (3 April 1968)" in A Testament of Hope, 279–88.

"I See The Promised Land (3 April 1968)." In A Testament of Hope, 279–88. Reprinted as "I've Been to the Mountaintop," in Critical Dialogues on Significant Episodes in American Political Rhetoric, edited by Michael C. Leff and Fred J. Kauffeld, 311–21. Davis, Calif.: Hermagoras Press, 1989.

"Letter from Birmingham [City] Jail (1963)." In A Testament of Hope, 289–303; Why We Can't Wait, 76–95; and Christian Century 80 (1963): 767–73.

"Love, Law, and Civil Disobedience (1961)." In A Testament of Hope, 43–53.

Martin Luther King Treasury. Yonkers, N.Y.: Educational Heritage, 1964.

"Nonviolence: The Only Road to Freedom (1966)." In A Testament of Hope, 54–62.

"On Police Brutality." Audio-recording on We Shall Overcome! Martin Luther King, Jr. Phoenix 10 Records, 1984.

"Pilgrimage to Nonviolence (1960)." In Stride Toward Freedom, 90–107; and A Testament of Hope, 35–40.

"Playboy Interview: Martin Luther King, Jr., (1965)." In A Testament of Hope, 340–77.

"Speech to Alabama Christian Movement for Human Rights (1963)." Birmingham Public Library Archives, Birmingham, Alabama.

Strength of Love. 1963. Philadelphia: Fortress, 1981.

Stride Toward Freedom. New York: Harper, 1958.

A Testament of Hope: The Essential Writings of Martin Luther King, Jr. Edited by James Melvin Washington. San Francisco: Harper and Row, 1986.

"A Time to Break Silence (1967)." In A Testament of Hope, 231–44.

"Transcript of 'Face to Face' Television News Interview (1967)." In A Testament of Hope, 394–416.

"We Shall Overcome." On We Shall Overcome! Martin Luther King, Jr. Phoenix 10 Records, 1984.

Where Do We Go from Here: Chaos or Community? New York: Harper and Row, 1967.

Why We Can't Wait. New York: Harper and Row, 1963.

Interviews

Borders, William Holmes. Interview with Keith D. Miller. King Center Archives, Atlanta, Georgia, July 1987, July 1988.

Drew, Addine. Telephone interview with E. Culpepper Clark, 27 June 1988.

Edwards, J. H. Interview with Keith D. Miller. King Center Archives, Atlanta, Georgia, June 1987, July 1988.

English, Jethro. Interview with Keith D. Miller. King Center Archives, Atlanta, Georgia, July 1988.

Garrow, David. Telephone interview with E. Culpepper Clark, 2 June 1988.

Grafman, Rabbi Milton. Interview with E. Culpepper Clark. Birmingham, Alabama, 22 June 1988.

Henderson, Arthur and Laura. Interview with Keith D. Miller. King Center Archives, Atlanta, Georgia, July 1987.

Jones, Clarence. Telephone interview with E. Culpepper Clark, 20 June 1988.

Kemp, James. Interview with Keith D. Miller. King Center Archives, Atlanta, Georgia, July 1988.

King, Coretta Scott. Interview with Robert and Linda Harrison, Atlanta, Georgia, 10 January 1988.

Reed, Sarah. Interview with Keith D. Miller. King Center Archives, June 1987.

Shores, Arthur. Telephone interview with E. Culpepper Clark, 20 June 1988.

Taylor, Gardner. Telephone interview with Keith D. Miller, January 1987.

Walker, Wyatt T. Telephone interview with E. Culpepper Clark, 12 July 1988.

Private Papers and Collections

Boutwell, Albert. Papers. Birmingham Public Library Archives, Birmingham, Alabama.

Chalmers, Alan Knight. Papers. Mugar Memorial Library, Boston University, Boston, Massachusetts.

Connor, Eugene T. "Bull." Papers. Birmingham Public Library Archives, Birmingham, Alabama.

Johnson, Lyndon B. Presidential Papers. White House Central Files, Johnson Library, Austin, Texas.

King, Martin Luther, Jr. Papers, 1954–68. Mugar Memorial Library, Boston University, Boston, Massachusetts.

King, Martin Luther, Jr. Papers, 1950–68. Library and Archives, Martin Luther King, Jr., Center for Nonviolent Social Change, Atlanta, Georgia.

Marshall, Burke. Papers. John Fitzgerald Kennedy Presidential Library, Waltham, Massachusetts.

Missouri Valley Collection. Brister Library, Memphis State University, Memphis, Tennessee.

National Association for the Advancement of Colored People. Papers, 1909–65. Library of Congress, Washington, D.C.

Southern Regional Council. Papers. Birmingham Public Library Archives, Birmingham, Alabama.

Audio and Video Recordings

Franklin, C. L. *Eagle Stirs Her Nest.* Jewel LPS 0083, 1973 (record).

———. *Moses at the Red Sea.* Chess LP 19, mid-1950s (record).

Free At Last. Gordy GLP 928, n.d. (record).

Freedom Songs: Selma, Alabama. Folkway Records FH5594, n.d. (record).
Gates, J. M. *Dry Bones in the Valley.* Victor 1, 35810 A, DLC 0242/1594, n.d. (record).
———. *Eagle Stirs Her Nest.* Okey 8582, n.d. (record).
———. *Moses in the Wilderness.* Matrix, 3649-1, Victor 20421, 1926 (record).
Georgia Sea Island Songs. New World Records, n.d. (record).
Great March on Washington. Gordy 908, n.d. (record).
I Have a Dream: Martin Luther King and the Nonviolent Crusade. Chelsea House, n.d. (videotape).
In Search of Freedom. Mercury MCR-461170, n.d. (record).
King, Martin Luther Jr. *Dimensions of a Complete Life Delivered at Yale University.* Pacifica Tape Library ASW 1011, n.d. (audiotape).
———. *I Believe I've Got to Go Back to the Valley.* G. Robert Vincent Voice Library, Michigan State University, M1647, n.d. (audiotape).
———. *I Have a Dream.* Pacifica Tape Library AS 1166, n.d. (audiotape). See *Montgomery to Memphis* for a video recording of this speech.
———. *Martin Luther King at Berkeley.* Pacifica Tape Library A 2005, n.d. (audiotape).
———. *Martin Luther King at Santa Rita.* Pacifica Tape Library A 2043, n.d. (audiotape).
———. *Martin Luther King at Stanford.* Pacifica Tape Library A 2043, n.d. (audiotape).
———. *Martin Luther King on the Future of Integration.* Pacifica Tape Library AS 1005, n.d. (audiotape).
———. *Remaining Awake Through a Revolution.* Creed 3024, n.d. (record).
———. *The Sickness of America.* Pacifica Tape Library BB 4661, n.d. (audiotape).
———. *Speech to Alabama Christian Movement for Human Rights, 3 May 1963.* Birmingham Public Library Archives, n.d. (audiotape).
———. *We Shall Overcome! Martin Luther King, Jr.* Phoenix 10 Records, n.d. (record).
———. *Who Is the Least of These.* G. Robert Vincent Voice Library, Michigan State University, M1647, n.d. (audiotape).
Ladysmith Black Mambazo. *Inala.* Shanachic Records Corp., n.d. (record).
Montgomery to Memphis. Martin Luther King, Jr., Center for Nonviolent Social Change, Atlanta, Georgia, n.d. (videotape).

Secondary Documents

Books and Book Chapters

Abernathy, Ralph. *And the Walls Came Tumbling Down.* New York: Harper, 1989.
Ahmann, Mathew, ed. *Race: Challenge to Religion.* Chicago: Henry Regnery Co., 1963.

Allen, Richard. "An Address to Those Who Keep Slaves . . ." In *The Life Experience and Gospel Labors of the Right Reverend Richard Allen*. New York: Abingdon, 1960.

Anderson, James D. "Black Cultural Equality in American Education." In *Equality and Social Policy*, edited by Walter Feinberg, 42–65. Urbana: University of Illinois Press, 1978.

Ansbro, John. *Martin Luther King, Jr.: The Making of a Mind*. Maryknoll, N.Y.: Orbis, 1982.

Antczak, Frederick J. "Discursive Community and the Problem of Perspective in Ethical Criticism." In *Conversations on Communication Ethics*, edited by Karen Joy Greenberg, 75–85. Norwood, N.J.: Ablex Press, 1991.

Asante, Molefi Kete. *Afrocentricity: The Theory of Social Change*. Buffalo, N.Y.: Amulefi Press, 1980.

———. *The Afrocentric Idea*. Philadelphia: Temple University Press, 1987.

Baldwin, Lewis V. *There Is a Balm in Gilead: The Cultural Roots of Martin Luther King, Jr.* Minneapolis: Fortress Press, 1991.

Bauman, Richard. *Verbal Art as Performance*. Prospect Heights, Ill.: Waverly Press, 1977.

Beifuss, Joan Turner. *At the River I Stand: Memphis, the 1968 Strike, and Martin Luther King*. Memphis: B & W Books, 1985.

Bellah, Robert N. *The Broken Covenant: American Civil Religion in Time of Trial*. New York: Seabury Press, 1975.

Belz, Herman. *Equality Transformed: A Quarter-Century of Affirmative Action*. New Brunswick, N.J.: Transaction Press, 1991.

Bennett, Lerone. *Confrontation: Black and White*. Chicago: Johnson, 1965.

Bercovitch, Sacvan. *The American Jeremiad*. Madison: University of Wisconsin Press, 1978.

Berry, Mary Frances, and John Blassingame. *Long Memory: The Black Experience in America*. New York: Oxford University Press, 1982.

Black, Edwin. "The 'Vision' of Martin Luther King." In *Literature as Revolt and Revolt as Literature: Three Studies in the Rhetoric of Non-Oratorical Forms: Proceedings of the Fourth Annual University of Minnesota Spring Symposium in Speech Communication, May 3, 1969*. Minneapolis: University of Minnesota Press, 1970.

Blankenship, Jane. "The Search for the 1972 Democratic Nomination: A Metaphorical Perspective." In *Methods of Rhetorical Criticism: A Twentieth-Century Perspective*, 2d ed., edited by Bernard L. Brock and Robert L. Scott, 321–45. Detroit: Wayne State University Press, 1980.

Booth, Wayne C. *Critical Understanding: The Powers and Limits of Pluralism*. Chicago: University of Chicago Press, 1979.

———. *The Company We Keep: An Ethics of Fiction*. Berkeley: University of California Press, 1988.

Branch, Taylor. *Parting the Waters: America in the King Years, 1954–63*. New York: Simon and Schuster, 1988.

Broderick, Francis, and August Meier, ed. *Negro Protest Thought in the 20th Century*. Indianapolis: Bobbs-Merrill Co., 1965.

Brooks, Tilford. *America's Black Musical Heritage*. Englewood Cliffs, N.J.: Prentice-Hall, 1984.

Bultmann, Rudolph. *Theology of the New Testament.* Vol. 2. Translated by Kendrick Grobel. New York: Charles Scribner's Sons, 1955.

Burke, Kenneth. *Permanence and Change.* 1935. Reprint. Berkeley: University of California Press, 1984.

———. *The Philosophy of Literary Form: Studies in Symbolic Action.* 1941. Reprint. 3d ed. Berkeley: University of California Press, 1973.

———. *A Grammar of Motives.* 1945. Reprint. Berkeley: University of California Press, 1969.

———. *A Rhetoric of Motives.* 1950. Reprint. Berkeley: University of California Press, 1962.

———. *Language as Symbolic Action: Essays on Life, Literature, and Method.* Berkeley: University of California Press, 1966.

———. *The Rhetoric of Religion: Studies in Logology.* Berkeley: University of California Press, 1970.

Cleveland, E. O. S. *The Eagle Stirring in Her Nest.* N.p., 1946.

Colaiaco, James A. *Martin Luther King, Jr.: Apostle of Militant Non-violence.* New York: St. Martin's Press, 1988.

Condit, Celeste Michelle, and John Louis Lucaites. *Crafting Equality: America's Anglo/African Word.* Chicago: University of Chicago Press, 1993.

Cone, James H. *Martin & Malcolm & America: A Dream or a Nightmare.* Maryknoll, N.Y.: Orbis Books, 1991.

Coppin, L. J. *Fifty Years of Religious Progress: An Emancipation Sermon.* Philadelphia: African Methodist Episcopal Book Co., 1913.

Cotman, John Walton. *Birmingham, JFK and the Civil Rights Act of 1963.* New York: Peter Lang, 1989.

Cox, J. Robert. "The Fulfillment of Time: King's 'I Have a Dream' Speech (August 28, 1963)." In *Texts in Context: Critical Dialogues on Significant Episodes in American Political Rhetoric,* edited by Michael C. Leff and Fred J. Kauffeld, 181–204. Davis, Calif.: Hermagoras Press, 1989.

Culler, Jonathon. *The Pursuit of Signs: Semiotics, Literature, Deconstruction.* Ithaca, N.Y.: Cornell University Press, 1981.

Cummings, Melbourne S., and Jack L. Daniel. "Scholarly Literature on the Black Idiom." In *International Conference on Black Communication,* edited by Bruce E. Williams and Orlando L. Taylor, 97–144. Bellagio, Italy: Rockefeller Foundation, 1980.

Dodd, C. H. *The Apostolic Preaching and Its Developments.* New York: Harper and Row, 1964.

Douglass, Frederick. *The Life and Times of Frederick Douglass.* 1892. Reprint. London: Collier-Macmillan, 1962.

Du Bois, W. E. B. *The Souls of Black Folks.* 1903. Reprint. New York: Fawcett, 1961.

Duncan, Hugh Dalziel. *Symbols in Society.* Oxford: Oxford University Press, 1968.

Ehninger, Douglas, and Gerard A. Hauser. "Communication of Values." In *Handbook of Rhetorical and Communication Theory,* edited by Carroll C. Arnold and John Waite Bowers, 720–48. Boston: Allyn and Bacon, 1984.

English, James. *The Prophet of Wheat Street: The Story of William Homes Borders, a Man Who Refused to Fail.* Elgin, Ill.: Cook, 1973.

Fairclough, Adam. *To Redeem the Soul of America: The Southern Christian Leadership Conference and Martin Luther King, Jr.* Athens: University of Georgia Press, 1987.

Fisher, Miles Mark. *Negro Slave Songs in the United States.* New York: Citadel, 1969.

Flew, Andrew. *The Politics of Procrustes: Contradictions of Enforced Equality.* Buffalo, N.Y.: Procrustes Books, 1981.

Franklin, C. L. "Dry Bones in the Valley." In *Give Me This Mountain*, edited by Jeff Todd Tilton, 80–88. Urbana: University of Illinois Press, 1989.

Frazier, E. Franklin. *The Negro Church in America.* 1964. Reprint. New York: Schocken Books, 1974.

Frye, Northrop. *Anatomy of Criticism: Four Essays.* Princeton: Princeton University Press, 1973.

Garrow, David J. *Bearing the Cross: Martin Luther King, Jr., and the Southern Christian Leadership Conference.* New York: William Morrow, 1986.

————, ed. *Martin Luther King, Jr.: Civil Rights Leader, Theologian, Orator.* 3 vols. Brooklyn, N.Y.: Carlson, 1989.

Gates, Henry Louis, Jr. *The Signifying Monkey: A Theory of Afro-American Literary Criticism.* New York: Oxford University Press, 1988.

Genovese, Eugene. *Roll, Jordan, Roll: The World the Slaves Made.* New York: Vintage, 1976.

Graber, Doris. *Politics and Verbal Behavior.* Urbana: University of Illinois Press, 1976.

Hamilton, Charles. *Black Preacher in America.* New York: Morrow, 1972.

Hanigan, James P. *Martin Luther King, Jr., and the Foundations of Nonviolence.* Lanham, Md.: University Press of America, 1984.

Hariman, Robert. "Time and the Reconstitution of Gradualism in King's Address: A Response to Cox." In *Texts in Context: Critical Dialogues on Significant Episodes in American Political Rhetoric*, edited by Michael C. Leff and Fred J. Kauffeld, 205–17. Davis, Calif.: Hermagoras Press, 1989.

Hart, Roderick P. *The Political Pulpit.* West Lafayette, Ind.: Purdue University Press, 1977.

————. "The Functions of Human Communication in the Maintenance of Public Values." In *Handbook of Rhetorical and Communication Theory*, edited by Carroll C. Arnold and John Waite Bowers, 749–91. Boston: Allyn and Bacon, 1984.

Hebdige, Dick. *Cut'N'Mix: Culture, Identity, and Caribbean Music.* New York: Metheun, 1987.

Heilbut, Tony. *Gospel Sound.* New York: Simon and Schuster, 1971.

Higginson, Thomas. "Negro Spirituals, 1867." In *The Negro and His Folklore in Nineteenth-Century Periodicals*, edited by Bruce Franklin. Austin: University of Texas Press, 1987.

Holt, Grace Sims. "Stylin' Outta the Black Pulpit." In *Rappin' and Stylin' Out*, edited by Thomas B. Kochman, 189–204. Urbana: University of Illinois Press, 1972.

Howard-Pitney, David. *The Afro-American Jeremiad: Appeals for Justice in America.* Philadelphia: Temple University Press, 1990.

Jackson, Mahalia (with Evan Wylie). *Movin' On Up.* New York: Hawthorn, 1966.

Jefferson, Thomas. *The Papers of Thomas Jefferson.* Edited by Julian P. Boyd. Princeton: Princeton University Press, 1950.

———. *The Writings of Thomas Jefferson: Memorial Edition.* Edited by Albert Ellery Bergh. Washington, D.C.: Thomas Jefferson Memorial Association of the United States, 1904.

Jewett, Robert, and John Shelton Lawrence. *The American Monomyth.* Lanham, Md.: University Press of America, 1988.

Johannesen, Richard L. *Ethics in Human Communication,* 2d ed. Prospect Heights, Ill.: Waveland Press, 1983.

Johannesen, Richard L., Ronald Allen, and Wil A. Linkugel, eds. *Contemporary American Speeches.* 6th ed. Dubuque, Iowa: Kendall-Hunt, 1988.

Johnson, Lyndon B. "Voting Rights Address of March 15, 1965." In *Great Issues in American History,* 3 vols., edited by Richard and Beatrice Hofstadter, 3:459–61. New York: Random House, 1982.

Jones, LeRoi. *Blues People.* New York: William Morrow, 1969.

Kennedy, George A. *Greek Rhetoric Under Christian Emperors.* Princeton: Princeton University Press, 1983.

Kennedy, John F. *Public Papers of the Presidents of the United States: John Fitzgerald Kennedy.* 3 vols. Washington, D.C.: Government Printing Office, 1962–64.

King, Coretta Scott. *My Life with Martin Luther King, Jr.* New York: Holt, Rinehart, and Winston, 1969.

King, Martin Luther, Sr. (with Clayton Riley). *Daddy King: An Autobiography.* New York: William Morrow, 1980.

King, Mary. *Freedom Song: A Personal Story of the 1960s Civil Rights Movement.* New York: William Morrow, 1987.

Kittel, Gerhard. *Theological Dictionary of the New Testament.* Vol. 2. Translated by Geoffrey W. Bromiley. Grand Rapids, Mich.: Wm. B. Eerdmans, 1964.

Kluckhohn, Clyde. "Values and Value-Orientation in the Theory of Action: An Exploration in Definition and Classification." In *Toward a General Theory of Action,* edited by Talcott Parsons and Edward A. Shils, 388–433. Cambridge: Harvard University Press, 1951.

LaFrance, Marianne, and Clara Mayo. *Moving Bodies: Nonverbal Communication in Social Relationships.* Monterey, Calif.: Brooks/Cole-Wadsworth, 1978.

Lakoff, George, and Mark Johnson. *Metaphors We Live By.* Chicago: University of Chicago Press, 1980.

Landau, George. *Victorian Types, Victorian Shadows.* Boston: Routledge, 1980.

Larson, Barbara A. *Prologue to Revolution: The War Sermons of Reverend Samuel Davies—A Rhetorical Study.* Falls Church, Va.: Speech Communication Association, 1978.

Leff, Michael C., and Fred J. Kauffeld, eds., *Texts in Context: Critical Dialogues on Significant Episodes in American Political Rhetoric.* Davis, Calif.: Hermagoras Press, 1989.

Lentz, Richard. *Sixty-Five Days in Memphis: A Study of Culture, Symbols, and the Press.* Journalism Monographs, no. 98. August 1986.

———. *Symbols, the News Magazines, and Martin Luther King.* Baton Rouge: Louisiana State University Press, 1990.

Levine, Lawrence. *Black Culture and Black Consciousness.* New York: Oxford University Press, 1977.

Lewis, David L. *King: A Critical Biography.* Urbana: University of Illinois Press, 1970.

Lincoln, C. Eric. *The Black Church Since Frazier.* New York: Schocken Books, 1974.

Lomax, Alan. *The Folk Songs of North America.* Garden City, N.Y.: Doubleday, 1960.

Lovell, John. *Black Song.* New York: Macmillan, 1972.

Lucaites, John Louis. "Constitutional Argument in a National Theater: The Impeachment Trial of Dr. Henry Sacheverell." In *Popular Trials: Rhetoric, Mass Media, and the Law,* edited by Robert Hariman, 31–54. Tuscaloosa: University of Alabama Press, 1990.

Lucaites, John Louis, and Celeste Michelle Condit. "The Rhetorical 'Foundation' of Equality in American Political Discourse." In *Taking Political Talk Seriously,* edited by John Nelson. Forthcoming.

Lucas, Stephen E. "Justifying America." In *American Rhetoric: Context and Criticism,* edited by Thomas W. Benson, 67–130. Carbondale: Southern Illinois University Press, 1989.

Lyell, Charles. "A Negro Church in Savannah." In *The Negro American: A Documentary History,* edited by Leslie Fishel and Benjamin Quarles. Glenview, Ill.: Scott, Foresman, 1967.

McClendon, James. *Biography as Theology.* New York: Abingdon Press, 1974.

McCrum, Robert, William Cran, and Robert MacNeil. *The Story of English.* New York: Elizabeth Sifting Books–Viking, 1986.

McGee, Michael Calvin. "A Materialist's Conception of Rhetoric." In *Explorations in Rhetoric: Studies in Honor of Douglas Ehninger,* edited by Ray E. McKerrow, 23–48. Glenview, Ill.: Scott, Foresman, 1982.

Malcolm X. "The Ballot or the Bullet" (3 April 1964). In *Malcolm X Speaks,* edited by George Breitman, 23–44. New York: Grove Press, 1966.

———. "The Black Revolution" (8 April 1964). In *Malcolm X Speaks,* edited by George Breitman, 45–57. New York: Grove Press, 1966.

———. "To Mississippi Youth" (31 December 1964). In *Malcolm X Speaks,* edited by George Breitman, 137–46. New York: Grove Press, 1966.

———. *Malcolm X and the American Negro Revolution: The Speeches of Malcolm X,* edited by Archie Epps. London: Peter Owen, 1968.

Malcolm X, and Alex Haley. *The Autobiography of Malcolm X.* New York: Grove Press, 1966.

Malone, Dumas. *Jefferson: The Virginian.* Boston: Little, Brown, 1948.

Marable, Manning. *Race, Reform and Rebellion: The Second Reconstruction in Black America, 1945–1982.* Jackson: University Press of Mississippi, 1985.

Margenau, Henry. "The Scientific Basis of Value." In *New Knowledge in Human Values,* edited by Abraham H. Maslow, 38–51. New York: Harper and Row, 1959.

Mayer, Lyle V. *Fundamentals of Voice and Diction.* 7th ed. Dubuque, Iowa: William C. Brown, 1985.

Miller, Keith D. *Voice of Deliverance: The Language of Martin Luther King, Jr., and Its Sources.* New York: Free Press, 1992.

Miller, William R. *Martin Luther King, Jr.: His Life, Martyrdom and Meaning for the World.* New York: Weybright and Talley, 1968.

———. *Martin Luther King, Jr.* New York: Avon, 1969.

Miner, Earl. *Literary Uses of Typology: From the Late Middle Ages to the Present.* Princeton, N.J.: Princeton University Press, 1977.

Mitchell, Henry. *Black Preaching.* New York: J. B. Lippincott, 1970.

Moltmann, Jürgen. *The Theology of Hope.* New York: Harper and Row, 1967.

Morris, Aldon. *The Origins of the Civil Rights Movement.* New York: Free Press, 1984.

Murphy, James J. *Rhetoric in the Middle Ages: A History of Rhetorical Theory from St. Augustine to the Renaissance.* Berkeley: University of California Press, 1974.

Myrdal, Gunnar. *An American Dilemma: The Negro Problem and Modern Democracy.* 2 vols. 1944. Reprint. New York: Pantheon Books, 1972.

Nelson, John S. "Political Foundations for Rhetoric of Inquiry." In *The Rhetorical Turn,* edited by Herbert W. Simons, 258–89. Chicago: University of Chicago Press, 1990.

Norrell, Robert. *Reaping the Whirlwind: The Civil Rights Movement in Tuskegee.* New York: Random House, 1986.

Oates, Stephen B. *Let the Trumpet Sound: The Life of Martin Luther King, Jr.* New York: Harper and Row, 1982.

Ong, Walter J. *Interfaces of the Word: Studies in the Evolution of Consciousness and Culture.* Ithaca, N.Y.: Cornell University Press, 1977.

———. *Orality and Literacy: The Technologizing of the Word.* London: Metheun, 1982.

O'Reilly, Kenneth. *"Racial Matters": The FBI's Secret File on Black America, 1960–1972.* New York: Free Press, 1989.

Ortega y Gassett, Jose. *Men and People.* Translated by Willard R. Trask. New York: W. W. Norton, 1957.

Osborn, Michael. *Orientations to Rhetorical Style.* Chicago: Science Research Associates, 1976.

———. "Rhetorical Depiction." In *Form, Genre, and the Study of Political Discourse,* edited by Herbert W. Simons and Aram A. Aghazarian, 79–107. Columbia: University of South Carolina Press, 1986.

Pasteur, Alfred B., and Ivory L. Toldson. *Roots of Soul.* Garden City, N.Y.: Anchor Press/Doubleday, 1982.

Perelman, Chaim. *The New Rhetoric and the Humanities.* Dordrecht, Holland: D. Reidel, 1979.

Perelman, Chaim, and L. Olbrechts-Tyteca. *The New Rhetoric: A Treatise on Argumentation*. Translated by John Wilkinson and Purcell Weaver. Notre Dame, Ind.: University of Notre Dame Press, 1969.

Pipes, William. *Say Amen, Brother!: Old-Time Negro Preaching*. Westport, Conn.: Negro Universities Press, 1951.

Pole, J. R. *The Pursuit of Equality in American History*. Berkeley: University of California Press, 1978.

Raboteau, Albert. *Slave Religion*. New York: Oxford University Press, 1978.

Raines, Howell. *My Soul Is Rested: Movement Days in the Deep South Remembered*. New York: G. P. Putnam's Sons, 1977.

Rawick, George P. *From Sundown to Sunup: The Making of the Black Community*. Westport, Conn.: Greenwood Press, 1972.

Rawls, John. *A Theory of Justice*. Cambridge, Mass.: Belknap Press, 1971.

Reid, John Phillip. *The Concept of Liberty in the Age of the American Revolution*. Chicago: University of Chicago Press, 1988.

Riffaterre, Michael. *The Semiotics of Poetry*. Bloomington: Indiana University Press, 1978.

Ritter, Kurt W., and James R. Andrews. *The American Ideology: Reflections of the Revolution in American Rhetoric*. N.p.: Speech Communication Association, 1978.

Robertson, James Oliver. *American Myth, American Reality*. New York: Hill and Wang, 1980.

Rohler, Lloyd E. "Martin Luther King's 'I Have a Dream.'" In *Great Speeches for Criticism and Analysis*, edited by Lloyd E. Rohler and Roger Cook, 329–36. Greenwood, Ind.: Alistair Press, 1988.

Rokeach, Milton M. *Beliefs, Attitudes, and Values*. San Francisco: Jossey-Bass, 1968.

Rosenberg, Bruce. *Art of the American Folk Preacher*. New York: Oxford University Press, 1970.

Rosenfield, Lawrence W. "The Practical Celebration of Epideictic." In *Rhetoric in Transition: Studies in the Nature and Uses of Rhetoric*, edited by Eugene White, 131–56. University Park, Pa.: Pennsylvania State University Press, 1980.

Rueckert, William H. *Kenneth Burke and the Drama of Human Relations*. Minneapolis: University of Minnesota Press, 1963.

Schlesinger, Arthur M. Jr. *Robert Kennedy and His Times*. Boston: Houghton Mifflin, 1978.

Schulke, Flip, and Penelope O. McPhee. *King Remembered*. New York: W. W. Norton, 1986.

Sennett, Richard, and Jonathon Cobb. *The Hidden Injuries of Class*. New York: Vintage Books, 1972.

Shaw, Anna Howard. "The Fundamental Principle of a Republic." In *Anna Howard Shaw: Suffrage Orator and Social Reformer*, edited by Wil A. Linkugel and Martha Solomon, 147–64. New York: Greenwood Press, 1991.

Sidran, Ben. *Black Talk*. New York: Holt, Rinehart, and Winston, 1971.

Sithole, Elkin. "Black Folk Music." In *Rappin' and Stylin' Out*, edited by Thomas B. Kochman, 65–82. Urbana: University of Illinois Press, 1972.

Sitkoff, Harvard. *The Struggle for Black Equality.* New York: Hill and Wang, 1981.

Smith, Arthur L. *Rhetoric of Black Revolution.* Boston: Allyn and Bacon, 1969.

————, ed. *Language, Communication and Rhetoric in Black America.* New York: Harper and Row, 1972.

Smith, Arthur L., and Stephen Robb, eds. *The Voice of Black Rhetoric.* Boston: Allyn and Bacon, 1971.

Smith, Kenneth, and Ira Zepp, Jr. *Search for the Beloved Community.* Valley Forge, Pa.: Judson, 1974.

Smitherman, Geneva. *Talkin and Testifyin: The Language of Black America.* Detroit: Wayne State University Press, 1977.

Sorensen, Theodore C. *Kennedy.* New York: Harper and Row, 1965.

Southern, David W. *Gunnar Myrdal and Black-White Relations: The Use and Abuse of an American Dilemma, 1944–1969.* Baton Rouge: Louisiana State University Press, 1987.

Stuckey, Sterling. *Slave Culture: Nationalist Theory and the Foundations of Black America.* New York: Oxford University Press, 1987.

Tawney, R. H. *Equality.* 1931. Reprint. London: George Allen and Unwin, 1964.

Thompson, Daniel C. *The Negro Leadership Class.* Englewood Cliffs, N.J.: Prentice-Hall, 1963.

Tillich, Paul. "Is a Science of Human Values Possible?" In *New Knowledge in Human Values,* edited by Abraham H. Maslow, 189–96. New York: Harper and Row, 1959.

Tindall, George Brown. "The Central Theme Revisited." In *The Southerner as American,* edited by Charles Grier Sellers, Jr., 104–29. Chapel Hill: University of North Carolina Press, 1960.

Turner, Bryan. *Equality.* London: Tavistock, 1986.

Tutu, Desmond. *Hope and Suffering.* Grand Rapids, Mich.: Eerdman's, 1985.

U.S. Congress. House. Select Committee on Assassination. *Investigation of the Assassination of Martin Luther King, Jr.: Hearings—No. 17, 20, and 21.* 95th Cong., 2d Sess., 1978.

Verba, Sidney, and Garry G. Orren. *Equality in America: The View from the Top Down.* Cambridge: Harvard University Press, 1985.

Walker, David. *One Continual Cry: David Walker's Appeal to the Colored Citizens of the World, 1829–1830.* Edited by Herbert Aptheker. New York: Humanities Press, 1965.

Walker, Wyatt. *Somebody's Calling My Name: Black Sacred Music and Social Change.* Valley Forge, Pa.: Judson, 1979.

Weatherby, W. J. *James Baldwin: Artist on Fire.* New York: Donald L. Fine, 1989.

Weaver, Richard M. *The Ethics of Rhetoric.* Chicago: Henry Regnery, 1953.

————. *Language Is Sermonic: Richard M. Weaver on the Nature of Rhetoric.* Edited by Richard L. Johannesen et al. Baton Rouge: Louisiana State University Press, 1970.

Westen, Peter. *Speaking of Equality: An Analysis of the Rhetorical Force of*

'Equality' in Moral and Legal Discourse. Princeton: Princeton University Press, 1990.

White, James Boyd. When Words Lose Their Meaning: Constitutions and Reconstitutions of Language, Character and Community. Chicago: University of Chicago Press, 1984.

———. Heracles' Bow: Essays on the Rhetoric and Poetics of the Law. Madison: University of Wisconsin Press, 1985.

Wildavsky, Aaron. The Rise of Radical Egalitarianism. Washington, D.C.: American University Press, 1991.

Williams, Bruce, and Orlando L. Taylor, eds. International Conference on Black Communication. Bellagio, Italy: Rockefeller Foundation, 1980.

Wills, Garry. Under God: Religion and American Politics. New York: Simon and Schuster, 1990.

Zepp, Ira G., Jr. The Social Vision of Martin Luther King, Jr. Brooklyn, N.Y.: Carlson, 1989.

Articles

Baldwin, Lewis V. "Martin Luther King, Jr., the Black Church, the Black Messianic Vision." Journal of the Interdenominational Theological Center 12 (Fall 1984/Spring 1985): 93–108.

———. "The Minister as Preacher, Pastor, and Prophet: The Thinking of Martin Luther King, Jr." American Baptist Quarterly 7 (1988): 79–97.

Benson, Thomas W. "Rhetoric and Autobiography: The Case of Malcom X." Quarterly Journal of Speech 60 (1974): 1–13.

Bitzer, Lloyd F. "The Rhetorical Situation." Philosophy and Rhetoric 1 (1968): 1–14.

Booth, Wayne C. " 'The Way I Loved George Eliot': Friendship with Books as a Neglected Critical Metaphor." Kenyon Review 2 (1980): 1–27.

Bosmajian, Haig. "Rhetoric of Martin Luther King's Letter from Birmingham Jail." Midwestern Quarterly 8 (1967): 127–43.

Bowers, John Waite, and Michael Osborn. "Attitudinal Effects of Selective Types of Concluding Metaphors in Persuasive Speeches." Speech Monographs 33 (1966): 147–55.

Brummett, Barry. "The Representative Anecdote as a Burkean Method Applied to Evangelical Rhetoric." Southern Speech Communication Journal 50 (1984): 1–23.

Bryant, Donald C. "Rhetoric: Its Functions and Scope." Quarterly Journal of Speech 39 (1953): 401–24.

Campbell, Finley C. "Voices of Thunder, Voices of Rage: A Symbolic Analysis of Malcolm X's Speech 'Message to the Grass Roots.'" Communication Education 19 (1970): 101–10.

Carson, Clayborne. "Martin Luther King, Jr.: Charismatic Leadership in a Mass Struggle." Journal of American History 74 (1987): 436–81.

———. "Documenting Martin Luther King's Importance—and His Flaws." Chronicle of Higher Education, 16 January 1991, A52.

Colaiaco, James A. "The American Dream Unfulfilled: Martin Luther King, Jr., and the 'Letter from Birmingham Jail.'" *Phylon* 45 (1984): 1–18.

————. "Martin Luther King, Jr., and the Paradox of Nonviolent Direct Action." *Phylon* 47 (1986): 16–28.

Condit, Celeste Michelle. "The Functions of Epideictic: The Boston Massacre Orations as Exemplar." *Communication Quarterly* 33 (1985): 284–99.

————. "Democracy and Civil Rights: The Universalizing Influence of Public Argumentation." *Communication Monographs* 54 (1985): 1–18.

————. "Crafting Virtue: The Rhetorical Construction of Public Morality." *Quarterly Journal of Speech* 73 (1987): 79–97.

Condit, Celeste Michelle, and John Louis Lucaites. "The Rhetoric of 'Equality' and the Expatriation of African-Americans, 1776–1826." *Communication Studies* 42 (1991): 1–24.

Cone, James H. "Martin Luther King, Jr.: Black Theology—Black Church." *Theology Today* 41 (1984): 409–20. (Reprinted in Garrow, ed., *Martin Luther King, Jr.: Civil Rights Leader, Theologian, Orator.* 3 vols. 1:409–20. Brooklyn, N.Y.: Carlson, 1989).

————. "The Theology of Martin Luther King, Jr." *Seminary Quarterly Review* 40 (1986): 21–39.

Conrad, Charles. "Agon and Rhetorical Form: The Essence of 'Old Feminist' Rhetoric." *Central States Speech Journal* 32 (1981): 45–53.

Cook, Anthoney E. "Beyond Critical Legal Studies: The Reconstructive Theology of Dr. Martin Luther King, Jr." *Harvard Law Review* 103 (1990): 985–1040.

Crosswhite, James. "Universality in Rhetoric: Perelman's Universal Audience." *Philosophy and Rhetoric* 22 (1989): 157–73.

Dance, Frank E. X. "Ong's Voice: 'I,' the Oral Intellect, You, and We." *Text and Performance Quarterly* 9 (1989): 185–98.

Daniel, Jack L., and Geneva Smitherman. "How I Got Over: Communication Dynamics in the Black Community." *Quarterly Journal of Speech* 62 (1976): 26–39.

DePalma, Anthony. "Plagiarism Seen by Scholars in King's Ph.D. Dissertation." *New York Times,* 10 November 1990, 1ff.

Eubanks, Ralph T., and Virgil L. Baker. "Toward an Axiology of Rhetoric." *Quarterly Journal of Speech* 48 (1962): 151–63.

Fairclough, Adam. "Was Martin Luther King a Marxist?" *History Workshop Journal* 15 (1983): 117–25.

Fisher, Walter R. "Reaffirmation and Subversion of the American Dream." *Quarterly Journal of Speech* 59 (1973): 160–67.

————. "Narration as a Human Communication Paradigm." *Communication Monographs* 51 (1984): 1–22.

Flick, Hank. "An Historical Perspective on Malcolm X." *North Carolina Journal of Speech and Drama* 11 (1977): 1–12.

Fulkerson, Richard P. "The Public Letter as a Rhetorical Form: Structure, Logic, and Style in King's 'Letter from Birmingham Jail.'" *Quarterly Journal of Speech* 65 (1979): 121–36.

Garrow, David J. "King's Plagiarism: Imitation, Insecurity, and Transformation." *Journal of American History* 78 (1991): 86–92.

Graves, Michael P. "Function of Key Metaphors in Early Quaker Sermons, 1671–1700." *Quarterly Journal of Speech* 69 (1983): 364–78.

Hart, Roderick P. "Contemporary Scholarship in Public Address: A Research Editorial." *Western Journal of Speech Communication* 50 (1986): 283–95.

Hastings, Arthur. "Metaphor in Rhetoric." *Western Speech* 34 (1970): 181–94.

Hecht, Michael L., Sidney Ribeau, and J. K. Alberts. "An Afro-American Perspective on Interethnic Communication." *Communication Monographs* 56 (1989): 385–410.

Henry, David. "The Rhetorical Dynamics of Mario Cuomo's 1984 Keynote Address: Situation, Speaker, Metaphor." *Southern Speech Communication Journal* 53 (1988): 105–20.

Higham, John. "Habits of the Cloth and Standards of the Academy." *Journal of American History* 78 (1991): 106–11.

Huggins, Nathan Irvin. "Martin Luther King, Jr.: Charisma and Leadership." *Journal of American History* 74 (1987): 477–81.

Illo, John. "The Rhetoric of Malcolm X." *Columbia University Forum* 9 (1964): 5–12.

Jamieson, Kathleen Hall. "The Metaphoric Cluster in the Rhetoric of Pope Paul VI and Edmund G. Brown, Jr." *Quarterly Journal of Speech* 66 (1980): 51–72.

Jordan, William J. "A Reinforcement Model of Metaphor." *Speech Monographs* 39 (1972): 223–26.

Jordan, William J., and Margaret L. McLaughlin. "The Metaphorical Dimension in Descriptive Language." *Human Communication Research* 2 (1976): 182–91.

Karst, Kenneth. "Why Equality Matters." *Georgia Law Review* 17 (1983): 245–89.

Kirkwood, William G. "Storytelling and Self-Confrontation: Parables as Communication Strategies." *Quarterly Journal of Speech* 69 (1983): 58–74.

———. "Parables as Metaphors and Examples." *Quarterly Journal of Speech* 71 (1985): 422–40.

Klein, Mia. "The Other Beauty of Martin Luther King, Jr.'s 'Letter from Birmingham Jail.'" *College Composition and Communication* 32 (1981): 30–37.

Lee, Ronald E. "The Rhetorical Construction of Time in Martin Luther King, Jr.'s 'Letter from Birmingham Jail.'" *Southern Communication Journal* 56 (1991): 279–88.

Lischer, Richard. "The Word That Moves: The Preaching of Martin Luther King, Jr." *Theology Today* 46 (1989): 169–82.

Logue, Cal M. "Transcending Coercion: The Communicative Strategies of Black Slaves on Antebellum Plantations." *Quarterly Journal of Speech* 67 (1981): 31–46.

Lucaites, John Louis, and Celeste Michelle Condit. "Reconstructing <Equality>: Culturetypal and Counter-Cultural Rhetorics in the Martyred Black Vision." *Communication Monographs* 57 (1990): 5–24.

———. "Malcolm X: The Limits of the Rhetoric of Revolutionary Dissent." *Journal of Black Studies* 23 (1993): 291–313.

McGee, Michael C. "In Search of 'the People': A Rhetorical Alternative." *Quarterly Journal of Speech* 61 (1975): 235–49.

———. "The Fall of Wellington: A Case Study of the Relationship Between Theory, Practice, and Rhetoric." *Quarterly Journal of Speech* 63 (1977): 28–42.

McGee, Michael Calvin. " 'Not Men, But Measures': The Origins and Import of an Ideological Principle." *Quarterly Journal of Speech* 64 (1978): 141–55.

———. "The 'Ideograph': A Link Between Rhetoric and Ideology." *Quarterly Journal of Speech* 66 (1980): 1–16.

Martin Luther King, Jr., Papers Project. "The Student Papers of Martin Luther King, Jr.: A Summary Statement on Research" and "Appendix." *Journal of American History* 78 (1991): 23–40.

Miller, Keith D. "Martin Luther King, Jr., Borrows a Revolution." *College English* 48 (1986): 249–65.

———. "Voice Merging and Self-Making: The Epistemology of 'I Have a Dream.' " *Rhetoric Society Quarterly* 19 (1989): 23–52.

———. "Composing Martin Luther King, Jr." *Publication of the Modern Languages Association* 105 (1990): 70–82.

———. "Martin Luther King, Jr., and the Black Folk Pulpit." *Journal of American History* 78 (1991): 120–23.

Miller, William Robert. "Gandhi and King: Trail Blazers in Nonviolence." *Fellowship* 35 (1969): 5–7.

Mott, Wesley T. "The Rhetoric of Martin Luther King, Jr.: Letter from Birmingham Jail." *Phylon* 36 (1975): 411–21.

Neuhaus, Richard John. Letter to the Editor. *Commonweal* 88 (1968).

Ortner, Sherry B. "On Key Symbols." *American Anthropologist* 75 (1973): 1338–46.

Osborn, Michael. "Archetypal Metaphor in Rhetoric: The Light-Dark Family." *Quarterly Journal of Speech* 53 (1967): 115–26.

———. "The Evolution of the Archetypal Sea in Rhetoric and Poetic." *Quarterly Journal of Speech* 63 (1977): 347–63.

Reagon, Bernice Johnson. " 'Nobody Knows the Trouble I See'; or 'By and By I'm Gonna Lay Down My Heavy Load.' " *Journal of American History* 78 (1991): 111–19.

Reinsch, M. Lamar, Jr. "An Investigation of the Effects of Metaphor and Simile in Persuasive Discourse." *Speech Monographs* 38 (1971): 142–45.

Rickert, William E. "Winston Churchill's Archetypal Metaphors: A Mythopoetic Translation of World War II." *Central States Speech Journal* 28 (1977): 106–12.

Scott, Robert L. "Justifying Violence: The Rhetoric of Militant Black Power." *Central States Speech Journal* 19 (1968): 96–104.

Sellers, James. "Love, Justice and the Non-Violent Movement." *Theology Today* 18 (1962): 65–69.

Smith, Arthur L. "Socio-Historical Perspectives of Black Oratory." *Quarterly Journal of Speech* 56 (1970): 264–69.

———. "Markings of an African Concept of Rhetoric." *Today's Speech* 19 (1971): 13–17.

Smith, Donald H. "Martin Luther King, Jr.: In the Beginning from Montgomery." *Southern Speech Communication Journal* 34 (1968): 8–17.

Snow, Malinda. "Martin Luther King's 'Letter from Birmingham Jail' as Pauline Epistle." *Quarterly Journal of Speech* 71 (1985): 318–34.

Solomon, Martha. "The Positive Woman's Journey: A Mythic Analysis of the Rhetoric of STOP ERA." *Quarterly Journal of Speech* 65 (1979): 262–74.

Spillers, Hortense J. "Martin Luther King and the Style of the Black Sermon." *Black Scholar* 3 (1971): 14–27.

Steele, Edward D. "Social Values in Public Address." *Western Journal of Speech Communication* 22 (1958): 38–42.

"Symposium: Value Theory and Rhetoric." *Western Journal of Speech Communication* 26 (1962): 70–91, 133–45.

Thelen, David. "Becoming Martin Luther King, Jr.: An Introduction." *Journal of American History* 78 (1991): 11–22.

Vatz, Richard E. "The Myth of the Rhetorical Situation." *Philosophy and Rhetoric* 6 (1973): 154–61.

Wainwright, Loudan. "Martyr of the Sit-Ins." *The Negro History Bulletin* 24 (1961): 147–51.

Waldman, Peter. "To Their Dismay, King Scholars Find a Troubling Pattern." *Wall Street Journal,* 9 November 1990, 1ff.

Wallace, Karl R. "The Substance of Rhetoric: Good Reasons." *Quarterly Journal of Speech* 49 (1963): 239–49.

Ware, B. L., and Wil A. Linkugel. "They Spoke in Defense of Themselves: On Generic Criticism of Apologia." *Quarterly Journal of Speech* 59 (1973): 273–83.

Wills, Garry. "Martin Luther King: Blessed Be the Name of De Lawd." *Esquire,* August 1968, 124–28.

Wright, Erik Olin. "Race, Class, and Income Inequality." *American Journal of Sociology* 83 (1978): 1368–97.

Unpublished Material

Bakke, John. "A Study of Establishment Rhetoric During the Sanitation Strike in Memphis, 1968." Missouri Valley Collection, Brister Library, Memphis State University, Memphis, Tennessee, n.d.

Lucaites, John Louis. "Flexibility and Consistency in Eighteenth-Century Anglo-Whiggism: A Case Study of the Rhetorical Dimensions of Legitimacy." Ph.D. diss., University of Iowa, 1984.

Osborn, Michael. "A Philosophy of Criticism." Paper presented at the annual meeting of the Eastern Communication Association, April 1988.

Rosteck, Thomas. "'I've Been to the Mountaintop': The Linkage of Narrative, Metaphor and Argument in Martin Luther King's Final Speech." Paper presented at the Speech Communication Association Conference, 1985.

Smith, Donald H. "Martin Luther King, Jr.: Rhetorician of Revolt." Ph.D. diss., University of Wisconsin, 1964.

Contributors

Frederick J. Antczak is associate professor and chair-elect of the Department of Rhetoric at the University of Iowa. He has research interests in American public address and the ethics of rhetoric. His *Thought and Character: The Rhetoric of Democratic Education* won a Phi Beta Kappa Award in 1986. He has also received the Thomas Jefferson Teaching Award in 1985 and the Karl Wallace Memorial Award in 1987. He is currently editor of *Iowa Journal of Speech Communication,* is editing a collection of essays on ethical criticism, and is at work on a book on Lincoln and King.

Carolyn Calloway-Thomas is associate professor of speech communication and associate dean of the faculties at Indiana University, where she teaches courses in African-American rhetoric and in cross-cultural communication. Her essays on the relationship between social change and African-American communication have appeared in *Communication Quarterly, Rhetoric Society Quarterly, Journal of Black Studies,* and *Southern Speech Journal.* She has also written *What If I Am a Woman: The Rhetoric of Sisterhood and Struggle, 1830–1970* (forthcoming). In 1990 she received a Fulbright Award to Nigeria, West Africa.

E. Culpepper Clark is professor of speech communication and executive assistant to the president at the University of Alabama. A past president of the Southern States Communication Association,

Clark's latest book is *The Schoolhouse Door: Segregation's Last Stand at the University of Alabama* (1993).

Celeste Michelle Condit is associate professor of speech communication at the University of Georgia. She is author of *Decoding Abortion Rhetoric* (1990) and the coauthor of *Crafting Equality: America's Anglo-African Word* (1993). She has written essays on Malcolm X, Martin Luther King, Jr., and the civil rights movement, as well as on the general process of social change, in *Communication Monographs, Quarterly Journal of Speech, Critical Studies in Mass Communication,* and *Buffalo Law Review.*

Linda K. Harrison is an artist. She has a background in communication and a long-standing interest in black history and communication.

Robert D. Harrison is assistant professor of communication arts at Gallaudet University. His research interests include the dynamics of speaker-audience interaction, family communication, black history, and communication.

Judith D. Hoover is associate professor of communication at Western Kentucky University. She has published articles on the relationship between values and communication in *Southern Quarterly* and *Southern States Communication Journal* and on the Kennedy press conferences as an early use of television as a political tool in *Journal of Popular Film and Television.*

John Louis Lucaites is assistant professor of speech communication at Indiana University. He teaches courses on rhetoric and social theory. He is the coeditor of *Great Speakers and Speeches* (1992) and the coauthor of *Crafting Equality: America's Anglo-African Word* (1993). His published essays examining the relationship between rhetoric and ideology appear in both national and international journals, including *Quarterly Journal of Speech, Communication Monographs, Canadian Journal of Social and Political Theory,* and *Informal Logic.* He is currently writing a book on the impact of documentary photography on the development of twentieth-century liberal, public argumentation.

Keith D. Miller is associate professor of English at Arizona State University. His essays and reviews about the language of Martin Luther King, Jr., have appeared in *PMLA, College English, Rhetoric Society Quarterly, Journal of American History,* and *New York*

Times. His book *Voice of Deliverance: The Language of Martin Luther King, Jr., and Its Sources* was published in 1992 by the Free Press.

Michael Osborn is professor of communication arts at Memphis State University. He is a past president of the Southern States Communication Association and the Speech Communication Association. His research, focused on rhetorical figuration and depiction, has been honored by SCA's Golden Anniversary Monograph Award, by the Douglas Ehninger Distinguished Rhetorical Scholar Award, and by the Distinguished Research Award from Memphis State University.

John H. Patton is associate professor in the Department of Communication and a fellow of Newcomb College at Tulane University, New Orleans. He has published articles and book chapters on political communication and presidential rhetoric, issues in rhetorical theory and criticism, and the rhetoric of Martin Luther King, Jr. He has served on the editorial boards of *Quarterly Journal of Speech, Central States Speech Journal,* and *Southern Communication Journal.* He is currently doing research and teaching on the rhetoric of civil rights, political persuasion, and rhetoric and cultural identity in the Caribbean.

Martha M. Solomon is professor in the Department of Speech Communication at the University of Maryland, College Park. She has published articles on the rhetoric of social movements, women's rhetoric, and rhetoric and social change in the major journals in the field of speech communication. In addition, she has written rhetorical biographies of Emma Goldman (Twayne, 1987) and Anna Howard Shaw (with Wil Linkugel, Greenwood, 1990). She is past editor of *Southern Speech Communication Journal* and *Quarterly Journal of Speech.*

Index

sentative anecdote," 68; "terministic screen," 83; "identification," 118
Burkeian theory, 68

Cadence, 173–74, 175, 177; defined, 173
California, 170
Call-response, 17, 122, 162–78, 210 (n. 28); cultural roots of, 164–68; definition of, 164–65; history of, 165; in the black church, 167; in the classroom, 178; in communication forms, 166; in spirituals, 167; sense of community in, 166; spontaneity in, 174
Calypso, West Indian, 122
Calypso music, 122
Cambodia, 140
Canaan, 22
Carey, Archibald, Jr., 130
Carlyle, Thomas, 18, 28
Carmichael, Stokely, 88, 131, 132
Carpenter, C. C. J., 39
Cathedral of Saint John the Divine, 26
Characterizations, rhetorical, 201 (n. 37)
Charlotte, North Carolina, 111
Chicago, Illinois, 10, 41, 130, 131, 132, 135, 150
Children, 55, 64, 74, 86, 99, 114, 116, 125, 133, 178
Children of Israel, 153, 156, 157, 158
China, 130, 144
Christian Century, 35
Christianity, 14, 27, 34, 35, 59, 79, 94, 96, 99, 100–101, 102; conception of justice, 97, 98; guaranteeing salvation, 94; moral heritage of, 138
Christians, 44, 64; early, 54
Cicero, 150
Circulating sermons, 11, 22–23, 184 (n. 22)
Civil disobedience, 43–44, 45, 48, 85, 124; of Socrates, 54
Civil liberties, 71
Civil rights, 69, 71, 72, 76, 91, 99, 108, 110, 111, 113–16, 119, 120, 123, 125, 129, 130, 144, 169, 177, 192 (n. 46)
Civil Rights Act of 1964, 29
Civil rights legislation, 60, 76, 79, 118
Civil rights movement, 7, 8, 10, 11, 13, 15, 25, 27, 28, 30, 50–53, 59, 60, 64, 83, 85, 87, 90, 99, 102, 119–21, 124, 135, 142, 210 (n. 28)

Clark, Jim, 116, 131
Clark, Septima, 26, 36–37
Cleaver, Eldridge, 88
Clergy and Laymen Concerned, 134
Cleveland, E. O. S., 22, 23; "I Know How to Fly," 23
Cleveland, Ohio, 131
Colorado, 170
Common sense, 51, 60, 63
Communal existence, 3, 5–6, 9
Communal identification, 3–6, 117. *See also* Sermonic function
Communal values, 3–6, 96. *See also* Sermonic function
Communism, 59, 143
Communist Party, 59
Communists, 134, 142, 181 (n. 24)
Community, 5, 6, 101–102, 133, 169, 181 (n. 16), 209 (n. 4); American, 138, 144; congregational, 167; of critical discourse, 146; "discursive," 137; human, 100; "generative power of," 163; national, 86; of minds, 118; performance of, 164; rhetorical, 141, 207 (n. 39); sense of, in call-response, 166, 169. *See also* "Beloved community"
Condit, Celeste Michelle, 13–14
Cone, James, 107
Congress, 64, 76
Congress of Racial Equality (CORE), 37, 131
Connor, Eugene "Bull," 29, 37–39, 45, 57, 131, 153
Conscience: national, 160; rhetoric of, 196 (n. 2)
Constitution, U.S., 5, 7, 8, 33, 58, 62, 69, 70, 71, 72, 77, 79, 90, 102, 120, 123, 155
"Contagion of liberty," 33
Coppin, L. J., 21, 27
Core communal values, 3–4, 8, 9, 15, 17. *See also* Sermonic function
Core statement, 67, 69
Court decisions, 60
Covenant: Declaration of Independence and Constitution as, 69, 70, 71, 72–73, 74, 75, 78, 79, 80, 81; choice of word, 195 (n. 20); rhetorical appeal, 79, 82, 83
"Creative extremism," 52, 53
"Creative protest," 196 (n. 2)
"Creative suffering," 100

Jamieson, Kathleen Hall, 194 (n. 7)

Jefferson, Thomas, 43, 53, 58, 86, 197 (n. 6)

Jericho, 154

Jerusalem, 154

Jesus Christ, 20, 21, 25, 27, 30, 31, 32, 41, 53, 105, 110, 154

Jews, 44, 54, 74, 110, 170

Johannesburg, South Africa, 151

Johannesen, Richard L., 60

Johnson, Haynes, 132

Johnson, Lyndon B., 8, 46, 120, 129, 130, 132, 134; administration, 15

Johnson, Mark, 68

Jones, Charles Colcock, 36, 39

Jones, Clarence, 34, 40

Jones, LeRoi, 165

Jordan, Barbara, 87

Jordan River, 20

Joshua, 20

Journal of American History, 107

Journey, 75, 79–80

Judeo-Christian: culture, 79; ethic, 16–17; heritage, 62, 65; sermon, 179 (n. 5); tradition, 13, 48–49, 65, 104

Justice, 9, 13, 44, 46, 54, 61, 63, 69, 70, 73, 74, 80, 91, 94, 97–101, 113, 114, 115, 119, 123, 125, 128, 142, 143

Justice Department, 59

Justification, 52, 54

Kennedy, John F., 8, 46, 48, 52, 59, 60, 76, 77, 118–19, 192 (n. 46); administration, 35, 38, 41, 42, 45, 51, 118–19

Kennedy, Robert, 8, 41, 59, 60, 118

Kenya, 151

Key phrases, repetition of, 115, 118

King, A. D., 55, 56

King, Coretta Scott, 117, 129, 168, 176, 177, 205 (n. 22)

King, Martin Luther ("Daddy"), 6, 24, 25, 39, 107

KING, MARTIN LUTHER, JR.: background, 9; early years, 121; academic training, 18–19, 24–25, 32, 43, 107, 108, 109; at Dexter Avenue Church, 106; as activist, 31; as cultural hero, 11; as dynamic conservator, 138–40; as historian/scholar, 43; as idealist, 64; as leader of civil rights movement, 7, 8, 9–10, 46, 53, 76, 83, 90, 163; as moral and political leader, 1–2, 7, 8, 17, 45, 102–103; 124; as Moses, 26, 34, 38, 74, 112, 124, 152; as great orator, 1, 95, 106, 156, 158, 163; as prophet calling to his people, 49; as a preacher/ minister, 2, 16, 25, 32, 72, 106, 160; as kerygmatic preacher, 111; as social critic, 15; effect of on audience, 25, 32, 128; sensitivity to audience, 106, 111; inspired by audience response, 176, 195 (n. 31); and "beloved community," 2, 6–10, 11, 13, 15, 87, 93, 98; commitment of to Christianity, 14, 41, 107, 112, 113, 119; and Christian concept of moral power, 94; religious values and beliefs, 72, 83; and sense of mission, 108; compared to Paul, 41; thought of, 104; development of civil disobedience, 85; and class orientation, 205 (n. 22); criticisms of, 39, 76, 134–35, 150; theme of deliverance in works of, 25; dream of, 73, 91, 101; democratic heritage of, 65, 14, 41; eloquence/ delivery of, 25, 128; and equality, 87–89, 96, 102; hearing the words of, rather than reading them, 156; in jail in Birmingham, 39, 40, 51, 57; and a positive prediction for Birmingham, 48; use of language, 109, 114, 115, 120–21; and revolution in language, 137–46; and definition of (agape) *love,* 100; disparate metaphors in language of, 66; contrasted with Malcolm X, 90–95; rejection of black supremacy, 47; and "marvelous new militancy," 94, 102; and philosophy of nonviolence, 57, 77, 117, 129; political philosophy of, 70, 71, 72, 83; plagiarism, 11, 107, 108–109, 183 (n. 36); oral performance of, 108; oratory of, 162–78; call-response in oratory of, 164, 169–77; power of oratory, 175–77; persuasive power of, 15, 39, 81, 163, 164; public character of, 128; public life of, 16; public discourse of, 8, 10, 11, 19, 83, 93, 107, 117, 128, 171; rhetoric of, 83, 112; rhetorical power/skill, 68, 81; ethical quality of rhetoric, 128; anti-war rhetoric of, 129–30; sermons, 11, 25, 105, 106–107; thematic development in sermons of, 11; use of slave theology and typology in speeches,

Self-making: in the black folk pulpit, 22–24; in Dr. King's speeches, 25, 32
Selma, Alabama, 30, 32, 116, 120, 155, 175
Separation, 100
Sermon, 17, 22–25, 184–85 (n. 22); black, 117; circulating, 22–23, 184 (n. 22); defined, 3; embedding lyrics, 23–24. *See also* Black folk preachers; Preachers/preaching
Sermonic function: of call-response, 17; of public discourse, 3–6; identifying core values, 3–4; structuring hierarchy of values, 4–5; performing communal existence, 5–6. *See also* Values
Sermon on the Mount, 13
Setting, 169
Shakespeare, William, 18, 28
Shaw, Anna Howard, 71
Shores, Arthur, 40
Shuttlesworth, Fred Lee, 38, 39, 42, 45, 46, 48, 56
Sidran, Ben, 167
Silence, 130
Sit-ins, 55, 59, 62, 155
Sitkoff, Harvard, 18
Sixteenth Street Baptist Church (Birmingham), 116, 152
Sixty-Five Days in Memphis (Lentz), 148
Slavery, 22, 27, 29, 33, 166, 167
Slaves, 19, 25, 27, 29, 30, 32, 34, 36, 70, 114, 122, 157, 165, 166, 167; religion/ theology of, 11, 19, 21, 25; sense of sacred time, 20; typology of, 19, 20, 22, 25
Smith, Arthur L. *See* Asante, Molefi Kete
Smith, Donald Hugh, 195 (n. 31)
Smith, Kenneth, 18
Smith, M. H., 56
Smitherman, Geneva, 164, 168, 171, 178
Snow, Malinda, 50, 59, 157
Social gospel, 24
Socrates, 42, 53, 54
Sorensen, Theodore C., 59
"Soul force," of the dream, 122
South, the, 43, 55, 59, 62, 90, 155, 159
South Africa, 33, 47, 143, 151
South America, 164
South Carolina, 75, 101
Southeast Asia, 141

Southern Christian Leadership Conference (SCLC), 7, 8, 10, 15, 36–39, 41, 48, 53, 56, 130, 134, 142
Southern Conference on Human Welfare, 37
Southern Regional Council, 39
Speaker, 96, 98–99, 112, 123, 157, 164–65, 166, 172; and audience, 5–6, 17, 124, 164, 172, 175, 176, 177
Spillers, Hortense, 117
Spirituals, 19, 20, 23–24, 25–26, 32, 167, 170, 184 (n. 5); double meaning of, 19
Spontaneity, 174
Stalin, Joseph, 47
States' rights, 71
Step (variations in pitch), 172–73, 175, 177; defined, 172. *See also* Call-response
Stone Mountain, Georgia, 73, 170
Stuckey, Sterling, 18
Student Nonviolent Coordinating Committee (SNCC), 8, 9, 37, 119, 131
Subject, 147
Suffering, 80, 100–101, 116, 129
Summerhill (Atlanta), 132
Supreme Court, 28
Symbolic environment, 10, 198 (n. 11)
Symbols, 99, 115, 116, 120, 121, 126; condensation, 68, 82; elaborating, 79; key, 67, 68, 78, 79; power of, 81
Synchronous kinesic and paralinguistic behaviors, 174–75, 177. *See also* Call-response
Synchrony, 174

Talmadge, Herman, 90
Taylor, Gardner, 21, 30
Tears of Love, 40
Tennessee, 73, 170
Tennyson, Alfred, 18, 28
Tenor, element of matrix metaphor, 68, 82
Tension, 42, 43, 61; productive, 114
Terrell, Mary Church, 87
Texts, multiple, 206 (n. 38)
Thailand, 140
Thelen, David, 109
Thematic unity, 66, 81
Theme, 123, 159; of perseverance, 115
Theology, 11, 104, 105, 114, 116–17, 126
Theory of Cognitive Dissonance, A (Festinger), 44

DATE DUE

SEP